T0330138

Towards Sustainable Project Development

Towards Sustainable Project Development

Edited by

Frank A. Wilson
Development and Project Planning Centre, University of Bradford, UK

Edward Elgar
Cheltenham, UK • Lyme, US

© Frank A. Wilson 1997

All rights reserved. No part of this publication may be reproduced, stored in a retrieval system or transmitted in any form or by any means, electronic, mechanical or photocopying, recording, or otherwise without the prior permission of the publisher.

Published by
Edward Elgar Publishing Limited
8 Lansdown Place
Cheltenham
Glos GL50 2HU
UK

Edward Elgar Publishing Company
1 Pinnacle Hill Road
Lyme
NH 03768
US

A catalogue record for this book
is available from the British Library

Library of Congress Cataloguing in Publication Data
Towards sustainable project development / edited by Frank A. Wilson.
    Includes bibliographical references.
    1. Sustainable development.   2. Economic development projects.
I. Wilson, Frank Arnal, 1942–
HC79.E5T694   1997
338.9—dc21   96–52675
                                                CIP

ISBN 1 85898 430 0

Typeset by Manton Typesetters, 5–7 Eastfield Road, Louth, Lincolnshire LN11 7AJ, UK.
Printed and bound in Great Britain by Biddles Ltd, Guildford and King's Lynn

Contents

List of figures   vii
List of tables   viii
List of contributors   ix
Acknowledgements   xi

Introduction: sustainability and development   xii

PART I   ENVIRONMENTAL SUSTAINABILITY

1 Integrating environment into development planning: where have we got to?   3
David Pearce
2 Hard methods for soft policies: environmental and social cost–benefit analysis   20
Arild Angelsen and Ussif Rashid Sumaila
3 Valuing environmental change: the contingent valuation method and project planning   43
Dominic Moran
4 Market liberalization and environmental assessment   56
Colin Kirkpatrick and Norman Lee

PART II   PROJECTS, PEOPLE AND PROCESS

5 Human resources, new growth theory and adjustment: implications for human resources projects   77
Rolph van der Hoeven
6 'Folk and pop' in the orchestration of development projects   97
Alan Rew
7 The ODA's process approach to projects: experience in India and lessons for project management   114
Ita O'Donovan
8 Process and blueprint in water resources development   127
Tom Franks and Ian Tod

9 Managerial skills and managerial effectiveness: an alternative to functionalism 137
Farhad Analoui

PART III TOWARDS SUSTAINABLE DEVELOPMENT:
PERSPECTIVES AND PRACTICE

10 Rural development via community participation: issues and lessons in project planning from the Sierra Leone experience 155
George Ola Williams
11 Learning big things from small countries: tales from the South Pacific with lessons for programme and project planners and managers elsewhere 167
Frank A. Wilson, M.T. Wilson and John Launder
12 Institutional capacity building for rural development: a case study from Zimbabwe 183
John Cusworth
13 Entrepreneurship development programmes in practice: a case study in evaluation 198
Malcolm Harper and Vijay Mahajan
14 Evaluating assistance to small enterprises: institutional financial sustainability and the survival and growth of borrowers 211
Patrick Ryan
15 Income generation and micro-enterprise projects: why do they not reach the poorest women? 235
Uschi Kraus-Harper

Index 247

Figures

4.1 Market liberalization and environmental assessment linkages 56
4.2 Overview of SEA 69

Tables

1.1	Applications of economic valuation studies	8
1.2	The economic costs of air pollution damage to human health	10
1.3	The economic costs of air pollution: UK and UNECE	12
1.4	The health cost of water pollution	14
2.1	The main steps of ESCBA	27
2.2	Overview of different valuation methods	30
7.1	Project task, environment and design	117
9.1	Perceived nature of managerial work	145
9.2	Perceived importance of the managerial skills, knowledge and the job-related aspects for increased effectiveness at work	147
9.3	Preferred managerial skills for increased effectiveness of senior officials in Zimbabwean public sector	148
9.4	Preferred managerial skills for increased effectiveness of senior officials in Indian railways	148
11A.1	Stabex transfer years: application years 1977–90	180
11A.2	Main projects/organizations receiving Stabex funding	181
14.1	SEDOM lending statistics, 1983–90	217
14.2	SEDOM total staff numbers, selected years	218
14.3	SEDOM's income and expenditure account	219
14.4	Distribution of term loans by broad ISIC categories	224
14.5	Survival rates by age of loans	224
14.6	Survival rates by activity category	226
14.7	Survival rates of new and existing enterprises	227
14.8	Survival rates of enterprises with full- and part-time entrepreneurs	228
14.9	Details of final sample by two-digit ISIC	229
14.10	Growth rate of surviving enterprises	231
14.11	Growth rates by ISIC category	231
14.12	Growth rate by region	232
15.1	Key elements of constructed types	238

Contributors

Farhad Analoui is Director of Professional Development and Training and a lecturer at the Development and Project Planning Centre, University of Bradford.

Arild Angelsen is a staff member of the Chr. Michelsen Institute, Bergen, Norway.

John Cusworth is Centre Director and senior lecturer at the Development and Project Planning Centre, University of Bradford.

Tom Franks is Director of Outside Programmes and a senior lecturer at the Development and Project Planning Centre, University of Bradford.

Malcolm Harper is an emeritus professor at Cranfield School of Management and a visiting faculty member of the Xavier Institute of Management, Bhubaneshwar, Orissa, India.

Colin Kirkpatrick is Professor of Development Economics at the University of Manchester.

Uschi Kraus-Harper is a UK based consultant and a visiting faculty member of the Xavier Institute of Management, Bhubaneshwar, Orissa, India.

John Launder is a lecturer at the Development and Project Planning Centre, University of Bradford.

Norman Lee is Director of the Environmental Impact Assessment Centre, Department of Economics, University of Manchester.

Vijay Mahajan is a consultant associate of Vikasoko Inc. New Delhi, India.

Dominic Moran is at the Centre for Social and Economic Research on the Global Environment, University College London and University of East Anglia, UK.

Ita O'Donovan is Director of Human Resources Management, Warwickshire County Council.

George Ola Williams is a consultant based in the UK.

David Pearce is Director of the Centre for Social and Economic Research on the Global Environment, University College London and University of East Anglia, UK.

Alan Rew is Director of the Centre for Development Studies and Professor of Development Policy and Planning at the University of Wales, Swansea.

Patrick Ryan is a lecturer at the Development and Project Planning Centre, University of Bradford.

Ussif Rashid Sumaila is a staff member of the Ch. Michelsen Institute, Bergen, Norway.

Ian Tod is a consultant based in the UK.

Rolph van der Hoeven works for the International Labour Office.

Frank A. Wilson is a senior lecturer and coordinator of the doctoral programme at the Development and Project Planning Centre, University of Bradford.

Thomas (MT) Wilson is an Overseas Development Institute Fellow working as an economic adviser in the South Pacific.

Acknowledgements

I am grateful to all the authors of the chapters contained in this book and in particular for their patience as they waited for their work to appear in edited and published form. Those concerned at Edward Elgar have also been patient but, more importantly, have been most constructive and encouraging.

The conference at which the papers were originally presented had financial support from the UK Overseas Development Administration. Pearl Golden and Mark Gargett assisted with the initial compilation of conference papers. Jean Hill has handled all the final word processing with her usual skill and cheerful cooperation.

On a more personal note, as this volume evolved out of a conference which celebrated 25 years of the Development and Project Planning Centre, I am able, as someone who joined the Centre only a few months after it was first established, to acknowledge the foresight and determination of four individuals: Professor 'Ted' Edwards, the first Vice-Chancellor of the University, Tony Bottomley, Professor of Economics, Ian Sanderson, later to be a most distinguished Registrar, and Dr Michael Gane, the Centre's first Director.

Frank A. Wilson
Bradford

Introduction: sustainability and development

The title of this book, *Towards Sustainable Project Development*, may appear tentative but is intended to reflect some of the current thinking and writing on the subject of sustainability insofar as it relates to the planning and management of development projects. In particular, the chapters in the book are meant to be illustrative of different dimensions and perceptions of sustainability and therefore extend well beyond what most scholars would recognize as the boundaries of economics. This is as it should be; after all botanists, meteorologists, geographers and environmental scientists (of all kinds) were concerned with issues of environmental sustainability long before economists began to apply their tools to the subject. In the same way, sociologists, management specialists and those with an interest and involvement in project implementation have also applied themselves, increasingly of late, to examining groups, institutions and organization structures and processes from sustainability perspectives.

This book evolved from papers first contributed to the twenty-fifth anniversary conference of the Development and Project Planning Centre, University of Bradford, UK which was held in 1995. The overall theme of the conference was 'Development Projects: Issues for the 1990s' and, as is the way with most conferences, the large number of presented papers ranged widely over a number of related topics. Edited versions of those papers are presented here and others have been included in a companion volume, *Cost Benefit Analysis and Project Appraisal in Developing Countries*, edited by Colin Kirkpatrick and John Weiss (also published by Edward Elgar).

The book is presented in parts which broadly follow three themes through which sustainable project development is explored. Part I contains chapters on environmental sustainability where the emphasis is on looking at ways in which environmental concerns can be more effectively incorporated into methodologies and policies. Pearce both sets the scene for other chapters in this section and cogently reviews and illustrates the arguments in favour of incorporating environmental concerns more effectively into development planning at project, programme and policy levels. Angelsen and Sumaila defend orthodox social cost–benefit techniques and show how it is methodologically possible to accommodate the effects on human welfare due to environmental degradation and also issues of inter- and intratemporal equity. Moran's contribution to this section concentrates on the explanation and illustration of the contingent valuation method of estimating environmental values, and Kirkpatrick and Lee complete this section of the book with a chapter which interestingly relates the development of environmental assessment methods with relatively recent trends towards market liberalization and structural change.

The second part is concentrated mainly on non-economic (analysis) determinants of project success and on some of the processes of project planning and management, set against a background of the concern for human resource development. The first chapter in this section, by van der Hoeven, paints a broad picture of the evolution of development policy with particular regard to human resource constraints as a key element in longer-term sustainable growth. Rew's contribution is concentrated on examining the ways and means by which we have been able to effectively build in social factors into our project constructs. He draws on his own research into a large number of project documents to investigate the extent to which sociocultural dimensions have been recognized by those involved in project planning, appraisal and evaluation. The two chapters which follow, by O'Donovan, and Tod and Franks, are concerned with examples of the extent to which it is proving possible to develop alternative approaches to project planning and management which are 'process' rather than 'blueprint' driven. In different ways, both chapters throw light on the extent to which the 'process' approach makes it more likely that projects will be more sustainable than those which are both less flexible and more externally influenced. The final chapter in this section, by Analoui, examines managerial effectiveness by drawing on research in Zimbabwe and India and points to ways in which we need to better understand the perceptions of managers if we are to translate project and programme ideas into long-term development.

The last six chapters, in Part III, are case studies or particular applications which all throw light on project and programme development and point to implications for longer-term sustainability which have wider relevance. Ola Williams draws on his own doctoral research for his chapter on the ways and means by which community participation was fostered in Sierra Leone. Wilson (F.A.), Wilson (M.T.) and Launder suggest that planners and managers can learn much from hard-earned lessons of externally funded interventions in the agricultural sector in two South Pacific countries. Cusworth draws on his considerable experience of rural development in Zimbabwe to examine ways in which a programme of UK assistance was able to approach institutional strengthening from an innovative perspective. The last three chapters look at related aspects of small and medium-scale enterprises. Harper and Mahajan present an enlightening (and encouraging) case study of an evaluation of entrepreneurship development in India. Ryan looks at the work of an aid-supported small enterprise promotion agency in Malawi and draws on his own detailed research to make valuable distinctions between survival and longer-term business and institutional growth. Kraus-Harper's contribution is an incisive analysis of the reasons why many projects which focus on small-scale income generation and microprojects appear to have very little impact on poorer women.

PART I

Environmental Sustainability

1. Integrating environment into development planning: where have we got to?

David Pearce

INTRODUCTION

The prime purpose of this chapter is to reflect on one aspect of development planning, namely how far we have got in terms of integrating environmental concerns in project appraisal. For some of us, arguing the case that we *should* achieve this integration has been a lifetime's work. Happily, I think we can say that, at last, the battle is won. What remains to be done is to extend our understanding of environmental economics to ensure that this victory is sustained and extended. I have selected only one area for assessment: the integration of environmental concerns into project appraisal. Elsewhere, my colleagues have shown how another important area has been influenced by this process of integration through the use of environmental indicators in macroeconomic planning. Essentially, this dimension of integrative thinking measures the economic value of environmental assets and their depreciation in order to secure a more truthful picture of a nation's 'genuine' rate of savings (Hamilton and Atkinson, 1995). For it is clear that we have all been misled by savings ratios that ignore the running down of natural capital assets. We may go further and argue that at least some part of the economic failure of continents such as Africa has arisen because of the 'mining' of renewable resources, from forests to elephants, to soil and water.

Nor should we neglect the other achievements of environmental economists, for example in what is now called 'economywide' policy, that is traditional macroeconomic guidance and planning. A recent publication from the World Bank gives an excellent summary of the insights that environmental economics has provided for policies of structural adjustment involving market liberalization (Munasinghe and Cruz, 1995) and I will not attempt to summarize its conclusions here. While much of what I have to say relates to development planning in the third world, I also have something to say about project appraisal in the rich world.

PROJECT APPRAISAL

Everyone is aware of the basic benefit–cost criterion for selecting projects, namely that, suitably discounted and converted to present value terms, benefits should exceed costs. This simple rule embodies the requirement of *economic efficiency*. Failure to honour it means that a fundamental requirement of economic development, the raising of real per capita incomes, will not be met. While it is fashionable to criticize economists for their preoccupation with economic efficiency, it remains worth reminding the critics that this preoccupation reflects the objective of real income growth without which the developing world will be locked into a poverty trap. Nonetheless, economists have not neglected other social objectives, especially distributive concerns. The early project appraisal manuals showed how, in principle, distributive concerns could be integrated into project appraisal through the use of *social prices* reflecting distributive weights (Squire and van der Tak, 1976). Indeed, many project appraisals were carried out using social rather than pure efficiency prices. It seems fair to say that this fashion died out fairly quickly, partly because of the complexity of making the adjustments, but also because it was never clear why projects should be an instrument for distributive fairness rather than other policy instruments. The point remains, however, that both efficiency and equity have always been addressed in cost–benefit rules.

The environment fared far less well in the development of project appraisal until recently. One of the problems, of course, is that there always has been some hostility to the idea of bringing environmental concerns into project appraisal. This hostility has tended to reflect two quite opposite viewpoints. What we might call the 'development first' school of thought has tended to argue that not only are environmental concerns not a priority for developing countries, but environmental regulations and investments actually act as a drag on economic growth and hence on the whole process of development. Regulations simply raise costs and reduce competitiveness, while environmental investments secure lower rates of return compared to development-oriented investments. A more recent manifestation of this approach has arisen with the abuse of what are known as 'environmental Kuznets curves', functions which trace out the relationship between environmental degradation and income growth in a manner analogous to the way Kuznets himself linked growth and income distribution (Grossman and Krueger, 1991; Cropper and Griffiths, 1994; Shafik, 1994; Pearson, 1994). Since some of the functions depicting this relationship appear as inverted 'U's, the implication is that environmental quality will inevitably worsen as development takes off but will improve later on as incomes rise. In fact, there is no *necessary* relationship between income growth and environmental quality. The econometric evidence on deforestation, for example, shows no clear links between income and deforestation (Brown and Pearce, 1994). More generally, there is no evidence to suggest that rates of return to environmental conservation are lower than rates of return to conventional development investments, although, unquestionably, some environmental investments have low rates of return because of poor selection and poor associated pricing of the environmental assets. We consider shortly some of the evidence suggesting that environmental improvements may in fact have very large rates of return.

I would argue, then, that the 'development first' school of thought is on very weak ground in arguing that the developing world can somehow wait for a better environment while they get on with the more important issues. The second argument against incorporating environment into development planning comes from the other end of the spectrum. This reflects the view of some environmentalists that the environment is somehow not the same kind of commodity as the ones we look at it investment appraisal. It is intrinsically different and is perhaps more akin to some kind of 'merit good' and hence is outside the province of economic assessment. Another version of this argument is that the environment is 'different' because environmental assets have intrinsic value unrelated to any concept of anthropocentric value. While it is possible to have considerable sympathy for the view that other species have moral value independently of humans, it is not at all clear how this view translates into practical decision making. Further, if it implies that there can never be trade-offs between environmental assets and other asset formation, this view quickly becomes sterile and unrelated to the real world (Pearce, 1994).

This second view mainly manifests itself in hostility to the monetization of environmental costs and benefits. Monetization is based on the idea of a preference-based decision rule, with the measure of preferences being individuals' willingness to pay in the market-place. As such, monetization, it is argued, is not consistent with a view that confers importance on the environment independently of what individuals want. An uncharitable view of this approach might suggest that what is being disputed is the relevance of others' preferences relative to those of the critic. A more generous view would focus on the critic's argument that monetization is not credible for many environmental assets. This aspect of the critic's approach is more tenable, but, as we shall see shortly, monetization may well provide very powerful arguments for environmental action where non-economic arguments have clearly failed.

If the relevance of preferences to environmental quality is acknowledged, then the cost–benefit rule needs a simple modification, namely:

$$\max \sum_t (B_t - C_t +/- E_t) (1 + s)^{-t}$$

where B is benefit, C is conventional cost, E is environmental cost or benefit, and t is time. The issue is, can we measure E in money terms and, if we can, does it turn out to be important? More specifically, even if the answer to these questions is 'yes' for developed countries, will the answer still be affirmative for the developing world? I shall argue that the answers to our questions are 'yes' (in general) for both developed and developing country contexts.

CAN WE MEASURE E?

The evidence that we can measure preferences for environmental quality in non-market contexts is now overwhelming. The methodologies are surveyed and developed in a number of modern texts (Pearce and Markandya, 1989; Pearce *et al.*, 1994; Freeman, 1993; Braden and Kolstad, 1991; Bentkover *et al.*, 1986; Johansson, 1987; Mitchell and Carson, 1989). The theory and practice relating to developed and developing country experience is reviewed extensively in Pearce *et al.* (1994), and the developing country experience is reviewed in Pearce *et al.* (1995). A few years ago, economic valuation of environmental impacts was commonplace in the developed world, especially in the USA; it was less popular in Europe and virtually unknown in the developing world. Now, valuation techniques are extensively applied throughout the world. Table 1.1 summarizes the experience. The general observation is that economic valuation techniques are in far more widespread use than might be imagined. In particular, they are being used at a rapidly accelerating rate in the developing world where, despite the existence of major market distortions, they are being applied very successfully.

IS THE ENVIRONMENT IMPORTANT?

Do the studies of the monetary value of the environment tell us anything about the importance of the environment in the developing world ? I would argue that they do and that the general, though not universal, message is that the environment is far more important to development planning than we thought hitherto. To illustrate this, Tables 1.2 and 1.3 assemble some of the evidence on the costs of urban air pollution to human health. Air pollution causes other damages, such as crop and forest loss, soiling and erosion of buildings, and general ecosystem impairment. But health looks as if it is of major importance within these categories of damage. Waterborne diseases are pervasive in the developing world and intuition would suggest that their economic cost is very high. What is more, the health of people has to be fundamental to the formation of human capital, which in turn is fundamental to the development process.

Table 1.2 suggests several conclusions with respect to air pollution control priorities. First, two air pollutants stand out in terms of damage: particulate matter and lead. The exact manner in which particulate matter may cause health damage is not known with any certainty, but statistical associations with respiratory illness and premature death are strong. The studies shown in Table 1.2 tend to use consensus dose response functions and hence overall damage costs will be mainly determined by the size of the population at risk and the unit economic values used to value symptoms and 'statistical life'. Costs per capita in developing countries appear fairly consistent in the range of $20–160, whilst the estimates for Bangkok suggest that overall damages could be very much higher. If the dose response function is linear through the origin, as much of the epidemiology for PM_{10} suggests, then per capita damage could be as high as $1000 in Bangkok ($209 is for a 20 per cent reduction). Lead damage is similarly high in the Bangkok study at $39–193 per capita. The Mexico and Jakarta studies show much lower per capita damages at around $8 per person. Lead health damage shows up in the form of reduced IQ scores in children, hypertension in adults (mainly males), coronary heart disease and mortality. Table 1.2 suggests that tropospheric ozone may rank as a significant health-damaging pollutant, with consistent per capita cost estimates of perhaps $5 per person. Ozone is a secondary pollutant, with the main precursors being NOx and volatile organic compounds (VOCs). In some studies, damage from VOCs is allocated to these two pollutants, although the allocation rule appears not to be generally agreed. Nitrogen oxides and sulphur oxide are generally revealed to be of limited relevance for health damage.

These observations bear on policy in important ways. They suggest that priority actions countries where Western ambient standards are not met should focus on particulate matter and lead. The former can be addressed by energy conservation and vehicle traffic countermeasures, especially the latter since inhalable particulate matter tends to be associated with vehicle emissions rather than stationary sources such as power stations. The practice requiring new power stations in Eastern Europe and developing countries to be fitted with flue gas desulphurization equipment (FGD) becomes questionable since SOx is not seen to be associated with significant health damage, although very high concentrations in 'black spots' probably do have health conse-quences. Lead emissions can be addressed primarily through the lead content of petrol. Overall, then, the air pollution studies suggest a focus on the transport sector rather than the traditional power station sector, although health damage from the latter can be significant.

The available studies suggest that health benefits are the major item in the overall benefit of air pollution control in cities in the developing world.

Table 1.1   Applications of economic valuation studies

(a)   Contingent valuation

Area of application	USA and Canada	Europe	Developing countries
Agriculture	Some	Few	
Air quality	Many	Many	
Climate change	Zero–few	Few	
Energy	Many	Few	Zero–few
Fishing: commercial	Some	Few	Zero–few
Fishing: recreational	Many	Few	
Forestry	Some	Many	
Health risks	Many	Many	
Recreational hunting	Many	Some	
Parks, nature reserves & wildlife	Many	Many	Some
Roads/transport	Few	Few	
Water quality	Many	Many	Some
Water supply & sanitation (including groundwater protection)	Many	Some	Many

Source: Carson *et al.* (1993) and author's estimates.

(b)   Hedonic property value studies

	USA	Europe	Developing countries
Agriculture	Few		
Air quality	Many	Some	
Health risks	Few		
Hunting	Few		
Noise	Many	Many	
Parks, nature reserves & wildlife	Many	Some	
Water quality	Few		
Water supply & sanitation	Few	Few	Few

However, other benefits, less easily quantified in some cases, also accrue, making air pollution control a 'multiple benefits' activity. Urban emissions of

Table 1.1   continued

(c)   *Travel cost models*

	USA	Europe	Developing countries
Fishing: recreational	Many	Many	
Parks, nature reserves & wildlife	Many	Many	Some
Water quality	Many	Some	Few
Water supply & sanitation		Few	Few

(d)   *Damage function studies*

	USA	Europe	Developing countries
Agriculture	Many	Some	Many
Air quality	Many	Many	Some
Fishing: commercial	Many	Few	Many
Health risks	Many	Some	Many*
Materials damage	Many	Many	
Water quality	Few	Few	Few
Water supply & sanitation		Few	Few

Note: *   inclusive of the economies of transition.

(e)   *Benefit transfer studies*

	USA	Europe	Developing countries
Forestry	Few		
Recreation	Many		
Water quality	Some		
Air quality	Few	Many	Many

NOx and SOx can travel extensive distances and may well cross national boundaries. Such transboundary pollution is implicated in acidification damage to lakes, rivers, soils and ecosystems generally, although links to forest damage remain controversial. Carbon dioxide emissions from fossil fuel

Environmental sustainability

Table 1.2   The economic costs of air pollution damage to human health in urban areas

(a) Particulate matter Coverage	Mortality cost (US$m)	Morbidity cost (US$m)	Total health cost (US$m)	Cost as % of GNP	Cost per capita US$
Costs of all exposure					
UK 1983[1]	11 800	9 400	21 200	2.7	848
China 1990[2]	41 670	19 300	60 970	11.1	52
Cairo 1990s[3]	186–992	157–472	343–1 464	n.a.	38 161
Jakarta 1990[4]	113	44	157	n.a.	19
Benefit of % reduction					
Mexico City 1990[5]	480	358	838	n.a.	50
58% reduction					
Bangkok 1989[6]	138–1 315	302–309	440–1 624	n.a.	57–209
20% reduction					
Santiago 1990s[7]	8	62	70	n.a.	15
15% reduction					
(b) Sulphur oxides					
Bangkok 1989[6]	0	0.2	0.2	n.a.	<1
20% reduction					
Santiago 1990s[7]	0	0.1	0.1	n.a.	<1
8% reduction					
(c) Nitrogen oxides					
Jakarta 1990[4]	0	1	1	n.a.	<1
Santiago 1990s[7]	0	1 or 17*	1 or 17	n.a.	<1 or 4
49% reduction					
(d) Ozone					
Cairo[3]	0	11	11	n.a.	1
50% reduction					
Mexico City 1990[5]	0	102	102	n.a.	6
21% reduction					
Bangkok 1990s[6]	0	9–36	9–36	n.a.	1–5
20% reduction					
Santiago 1990s[7]	0	33	33	n.a.	7
69% reduction in VOCs and 49% reduction in NOx					
(e) Lead					
Jakarta 1990s[4]	26	36	62	n.a.	8
All exposure					
Mexico 1989[5]	n.a.	125–130	125–130	n.a.	7–8
All exposure					
Bangkok 1990s[6]	291–1 470	6–8	297–1 478	n.a.	39–193
20% reduction					

Table 1.2   continued

Coverage	Mortality cost (US$m)	Morbidity cost (US$m)	Total health cost (US$m)	Cost as % of GNP	Cost per capita US$
(f) Total health damage costs of air pollution					
Cairo[3]	186–992	157–472	343–1 464	n.a.	38–161
All exposure, PM only					
Jakarta[4]	138	82	220	n.a.	27
All exposure, PM, lead, NOx					
Mexico[5]	480	590	1 070	n.a.	63
All exposure, lead, PM, ozone					
Bangkok[6]	429–2 785	317–353	746–3 138	n.a.	97–402
Benefits of 20% reduction in lead, PM, SOx and ozone					
Santiago[7]	8	96 or 112	104 or 120	n.a.	22–25
Benefits of package of measures					

Notes:

[1]   Pearce and Crowards (1995). Assumes a 'value of statistical life' of $2.25m and population at risk of 25.2 million. Damage done by PM_{10} only.

[2]   Florig (1993). Adjustments made to the original estimates to give a value of statistical life of $45 547 based on a US/UK VOSL of $2.25m multiplied by the ratio of GNP per capita in China to GNP per capita in USA. For a justification for using this ratio, see Alberini *et al.* (1995). Morbidity effects are restricted activity days (RADs) which are valued at a daily GNP per capita of $1.29.

[3]   Estimates of mortality and RADs taken from Chemonics International (1994). Value of statistical life taken to be $2.25m x GNP per capita Egypt/GNP per capita USA = $62 021. RADs valued at daily GNP per capita of $1.75 per day. Population taken to be 9.08 million. Estimates of hospital admissions valued at $260; minor restricted activity days and days of respiratory symptoms valued at $0.4, asthma attacks valued at $2.5.

[4]   World Bank (1994b). Value of statistical life of $75 000 and population at risk of 8.2 million. Morbidity effects include RADs, outpatient visits, hospital admissions, respiratory illness among children, asthma attacks and respiratory symptoms. See also Ostro (1994).

[5]   Margulis (1992). Value of statistical life of $75 000 assumed based on human capital approach. Population of 17 million assumed.

[6]   World Bank (1994c). Bangkok population of 7.67 million assumed. Value of statistical life of $336 000 based on compensating wage differentials in Bangkok for risky occupations.

[7]   World Bank (1994a). Estimates are based on dose-response functions for mortality and morbidity converted to workdays lost, each workday being valued at US$9.55. Population of Santiago taken to be 4.8 million. Control costs for this package of measures were estimated at $60m, so that, even without considering other pollutants, the benefits of reduced PM_{10} exceed the costs of control. Other benefits arise from the associated control of ozone, NOx and SOx. Alternative estimate for NOx in (c) (*) assumes NOx is credited with half the benefits of avoided ozone pollution damage.

burning are implicated in global warming damage. Estimating the economic cost of global warming is complex since both the science and the impacts are very uncertain. Recent work suggests that minimum estimates of economic damage from carbon dioxide amount to $20 per tonne of carbon (Fankhauser and Pearce, 1994; Fankhauser, 1995).

Table 1.3 shows the results of a study of the damage done by emissions from the UK (CSERGE/EFEC/Eyre, 1995). Here the damage to various 'receptors' has been estimated and expressed in an economic value per tonne of pollutant emitted. The UK study shows results for UK damage only and also for damage done by UK emissions to the UK and to the rest of the

Table 1.3   The economic costs of air pollution: UK and UNECE

(a)   Unit economic values for damage in the UK (US$ per tonne emission)

Impacts	SO	NO$_x$	Particulates	CO$_2$	CH$_4$	N$_2$O
Health	1 280	480	14 080	n.e.	n.e.	n.e.
Forests	160	160	n.e.	n.e.	n.e.	n.e.
Crops	16	16	n.e.	n.e.	n.e.	n.e.
Buildings	320	320	288	n.e.	n.e.	n.e.
Global warming	n.e.	n.e.	n.e.	6	112	960
Total	1 776	976	14 368	6	112	960

Note: n.e. = no effect.

(b)   Unit economic values for damage in the UK and the rest of the UNECE area (US$ per tonne emission)

Impacts	SO	NO$_x$	Particulates	CO$_2$	CH$_4$	N$_2$O
Health	2 080	640	14 080	n.e.	n.e.	n.e.
Forests	160	240	n.e.	n.e.	n.e.	n.e.
Crops	22	16	n.e.	n.e.	n.e.	n.e.
Buildings	432	288	288	n.e.	n.e.	n.e.
Global warming	n.e.	n.e.	n.e.	6	112	960
Total	2 694	1 184	14 368	6	112	960

Note: n.e. = no effect.

Source: CSERGE/EFEC/Eyre (1995).

Economic Commission for Europe region (traditional Europe, plus Scandinavia, plus Eastern Europe). Comparison of these two geographical boundaries shows that including transboundary effects raises damage from SOx by about 50 per cent and from NOx by 20 per cent. As the UK is a signatory of the UNECE region Second Sulphur Protocol (1994) and the First Nitrogen Protocol, these damages are relevant to UK emission control policy. The study also shows that, per tonne of pollutant, particulate matter has the highest damage cost and that health effects account for 90 per cent of this damage cost. Dose Response Functions for air pollution are discussed in the annexe.

The epidemiology of water pollution is well understood, but estimating dose response functions for waterborne pollution and human health remains very difficult. Contamination of water supplies has known health effects, but these effects can vary substantially according to personal hygiene behaviour and the amount of water available. It has been estimated that, in 1979, some 360–400 billion working days were lost in Africa, South America and Asia because of water-related diseases (Walsh and Warren, 1979). At even a nominal 50 cents per day, this suggests that these continents lost $180–200 billion in forgone GNP each year. The combined GNP of the three continents in 1979 was about $370 billion, so that GNP was a staggering 35 per cent below its potential value because of waterborne diseases alone (Pearce and Warford, 1993).

A review of over 80 studies of water quality and quantity reveals that improved water and sanitation can be expected to reduce diarrhoeal mortality by 55–60 per cent and morbidity by 25 per cent (Esrey, 1990). Table 1.4 assembles some estimates of water pollution control benefits for two cities and one country. The Mexico study suggests that the benefits of control could be substantial and on a par with those from the control of particulate matter air pollution and lead exposure. A review of past policies in Chile on typhoid suggests that the modest actions taken in 1984 were justified on benefit–cost grounds, while more drastic action might well have had costs in excess of benefits. In 1991 a cholera outbreak prompted quick and effective action on educating the public concerning the consumption of unwashed vegetables and the banning of sewage irrigation for growing vegetables. Benefit–cost analysis suggests a benefit–cost ratio of 5:1 in favour of the emergency actions, with most of the benefits coming from the avoided costs of restrictions on food exports. The limited analyses available on the control of water pollution in urban areas suggest that (a) economic damages to human health can be very large, and (b) benefit–cost ratios typically favour intervention in water quality treatment.

Environmental sustainability

Table 1.4   The health cost of water pollution

Coverage	Mortality cost US$m	Morbidity cost US$m	Total health cost US$m	Cost as % of GNP	Cost Per Capita US$
Jakarta[1] Faecal contamination	300	3	303	n.a.	37
Mexico[2] Intestinal disease	3 600	small	3 600	n.a.	212
Santiago[3] Typhoid					
(a) 1985–90	0.5	0.9	1.4	n.a.	<1
(b) 1991	0.2	0.7	0.9	n.a.	<1

Notes:
[1] World Bank (1994b). Value of statistical life of $75 000 and population at risk of 8.2 million. Assumes 7000 diarrhoea-related deaths per year. Improved water quality and sanitation can reduce such deaths by 55–60% per annum, so that 3800–4200 deaths could be avoided. Some 360 000 fewer diarrhoeal episodes per year are estimated to be saved by improved water quality.
[2] Margulis (1992). Value of statistical life of $75 000 assumed based on human capital approach and applied to the whole of Mexico.
[3] World Bank (1994a). Direct costs of typhoid only and based on forgone production, i.e. human capital approach. Indirect effects excluded from health effects include those on farm profitability from loss of exports of farm produce.

CONCLUSIONS

Economic valuation of environmental impacts has made major advances in recent years. Moreover, economic valuation in a cost–benefit context has made a discreet and effective foray into the developing world where, once upon a time, we might have thought it would have little relevance. The outcome of this research ought to put the minds of the environmentalists at rest: the environment turns out to be important in some rather elementary and basic ways. If we focus policy on securing health benefits from reducing pollution, many other environmental benefits will follow. We have pursued elsewhere the same issue with respect to the conservation of renewable resources such as tropical forests. The picture is the same. Potentially, the economic value residing in conserved natural assets is huge. The challenge continues to be one of measuring it, but the bigger challenge is its capture through the design of new institutions (Pearce, 1995).

So, where are we? Environmental economists have demonstrated the conceptual foundations for a process of integrating environment into development planning. In the context of project appraisal, the conceptual basis is elementary since the requirements of environmental valuation are predetermined by the widely accepted rules for carrying out benefit–cost studies. The practical challenge is also being met and we can look forward to the environment being an 'equal partner' in future development planning. It is about time: the environment really matters.

ANNEXE: DOSE RESPONSE FUNCTIONS FOR AIR POLLUTION

Health effects (H) are related to ambient air quality by

$$dH_i = b.POP_i. d_j. \tag{1A.1}$$

where

d	= change in
i	= health effect, I
b	= slope of dose response function
POP_i	= population at risk from health effect, I
A	= ambient air quality
j	= jth pollutant

Ambient air quality is related to emissions either through some diffusion model or through an approximation involving a relationship such as

$$dA_j/A_j = dE_j/E_j \tag{1A.2}$$

where E = emissions. Equation (1A.2) says that an x per cent change in emissions is associated with an x per cent change in ambient concentrations.

Each health effect, H_i, has a unit economic value P_i so that

$$P_i. dH_i = P_i. b.POP_i. dA_j. \tag{1A.3}$$

and the sum of damages, D, from pollutant j is:

$$D_j = \Sigma_i P_i.dH_i \tag{1A.4}$$

In equation (1A.1), b is the slope of the dose response function (DRF). The DRF could begin at some threshold value below which no damage is done.

No firm evidence for thresholds of air pollutants appears to be available. For this reason a working assumption is that the DRF begins at the origin. However, this working assumption is clearly open to further analysis.

The dose response function is illustrated here with respect to particulate matter since this appears to be the single most damaging pollutant in health terms in the urban environment. Health damage appears to be related to particulate matter of less than 10 microns diameter, that is PM_{10}. Particulates are associated with a wide range of respiratory symptoms. Long term exposure may be linked to heart and lung disease. Particulates may also carry carcinogens into the lungs.

Concentrations of particulate matter are measured in various ways, as total suspended particulates (TSP), sulphates and 'British Smoke' (BS) (or just 'smoke'). One problem is that the various measures need to be converted into units of PM_{10}, since it is PM_{10} that is implicated in health damage. The following conversions (all in $\mu g/m^3$) are suggested in the literature:

$$PM_{10} = 0.55 \text{ TSP} \tag{1A.5}$$

$$\text{Sulphates} = 0.14 \text{ TSP} \tag{1A.6}$$

hence

$$\text{Sulphates} = 0.25 \text{ } PM_{10} \tag{1A.7}$$

$$\text{BS} \approx PM_{10} \tag{1A.8}$$

The equivalence in (1A.8) appears to be disputed, with some authorities claiming that there is no direct link between BS and PM_{10} and others claiming that there is a link but a more complex one than is suggested by the simple equivalence in (1A.8). The conversion problem arises because of different ways of measuring particulate concentrations. The British approach has been to use the black smoke method whereby air is drawn through a filter. The darkness of the stain is then measured and is calibrated to indicate concentration. The darkness of the stain varies by the type of particle and what is in dispute is the link between this measure and those obtained by gravimetric techniques which essentially measure the weight of the particulate matter on the filter paper. Gravimetric approaches have been used in the UK only recently.

Based on meta-analysis of DRFs, a consensus DRF for *mortality* from particulate matter is

$$\%dH_{MT} = 0.096.dPM_{10} \tag{1A.9}$$

where dH_{MT} is the (central estimate of the) change in *mortality*.

The coefficient makes due allowance for other compounding factors such as smoking. Equation (1A.9) says that a $1\mu g/m^3$ change in PM_{10} concentrations is associated with a 0.1 per cent change in mortality, or a 10 $\mu g/m^3$ change in PM_{10} concentrations is associated with a 1 per cent change in mortality. Upper and lower bounds for equation (1A.9) are given as:

$$\%dH_{MT} = 0.130.dPM_{10} \tag{1A.10}$$

and

$$\%dH_{MT} = 0.062.dPM_{10} \tag{1A.11}$$

To get the absolute change in mortality, then, we require:

$$dH_{MT} = b.\ dPM_{10}.\ CMR.\ POP.1/100 \tag{1A.12}$$

where $b = 0.062$, 0.096 and 0.130, respectively for lower, central and upper bounds; and *CMR* is the crude mortality rate. The factor of 100 converts from percentages to absolute numbers.

The source of this annexe is Pearce and Crowards (1995).

REFERENCES

Alberini, A. *et al.* (1995) *Valuing Health Effects of Air Pollution in Developing Countries: the Case of Taiwan*, Washington, DC: Discussion Paper 95–01, Resources for the Future.

Bentkover, J.D., Covello, V. and Mumpower, J. (1986) *Benefits Assessment: The State of the Art*, Dordrecht: D. Reid.

Braden, J.B. and Kolstad, C.D. (1991) *Measuring the Demand for Environmental Quality*, Amsterdam: North-Holland.

Brown, K. and Pearce, D.W. (eds) (1994) *The Causes of Deforestation*, London: University College London Press.

Carson, R., Carson, N., Alberini, A., Flores, N. and Wright, J. (1993) *A Bibliography of Contingent Valuation Studies and Papers*, La Jolla, Cal.: Natural Resource Damage Assessment, Inc.

Centre for Social and Economic Research on the Global Environment, Economics for X Environment Consultancy, and Eyre Energy and Environment (1995) *Assessing the Environmental Costs and Benefits of Renewable Energy Technology in Scotland*, Edinburgh: Scottish Office.

Chemonics International and Associates (1994) *Comparing Environmental Health Risks in Cairo, Egypt, Vols 1 and 2*, Report to USAID, Egypt.

Cropper, M. and Griffiths, C. (1994) 'The Interaction of Population Growth and

Environmental Quality', *The American Economic Review: Papers and Proceedings,* **84**, (2), May, 250–54.

Esrey, S. (1990) *Health Benefits from Improvements in Water Supply and Sanitation: Survey and Analysis of the Literature on Selected Diseases,* Washington, DC: Report to USAID.

Fankhauser, S. (1995) *The Economic Costs of Climate Change,* London: Earthscan.

Fankhauser, S. and Pearce, D.W. (1994) 'The Social Costs of Greenhouse Gas Emissions', in Organisation for Economic Cooperation and Development (OECD), *The Economics of Climate Change,* Paris: OECD.

Florig, H.K. (1993) 'The Benefits of Air Pollution Reduction in China', mimeo, Washington, DC: Resources for the Future.

Freeman, A.M. (1993) *The Measurement of Environmental and Resource Values: Theory and Methods,* Washington, DC: Resources for the Future.

Grossman, G. and Krueger, A. (1991) *Environmental Impacts of a North American Free Trade Agreement,* Working Paper 3914, Cambridge, Mass.: National Bureau of Economic Research.

Hamilton, K. and Atkinson, G. (1995) 'Valuing Air Pollution in the National Accounts', mimeo, Centre for Social and Economic Research on the Global Environment, University College London and University of East Anglia.

Johansson, P.-O. (1987) *The Economic Theory and Measurement of Environmental Benefits,* Cambridge: Cambridge University Press.

Margulis, S. (1992) *Back of the Envelope Estimates of Environmental Damage Costs in Mexico,* Working Paper WPS 824, Country Department II, Latin America and the Caribbean Regional Office, World Bank.

Mitchell, R.B. and Carson, R.T. (1989) *Using Surveys to Value Public Goods: The Contingent Valuation Method,* Washington, DC: Resources for the Future.

Munasinghe, M. and Cruz, W. (1995) *Economywide Policies and the Environment: Lessons from Experience,* World Bank Environment Paper No. 10, Washington, DC: World Bank.

Ostro, B. (1994) *Estimating Health Effects of Air Pollution: a Methodology with an Application to Jakarta,* Washington, DC: PRDPE, World Bank.

Pearce, D.W. (1994) 'The Great Environmental Values Debate', *Environment and Planning,* **26**, 1329–1338.

Pearce, D.W. and Crowards, T. (1995) 'Assessing the Health Costs of Particulate Air Pollution in the United Kingdom', Centre for Social and Economic Research on the Global Environment, University College London and University of East Anglia.

Pearce, D.W. and Markandya, A. (1989) *The Benefits of Environmental Policy: Monetary Valuation,* Paris: OECD.

Pearce, D.W. and Warford, J. (1993) *World Without End: Economics, Environment and Sustainable Development,* New York and Oxford: Oxford University Press.

Pearce, D.W., Whittington D. and Georgiou, S. (1994) *Project and Policy Appraisal: Integrating Economics and Environment,* Paris: OECD.

Pearce, D.W., Whittington, D., Georgiou S. and Moran, D. (1995) *Economic Values and the Environment in the Developing World,* Aldershot: Edward Elgar.

Pearson, P. (1994) 'Energy, Externalities and Environmental Quality: Will Development Cure the Ills it Creates?', *Surrey Energy Economics Discussion Paper Series,* SEEDS 78, Department of Economics, University of Surrey, UK.

Shafik, N. (1994) 'Economic Development and Environmental Quality: an Econometric Analysis', *Oxford Economic Papers,* **46**, October, 757–73.

Squire, L. and van der Tak, H. (1976) *Economic Analysis of Projects*, Baltimore: Johns Hopkins University Press.

Walsh, J. and Warren, K. (1979) 'Selective Primary Health Care: An Interim Strategy for Disease Control in Developing Countries', *New England Journal of Medicine*, **301**, (18), 967–74.

World Bank (1994a) *Chile: Managing Environmental Problems – Economic Analysis of Selected Issues*, Environment and Urban Development Division, Country Department 1, Latin America and the Caribbean Region, Washington, DC: World Bank.

World Bank (1994b) *Indonesia: Environment and Development: Challenges for the Future*, Environment Unit, Country Department III, East Asia and Pacific Region, Washington, DC: World Bank.

World Bank, (1994c) *Thailand: Mitigating Pollution and Congestion Impacts in a High Growth Economy*, Country Operations Division, Country Department 1, East Asia and Pacific Region, Washington, DC: World Bank.

2. Hard methods for soft policies: environmental and social cost–benefit analysis

Arild Angelsen and Ussif Rashid Sumaila [1]

INTRODUCTION

Cost–benefit analysis (CBA) is facing strong criticism among environmentally concerned scholars (for example, Booth, 1994; Drepper and Månsson, 1993; Hanley, 1992; van Pelt, 1993; Schulze, 1994). We argue that a large share of the criticism of CBA is either misplaced or based on misunderstandings about the method. Furthermore, we show that through the application of a pragmatic approach, already available methods can be used to incorporate the main sustainability concerns into the existing CBA techniques.

While recognizing the many difficulties involved in applying CBA to project appraisal, and that other competing methods are available, we use CBA as our point of departure for several reasons. Generally, CBA provides a consistent methodology for project appraisal. In doing so, however, it raises certain problems which other methods also face, even if only implicitly. Typically, other 'softer' methods do not have much to offer when it comes to the hard choices: should, for instance, some environmental resources be sacrificed in order to increase the welfare of the poor living in a village? Whereas we do *not* believe that CBA, or even the expanded CBA, can provide precise answers to such questions, its merits lie in two areas. First, the trade-offs and hard choices involved are made explicit and confronted directly, and not assumed away implicitly. We believe that better choices can be reached only if the available alternatives are clearly stated and their consequences made as transparent as possible. Second, it provides a coherent framework within which the various arguments relating to the costs and benefits involved in such a trade-off can be assessed. Although we may not be able to quantify and value all effects, CBA will provide useful information on the relative merits of different projects, given what information is available.

A common argument against CBA relates to its apparent conflict with the notion of sustainability. In the next section, we discuss the two main definitions of sustainable development commonly found in the environmental economics literature, that is, the 'non-declining welfare' and the 'constant natural capital' approaches. In our view, neither of these approaches offers definitions or criteria that are very useful guides for project selection. We therefore identify two main concerns in the sustainability debate that can form reasonable bases for formulating such criteria. These are a concern for human welfare of the poor in both the present and future generations (distributional concern), and a concern that environmental degradation now may seriously hamper overall human welfare (environmental concern).

The challenge, then, is how to incorporate these concerns into a consistent framework for project assessment. A two-track strategy to improve the conventional methods of project evaluation is put forward: first, a proper valuation of the environmental effects of the projects, and second, a framework that gives higher value to benefits to the poor than to the rich, either now or in the future. Fortunately, most tools for such an approach are readily available in the economic literature, as shown in the third section. We label this approach the 'environmental and social cost–benefit analysis' (ESCBA). It is only in the special cases where the critical functions of the environment will be adversely affected by the project that the imposition of sustainability constraints is required as an addition to ESCBA.

This chapter is based on a study of ways to integrate the sustainability concern in project appraisal of development projects (Angelsen *et al.*, 1994). Thus our references and examples relate mainly to third world settings. This has some implications for the discussion; for example, valuation based on contingent valuation (CV) of recreational services provided by the environment – an issue receiving considerable attention in the valuation literature – is of much less importance in less developed countries (LDCs) than environmental changes that affect production directly. Indeed, there seems to be an inverse relationship between applicability in LDCs and the level of theoretical attention given to the various methods. Much of our optimism with regard to the possibilities for a successful application of CBA arises because the simplest methods would frequently be the most useful.

The fact that we relate our discussion to poor countries also implies that more hard choices have to be made: conflicts between increasing the material standard of living and environmental preservation are much more pressing than in the rich parts of the world where the material sacrifices necessary are often marginal compared to those involved in LDCs. One may in fact argue that applying CBA is more relevant and easier to defend for LDCs. Booth (1994, p. 251), who is in general critical of CBA, suggests a moral standard which 'implies that human beings take priority when the income they require to live decently is threatened, but that ecosystems have priority over income above this level'.

THE PROBLEM OF DEFINING SUSTAINABILITY

> It is very hard to be against sustainability. In fact, the less you know about it, the
> better it sounds. ... sustainability is an essentially vague concept, and it would be
> wrong to think of it as being precise, or even capable of being made precise.
> (Robert Solow, 1993, pp. 179–180, Nobel laureate in economics)

The concept of sustainable development was moved to the top of the international political agenda by the World Commission on Environment and Development (WCED, 1987). It captures the widespread concern for the negative
impacts of environmental degradation on human welfare and its development
into the future. The popularity of the 'sustainable development' idea should
be understood in several ways. There is no doubt that it expresses a genuine
concern with respect to the environment and the welfare of future generations. At the same time, the concept is sufficiently wide and vague to act as an
umbrella for a large number of movements with contradictory goals (Ruttan,
1994). It has acted as a mediating term between environmentalists and devel-
opers, who each have a stake in both the 'sustainable' and 'development'. For
analytical purposes, however, we will argue that the term is of limited use,
and a workable definition is yet to be formulated.

There are a number of concerns driving those marching under the
sustainability banner: the present generation's poor, the well-being of future
generations, the environment in itself (in particular, biodiversity), cultural
diversity, and so on. It is, however, possible to categorize the concerns that
seem to permeate them all into two broad groups: (1) the concern for human
welfare both present and future; this is known as the *instrumental view*, and
(2) the concern for the persistence of all components of the biosphere, even
those with no apparent benefits to humanity; this is the *deep ecological
view*.[2] Even though the ecological view has few followers in its pure version,
it has had far-reaching implications for environmental economists in their
effort to incorporate environmental values in the neoclassical paradigm. The
concept of *existence value* has been introduced to capture the non-use values
people assign to environmental resources. Thus, when it comes to the measurement of people's preferences (that is, environmental valuation), the distinction between the instrumental and the deep ecology view is not as sharp
as it appears: whether people assign values to environmental goods because
of their 'use' or 'existence' value is of minor theoretical importance, and both
should be included in a CBA.

It should also be noted that an instrumental view does *not* imply that terms
like 'rights of nature' or 'rights of future generations' are meaningless. The
essential point is that such rights (viewed as restrictions on current human
activities) are granted by *human beings in the present generation*. Rather than
viewing this as a very anthropocentric view, we take this to be the logical

consequence of the simple fact that nature or future generations cannot participate in the current decision-making process. Again, this problem would not be confined to CBA, as any criteria chosen and decision made would reflect our, that is, human beings of the present generation's, preferences.

Moving to the attempts at operationalizing the concept of sustainable development, a useful framework or typology is provided by, among others, Pearce *et al.* (1990), who consider development to be a vector of several desirable social objectives. Possible elements in the vector are increases in real income per capita, improvements in health and nutritional status, a 'fairer' distribution of income, and increases in basic freedoms. Development is said to occur if this vector increases and we have sustainable development if this pattern stretches over a long period of time.

This approach is in line with most definitions of sustainable development suggested in the economic literature, which can be summarized in the phrase 'non-declining welfare over time'. An early statement of this principle is Tietenberg (1984, p. 33): 'The sustainability criterion suggests that, at a minimum, future generations should be left no worse off than current generations.' However, definitions along this line – or any others, for that matter – do not address the more difficult issues:

- Which elements should be included in the 'development vector'?
- What weight should be given to each element?
- To what extent can a decline in one element be compensated for by an increase in others (substitution)? Must all components in the vector increase in order to have sustainable development?

It is exactly these kinds of questions that welfare economics and its applied branch, CBA, attempt to deal with. Thus the non-declining welfare approach to sustainability leads us directly into the core of CBA.

One noteworthy attempt towards operationalization of the concept is the *constant natural capital approach*. There are at least three different views on the relevance of the constant natural capital approach to sustainable development: first, some authors use this concept as the definition of sustainable development (Pearce *et al.*, 1990); second, others view it as a precondition and/or an essential step towards the operationalization of the *non-declining welfare approach*; third, there is the view that constant natural capital is not a necessary or sufficient condition for sustainable development. Some followers of this view would argue that the focus should be on the *total* capital stock: human, physical reproducible, technological and natural (Mähler, 1990).

The interpretation of the concept of constant natural capital stock in the literature usually takes the 'stock–flow' and the 'economic value–physical quantity' axis. The instrumental view and CBA are generally more concerned with the flows (which, of course, are closely related to the size of stocks) and more so with the value than the quantity of flows. This diverges from the more common interpretation of constant natural capital as constant physical stocks. At a glance, one would expect the latter to be easier to operationalize, but it faces problems and involves trade-offs to which there is no easy answer. Maintaining the physical quantity of (each kind of) natural capital stock *could* be interpreted as follows.

1. Always use renewable resources according to the following rule: (h) < (g), where (h) is the harvest rate of the resource and (g) its regenerative rate. Here the maximum sustainable yield (MSY) is frequently proposed as the main guide for the sustainable exploitation of the resource.
2. Always keep waste flows to the environment (w) at or below the assimilative capacity of the environment (a), that is, according to the rule: $w <$ a.
3. Never exploit non-renewable resources.

Some caveats to the rules above are necessary. The third rule is both unrealistic and impractical to abide by. The main solution to this problem seems to be that, insofar as non-renewable resources must be exploited, we must ensure that their reduced stock is compensated for by investments in renewable resources. The Hartwick (1977) rule tells us that, under certain assumptions, the consumption level may be sustained if the economic rent from the extraction of non-renewable resources is invested. Thus this rule allows for substitutability between renewable and non-renewable resources.

Secondly, the regenerative capacity of natural resources is not static. Renewable resources can also be managed so as to improve their sustained yield.[3] The meaning of MSY is also somewhat unclear when, for example, several ecologically dependent species are harvested, or more generally because environmental functions are interrelated. Then some weighted sum must be used, and the outcome depends crucially on the weighting system applied (Clark, 1990). Moreover, the MSY approach overlooks the costs of extraction and discounting. Cost considerations can in fact lead to higher stocks than would be predicted by a simple MSY rule. This is particularly so in the realistic case where harvest costs increase with declining stocks.

Thirdly, the waste assimilative capacity of the environment can be improved; for instance, river flows can be augmented to enhance their assimilative function. To further complicate matters, the idea of assimilative capacity in itself is not definite, as many ecological equilibria are possible.

Other factors that make the stipulation of conditions for sustainable development very difficult are the effects of population increases and of technological progress. The latter improves efficiency in the use of natural resources and increases the scope for substituting man-made capital for natural capital. Indeed, at the core of the debate between the 'growth disciples' and the 'limits-to-growth prophets' is their different views on the future role of technological progress. We do not pursue the controversy here for the reason given by Buchholz (1990, p. 58): 'Long-term forecasts regarding economic resources and technology require divine gifts, not degrees in economics.' Population growth, on the other hand, may make the constant natural capital rule insufficient, as constant natural capital per capita may be a necessary requirement for non-decreasing welfare per capita. Other problems arise from risk, uncertainty and irreversibility.[4]

Thus we can conclude that neither the 'non-declining welfare' nor the 'constant natural capital' approaches provides readily applicable definitions of (or conditions for) sustainable development, and we subscribe to the view of Solow in the opening quotation of this section. Whereas these concepts are *potentially* useful for guiding macro-level policies, they are even more difficult to translate into meaningful sustainability criteria at the project level. Any attempt to define a sustainability criteria at the micro level would lead us into situations where applying the criteria would be too rigid. Moreover, any sustainability criteria that may be designed would in many situations not guide us on how to spend available resources efficiently or on which project(s) to select. This is the background for the provocative statement by two of the founders of social CBA, Little and Mirrlees (1991, p. 365): 'Whether a project is sustainable has nothing to do with whether it is desirable.'

It is hard to imagine any decision rule that does not involve some balancing of costs and benefits. Given this, our approach is to look carefully at the underlying concern for sustainability and see how these can be integrated in a consistent framework for project appraisal, that is CBA. We interpret the quest for sustainable development to arise from two basic concerns: (1) a concern that current environmental degradation may seriously reduce human welfare, and the fact that present policies and practices do not take sufficient account of this effect (an *environmental* concern), and (2) a concern for human welfare of the poor in both the present and future generations (a *distributional* concern). In a broad sense, this interpretation is not new; for example, Veeman (1989) interprets sustainable development to consist of three critical sub-components: growth, distribution and environment. Policies and project appraisal practices have, conventionally, emphasized the growth component, often implicitly. The redirection suggested by the sustainability debate is to put more emphasis on distributional and environmental effects.

Generally, the economic literature on sustainability tends to limit sustainability to intergenerational justice. In line with the WCED (1987), we argue for the inclusion of intragenerational justice, that is the distribution *within* the present generation, in the concept for two reasons. First, our concern for the future is based on the real possibility that future generations may not enjoy the same level of welfare as the present generation. If this is so, there should be no reason why the present generation's poor should be excluded from the same consideration: 'There is something inconsistent about people who profess to be terribly concerned about the welfare of future generations but do not seem to be terribly concerned about the welfare of poor people today' (Solow, 1993, p. 185). Second, most environmental problems in the less developed countries (LDCs) are caused or escalated by poverty and the unequal intragenerational distribution of resources both nationally and globally. Thus, in order to solve the intergenerational problem, we must also address the present skewed intragenerational distribution.

INCLUDING ENVIRONMENTAL AND DISTRIBUTIONAL EFFECTS IN CBA

The main issue in this section, deriving from the above discussion, is how to incorporate the environmental and distributional concerns in the CBA methodology. CBA is a conceptual framework for the evaluation of the social desirability of a project. The CBA procedure attempts to quantify and value different types of costs and benefits, occurring at different points in time, into one common unit, that is, the net present value (NPV). Bojö *et al.* (1990, pp. 57–8) summarize the general understanding of the content of CBA:

> A coherent method to organize information about social advantages (benefits) and disadvantages (costs) in terms of a common monetary unit. Benefits and costs are primarily valued on the basis of individuals' willingness to pay for goods and services, marketed or not, as viewed through a social welfare ordering representing the preferences of the relevant decision-maker. The flow of monetary units over time is brought together to a net present value. Unvalued effects (intangibles) are described quantitatively or qualitatively and put against valued items.

As there exist a large number of excellent texts on CBA both in general and as applied to developing countries, we shall not go into further detail on the underlying principles of CBA.[5] One clarification may, nevertheless, be in order. Many people react against the idea of reducing the value of (the services from) the environment into monetary terms, or assume that economic criteria in themselves are biased against the environment and future generations: 'A large body of people are nervous about what they think economists are up to' (Winpenny, 1991b, p. 381). Much of this fear is based on the lack of distinction between two separate issues: the present economic policies and the interests of the economic power holders in many countries, on the one hand, and the principles of economic theory, on the other.

The use of monetary units as the unit of measurement (numéraire) does *not* imply any bias towards goods sold in a market, or a view that 'money is all that counts'. In principle, any numéraire could have been used, but a monetary measure is conveniently chosen as it is commonly used as a measure of value. Hence we disagree with the statement by van Pelt (1993, p. 29) that 'CBA's monetary numéraire is likely to be the major obstacle to the incorporation of environmental effects in efficiency measurement under broad welfare concepts.' Everything which is valued by people should, *in principle*, be included in a CBA.

Some costs and benefits are obviously more difficult to quantify, but this does not imply that they are less valuable. We have no problem realizing that *in practice* measurable costs and benefits have usually been given more attention. Besides the practical explanation regarding data availability, this also reflects an important aspect of the political economy of environmental degradation: measurable benefits of resource degradation will often be appropriated by the few (and powerful), whereas the more diffuse costs are shared by the many. While this practice does not derive any support from economic theory, it may be supported by powerful interest groups in society. It is not well founded, but well funded.

To facilitate the further discussion, we briefly outline in Table 2.1 below the main steps used to assess the environmental impacts of a project, using the CBA technique.[6] All the listed steps are important in the ESCBA we advocate; however, the processes in steps 4 and 5 assume greater emphasis here. Steps 2 to 4 capture our first main point that environmental effects of projects be properly identified, quantified and valued, while step 5 accommodates the concern for inter- and intragenerational equity – our second main point.

The identification of major environmental effects (step 2) is not unique to ESCBA, but necessary for most methods. The identification of major en-

Table 2.1   The main steps of ESCBA

---

1. Defining the alternatives (or projects)
2. Identification of the major environmental effects (costs and benefits)
3. Quantification in physical terms of the environmental effects
4. Valuation of the environmental effects
5. Weighing of the costs and benefits
    (a) between different income groups (intratemporal): distributional weights
    (b) in time (intertemporal): discounting
6. Sensitivity and risk analysis
7. Modifications of the project(s) and policy recommendations

---

vironmental effects is not an area where economists have their comparative advantage. Their contribution here may be in the selection of which effects need to be studied further, based on preliminary estimates on their relative importance to welfare. This selection, known as 'scoping' (Bisset, 1987, p. 5) will always be necessary as a result of resource and time constraints.

The quantification in physical terms of the environmental effects (step 3) raises more difficult problems than the identification. Still, in many situations relatively reliable estimates can be made. A number of ways to handle uncertainty have been suggested in the literature (see Angelsen *et al.*, 1994, for a discussion). A useful tool in the quantification process is the development of an *effect matrix*. The most well-known effect matrix is the Leopold *et al.* (1971) matrix, which is a horizontal list of development activities and a vertical list of environmental parameters. The effect matrix would often need to have several dimensions: it may be essential to differentiate between different effects in time, in space and between different income groups.

Steps 2 and 3 listed in Table 2.1 are often labelled as 'environmental impact assessment' (EIA), though the definition of EIA varies in the literature. Some use it to cover most methodologies applicable to the analysis of environmental consequences, including CBA and economic modelling (Biswas and Geping, 1987). Others would include in EIA measures for reducing or eliminating any negative environmental impacts, the implementation of these and the monitoring of the project (Therivel *et al.*, 1992, p. 13). For present purposes we will narrow the definition of EIA to cover the identification and physical quantification of the environmental consequences of projects, while CBA deals with the social valuation of these effects. This corresponds to the actual focus in the literature on EIA and CBA: the EIA term is mainly used by engineers and natural scientists, whereas economists use CBA. It also reflects an appropriate division of labour between the disciplines. The above definitions imply that EIA and CBA are not alternative but rather complementary methods: EIA should be considered as a part of the overall ESCBA process. Following Cooper (1981), we consider EIA to be a *specification technique* of the environmental consequences, whereas the bulk of CBA is concerned with *valuation techniques*.

The specification techniques would not vary too much between various methods for environmental assessment, and they form the basis for any valuation to be done. Schulze (1994, pp. 197–8) states that 'undervaluation of poorly understood impacts' is one of three biases of CBA. This is certainly true, but the same could be said about any method. No method could have captured the damage to the ozone layer caused by CFC emissions before science discovered the effect!

The distinction between specification and valuation techniques also reveals the main flaw with several of the methods suggested as alternatives to CBA:

they do not provide a consistent method or criteria for determining which projects are worthy of implementation. The same is true of multi-criteria analysis (MCA), which is more to be considered as an alternative to CBA. MCA does not provide a consistent procedure on how the different criteria should be weighted together in the overall analysis. *Most alternative methods are not wrong, per se, but simply insufficient.*

One possible escape route here is for the project analyst to leave the final weighting to the decision maker or the decision-making process. Indeed, one may argue that this is always the case in practice: results of the EIA, (ES)CBA or MCA would be but one of several inputs into the decision process. However, the EIA or MCA procedures for project selection are likely to be less consistent than if performed using a systematic application of the CBA technique. The result could be less environmental protection, less poverty reduction and/or less overall economic growth, because the weights given to these goals are likely to vary considerably between projects. The ESCBA provides a consistent framework for valuing environmental effects and balancing the growth, distributional and environmental objectives.

VALUATION OF ENVIRONMENTAL EFFECTS

The valuation of environmental effects involves putting prices or social values on the physical environmental changes. The prices used in CBA are *shadow prices*, which can be defined as the social value of one unit of a good, or the marginal effect on social welfare of a unit change in the quantity of the good. 'Economic benefits and costs of a project can be defined only by the effect of the project on some fundamental objectives of the economy' (Ray, 1984, p. 9). If the objective is to maximize total individual welfare in society, the classical utilitarian approach, then valuation should be based on individual preferences as expressed through their willingness to pay (WTP). Consequently, the phrase 'environmental valuation' is very misleading (Pearce, 1993, p. 4): economists 'only' try to measure preferences and thereby reveal people's valuation of the environment.

Market prices are often the most useful starting point for estimating shadow prices. To estimate shadow prices, from market prices, at least three modifications need to be made. First, they have to be corrected for any market distortions, that is cases where market prices do not reflect marginal valuation and marginal costs.[7] Second, estimation of prices for non-market goods must be undertaken (see below). Third, market prices need to be adjusted to give different weights to costs and benefits occurring to different groups, which has both an intra- and intertemporal aspect. This is a way to build in explicit policy objectives in the appraisal. A comparison between the ESCBA we advocate and the multi-criteria analysis (MCA) advocated by van Pelt (1993) reveals that the differences *in part* are only semantic: 'MCA is characterized by a weighting system involving relative priorities of policy-makers or any other group affected by projects' (van Pelt, 1993, p. 27). On the other hand, ESCBA uses weights that are determined partly by individual preferences (as approximated through adjusted market prices) and partly by the decision makers' preferences and priorities.

The most common valuation methods are listed in Table 2.2, and grouped according to the extent to which existing markets and the prices found in these can be used as a point of departure for the valuation (Bojö *et al.*, 1990). Space does not permit any detailed discussion of the various valuation methods. Winpenny (1991a) gives a comprehensive and accessible overview of valuation methods for projects in LDCs.

Table 2.2   Overview of different valuation methods

---

1. Valuation using conventional markets
    Effect on production (EOP)
    Human capital (HC)
    Preventive expenditure (avoid damage) (PE)
    Replacement costs (restore after damage) (RC)
2. Valuation using implicit markets
    Travel cost (TC)
    Hedonic prices (HP): property value (PV) & wage differentials (WD)
3. Valuation using artificial markets
    Contingent valuation (CV)

As Winpenny (1991a, 1991b) rightly observes, there seems to be a negative correlation between the usefulness of the methods applicable in LDCs and the space they receive in methodological writings. The simplest methods, that is the effect on production (EOP), the replacement costs (RC) and the preventive expenditure (PE), have proved to be the most useful. These methods are able to capture most costs affecting the local population from serious environmental problems like soil erosion and deforestation. On the other hand, the contingent valuation (CV), hedonic price (HP), travel cost (TC) and human capital (HC) methods, while receiving considerable attention in the literature, have more limited applicability in LDCs. The CV and TC methods have been developed primarily to deal with the valuation of non-market environmental goods in richer societies, for example recreational services which generally are highly income-elastic.

We would therefore recommend that efforts be concentrated on a more systematic application of EOP, RC and PE methods in the evaluation of environmental effects of development projects. Experimental studies of the four other methods would definitely be of interest, and of potential value in the future. As for the EOP, HC, RC and PE methods, lack of data seems to be a problem resulting mainly on the natural sciences side: estimates of the linkages between human activities and environmental changes are needed to carry out economic analysis, that is valuation of the environmental changes.

The weighting of the various costs and benefits should ideally provide a conclusion on the desirability of the project. Lack of or uncertain data is always a problem, especially in LDCs. The guiding rule should be to quantify and value the effects whenever reliable estimates can be made. The meaning of 'reliable' would, to some extent, be based on subjective judgements. One should avoid both 'number fetishism' (variables are quantified in spite of very unreliable data) and 'number phobia' (variables are not quantified because they are not commonly thought of in quantitative terms).

In the end, decision makers will base their conclusion on both quantitative and qualitative assessments. Even though it is hard to avoid some qualitative judgements, CBA can in a number of cases filter out either the very good or the very bad alternatives. And it is exactly in these cases that the costs of a wrong decision are highest: either to implement a very bad project or not to implement a very good one. For projects with a NPV around zero the cost in terms of reduced efficiency in the allocation of scarce resources is relatively small. CBA cannot provide precise answers, but can give a highly useful picture of the relative merits of the alternatives (Lind, 1982, p. 24).

DISTRIBUTIONAL WEIGHTS

The conventional CBA gives equal weight to marginal income changes to all individuals, regardless of their initial income. It is based on the Pareto criterion and the Kaldor–Hicks *potential compensation* principle. This is commonly considered a pure efficiency criterion, and the equity objective of society is ignored. One should, however, note that the term 'efficiency' has acquired a rather misleading interpretation in the economic literature. The term itself generally refers to the extent to which certain means attain the stated ends. Using the term without specifying the ends is therefore meaningless. The way the term is commonly used in the economics literature implicitly assumes that growth in total income (GNP) is the only objective; other goals such as distribution are ignored.

It is equally misleading when some, for example van Pelt *et al.* (1990) label the CBA without distribution weights 'economic CBA' (ECBA), as opposed to SCBA. There is nothing in welfare economics saying that income changes to all individuals should be given the same weight in a welfare assessment (project appraisal), though this has been the most common practice. The term 'social CBA' is therefore in many ways inappropriate. 'In the folklore of project work, the term "social" symbolizes loose thinking, and the term "efficiency" is nothing short of being a rallying cry' (Ray, 1984, p. 11). Indeed, we may put ourselves in a glasshouse by using 'ESCBA', as both environmental and social considerations should have been included in CBA in any case.

The reason why distributional effects are ignored may have several explanations, one being the assumption that the issue of distribution should be left to politicians after the economists have given their advice on how to maximize total income. 'Income-distributional ... aspects of any project or program, ... are not part of that package of expertise that distinguishes the professional economist from the rest of humanity', argues Harberger (1971, p. 785), one of the most outspoken defenders of the conventional approach. It follows, in this line of argument, that there are efficient policy instruments available to achieve the desired distribution. 'Let's first make the cake as big as possible, and then decide on how to share it' is a basic postulate.

We believe this position is wrong, for two reasons. First, there is a relationship between the size of the cake and how we cut it, so the distributional aspect cannot be separated from the objective of maximization of national income or welfare (cf. the long-standing discussion on the Kusnetz curve). Second, the means for redistribution of income are far from perfect. Thus, if society has a more equal income distribution as one of its objectives, distributional considerations should be a part of the criteria for project selection and design. The conventional two-step procedure often suggested in these circumstances, would *not* give an optimal solution. The growth and distribution issues must be solved simultaneously.

A second reason for conventional CBA giving little attention to distributional aspects is the fact that one has to introduce some rather rigid assumptions about the social welfare function and individual utility functions. To make interpersonal welfare comparisons, we need a cardinal measure of individual utility (cf. Arrow's (Im)possibility theorem). Measurable utility is not a part of the standard theory of consumer behaviour, where the ordinal theory is sufficient. The ordinal theory leaves us only with the Pareto criterion, which is not very helpful in most interesting cases. Cardinal or measurable utility is clearly a problematic concept. However, for a formal analysis of income distribution beyond the Pareto criterion, there is no escape route.

To single out the specific state among all the Pareto-optimal sets which gives us the highest welfare of the society, we need an indicator which makes it possible for us to assign different values (or weights) to marginal income increases accruing to different income groups. Such a framework is provided by social cost–benefit analysis (SCBA). A key parameter in SCBA is the distributional weights (d_i). This is the factor by which an income increase to a particular individual or group, i, should be multiplied in the overall welfare valuation. Under certain assumptions, this weight can be written as:[8]

$$d_i = \left(\frac{C^d}{C_i} \right)^n$$

where C^d is the average consumption level, used as a benchmark, and C_i denotes consumption of group I; $n \geq 0$ is the elasticity of marginal utility with respect to consumption, and a key parameter in the analysis. The higher the value of n, the higher the weight given to consumption increases of low-income groups (strong preferences for a more equal income distribution). For example, if $n = 1$, and individual P's consumption is only half of the average, a consumption increase to P is valued twice as much as the same monetary increase to a person at the average consumption level. If $n = 2$, the increase to the poor P is valued four times as much.

By applying distributional weights for different income groups, SCBA handles two social objectives: the total income growth, and the distribution of the income. The net present value (NPV) of the project is therefore estimated at *social* prices; that is, the distributional effects are taken into account.

If there is asymmetry between the distribution of costs and benefits, the use of SCBA instead of CBA can influence the outcome of the analysis significantly. One can argue that this is a major characteristic of many development projects with significant environmental effects: the environmental costs are commonly borne by the poor, whereas a smaller group of rich people get the benefits. This would typically be the case for large-scale resource extraction or land use projects in rural areas. The resource use by outside companies (government or private) will often compete with local uses. Therefore environmental degradation has effects not only on intergenerational distribution, but on intragenerational distribution as well.

Under such circumstances, using SCBA rather than the conventional CBA would not only select projects more beneficial to the poor, but also favour projects oriented towards conservation of natural resources. Negative environmental effects are given higher weights because the poor bear the costs. Similarly, the benefits would be given lower weights because the relatively richer groups reap the benefits, and income increases to the rich are valued relatively less in the analysis. The use of distributional weights as a possible way to promote sustainability in project appraisal has, to our knowledge, not been elaborated in the literature on SCBA and environmental assessment.

DISCOUNTING

> Economists did not – contrary to widespread opinion – invent short-sightedness
> and greed, but they have studied the weighing of future values as revealed by
> people's actual behaviour. Many economists have in fact looked upon discounting
> as (at least partially) an expression of human irrationality. (Bojö *et al.*, 1990,
> p. 66)

The general purpose of discounting is to make it possible to compare costs
and benefits at different points in time, and to transfer them into a common unit
of measurement – the NPV. The issue is unavoidable in project analysis: no
discounting implies a discount rate of zero per cent. Discounting is a complex
topic, often misunderstood, widely disputed and 'a subject exhibiting simultaneously a very considerable degree of knowledge and a very substantial level of
ignorance' (Baumol, 1968, p. 788). This is unfortunate, as the choice of discount rate may be crucial for the outcome of the analysis. Particularly when
there is a large lag in time between costs and benefits, the discount rate could
be the single most important factor in determining the sign of the NPV.

Discounting relates to the sustainability debate in at least two important
ways. First, it is directly related to the question of intergenerational justice.
Second, the discount rate may have important consequences for the environmental impacts of the project portfolio that passes the NPV test. Contrary to
popular belief there is no clear-cut relationship between the size of the
discount rate and environmental conservation. Consider a hydropower development project that requires high initial investments, to produce some benefits (electricity), but at the same time has some environmental costs. Lowering
the discount rate would in this case increase the NPV of the project, thereby
increasing the number of projects acceptable and the overall environmental
damage.[9] It is also argued that higher discount rates will 'slow down the
general pace of development through depressing effects on investment. ... the
demand for natural resources is generally less with high discount rates than
with lower ones' (Markandya and Pearce, 1988, p. 3).[10]

Even though one may argue that, for certain projects, a lower discount rate
will have a conservation effect, it is not valid as a general argument. Using
the discount rate to promote environmental conservation would be a *non-
target solution*, and would in many cases have the opposite effect. Further,
there is little theoretical foundation for arguing that the existence of large
environmental effects, per se, should make us lower the discount rate. This
does *not* suggest that the rates currently used should not be lowered. Neither
does it exclude environmental considerations from having an indirect bearing
on the level of the discount rate.

To derive the factors that should determine the level of the social discount
rate, we assume that the objective of economic policy is to maximize the

welfare of the society over time. By assumptions similar to the ones used for the derivation of distributional weights, one arrives at the following formula for the discount rate:[11]

$$i = ng + p$$

where i is the consumption rate of interest, that is the rate at which consumption should be discounted; n is, as before, the elasticity of marginal utility of consumption; g is the annual growth rate of consumption; and p is the rate of pure time preference. According to this formula, we have two basic reasons for discounting. First, we place less weight on future increases in consumption simply because we have become richer. As n is assumed to be positive, a marginal increase in the consumption of a rich consumer in a future generation entails less increase in welfare than the same increase to the relatively poor consumer of the present generation. This reason for discounting is parallel to the one used when discussing intragenerational distribution in SCBA. The discussions on the inter- and intragenerational distribution are closely linked: both are related to our preferences for consumption increases to the poor, as expressed through the parameter n. The considerations that underlie the concern for intergenerational equity also apply to intragenerational equity, which is our main argument for including intratemporal distribution in the sustainability concept.

The second reason for discounting is the pure time preference. The case when $p > 0$ implies that we have some impatience, and would prefer early consumption to later consumption, even if the consumption level is the same. The pure time preference is a controversial issue. There is little doubt that most people are impatient and have a positive rate of pure time preference. The main question is, however, whether *individual* myopia should have any bearing on *social* discount rates. As first shown by Strotz (1955/6), $p > 0$ represents an inconsistency if the individual's objective is lifetime welfare maximization. If pure time preference is a kind of irrationality, it is hard to justify that p should be positive and thereby have an impact on the social discount rate. The environmental debate has highlighted the problem of short-sightedness in public policy making, and conservationists will find support in the economic literature (Sen, 1961, 1982; Pearce and Nash, 1981; Markandya and Pearce, 1988).

If we conclude that pure time preferences are unacceptable in determining the social discount rate ($p = 0$), we are left with the first argument for discounting: consumption growth combined with diminishing marginal welfare of consumption increases. There are strong arguments for the case that future consumption growth will (or should) be significantly limited by environmental (and possibly also other) constraints. This is indeed already the case in many developing countries. The World Bank (1992) estimates the annual loss due to soil erosion for many developing countries to be in the range of 0.5–1.5 per cent of their GNP. If we have a negative rate of consumption growth ($g < 0$) and $p = 0$, the discount rate should be *negative*. This is consistent with a standard economic approach to discounting, yet most economists would hesitate to draw this conclusion. Most analysis would assume a positive rate of economic growth and therefore save the case for positive discount rates.

Note also that strong preferences for a more equal distribution among individuals today (high n) also implies a strong preference for consumption now rather than in future periods. If we generally give a relatively high value to consumption increases to the poor, the poor in an intergenerational perspective comprise the present generation, not the future ones (as long as g is positive). On the other hand, conventional CBA implicitly sets $n = 0$ when it comes to the use of distributional weights, which implies lower discount rates according to the formula above – a recommendation not followed in practice!

On the basis of the above framework, one may argue forcefully that the discount rates currently used are too high. A 10 per cent discount rate seems to have gained some universal acceptance in the analysis of development projects. The main reason is probably that it is a 'nice, round figure' and that a 'correct' rate could be in that range. Following our formula above, with $p = 0$ and $n = 1$ (which is often assumed – the Bernoulli case), the discount rate would equal the growth rate (g). This would for most countries imply much lower rates than the one currently used.[12]

Our analysis so far is based on the assumption that we can trace all the effects (costs and benefits) to changes in consumption, that is consumption is our numéraire. Most project analysis will only consider the direct effects in monetary terms, and these will generally affect both investments and consumption. A positive rate of return on investments (capital productivity) is commonly used as an argument for discounting. We have assumed here that any changes in investments are transformed into consumption changes, and a high capital productivity will be taken into account in that manner. If, however, we use the direct effects of a project in the analysis (that is, consumption is no longer the numéraire), we may need to adjust the discount rate. For example, the discount rate should be lowered if the decrease in investment due to a one dollar investment in a project (the crowding-out effect) is lower than the increase in other investments due to a one dollar output from the project (see Bradford, 1975, for a further discussion).

Another issue that causes some confusion is the use of the discount rate as a way to ration capital. Though widely used in many textbooks on CBA, this confuses two issues, namely the price of capital and the weighing of costs and benefits in different periods (discounting). As demonstrated by Markandya and Pearce (1988), using the discount rate to ration capital would generally *not* give an optimal resource allocation. Discounting applies to all types of costs and benefits in the project, whereas the price of capital itself should be used to reflect capital scarcity.

A final point is that the choice of discount rate must be seen in relation to other parts of the analysis. Some have argued for the use of a lower discount rate for environmental costs and benefits because the costs or benefits may increase over time, and future values should be given higher weights. There are good reasons why environmental costs or benefits may increase over time. However, the increasing value of environmental costs and benefits should be reflected in the future shadow prices used. Indeed, the effect of assuming increasing value of environmental costs or using a lower discount rate is, under certain assumptions, exactly the same (Porter, 1982). For clarity and consistency in the analysis, the adjustments should be made via the future shadow prices and *not* via the discount rates.

To summarize, the issue of intergenerational distribution should form the foundation for the choice of discount rate. Discount rates should *not* be lowered in an attempt to avoid environmental damage. However, the rates at present used are often too high. Furthermore, the discount rate used cannot be viewed in isolation: it depends on the unit in which the costs and benefits are measured (numéraire) and on how future costs and benefits are valued. The choice of discount rate also involves elements of political choice. The parameter n will, as in the discussion of distribution weights, be a politically determined parameter.

DO WE STILL NEED SUSTAINABILITY SCREENING?

The sustainability concern highlights two important issues. First, we need methods to quantify and value environmental changes in order to include them in the formal analysis and thereby make them comparable to other types of costs and benefits. Second, given that our concern for sustainability is basically a concern for the welfare of the poor, both in the present and future generations, this concern should be reflected in the weighting method applied. This relates in particular to the issues of distributional weights and discounting. The environmental and social CBA (ESCBA) put forward in this chapter would result in a project portfolio which is more environment- and poverty-oriented than the conventional approach.

Some would argue that, in spite of these extensions of the conventional practice of CBA, there may be a need for sustainability screening before projects are accepted. There are both theoretical and practical arguments in favour of this view. Regarding the former, it may be argued that there is no guarantee that sustainability will be achieved even in the ESCBA. This is correct, and the reason is *not* discounting, but the fact that one allows for substitution between goods. If one believes that meeting a sustainability criterion (however defined) is a 'must' for all projects, using only the ESCBA would be insufficient.

The obvious problem is to find a meaningful and operational criterion of sustainability. Simple criteria like 'always leave all kinds of natural resources at the pre-project level' would be too rigid and impossible to apply in all cases. Some trade-offs should be allowed, and that is exactly what economic analysis is about. ESCBA provides a consistent way of balancing the various costs and benefits involved. In our opinion, many writers treat the issue of defining meaningful sustainability criteria too lightly. An exception is Ruttan (1994, p. 216), who in his discussion of sustainable agricultural systems concludes that 'sustainability is appropriately viewed as a guide to future agricultural research agendas rather than a guide to practice'. Moreover, the ESCBA gives us a more immediate reason for seriously taking into account environmental effects, as we demonstrate how they will affect our present and future welfare. Even though we do not like the separation between environmental and economic effects, which is not based on the theory any-way, it is still important to decision makers. A clear demonstration of the costs of environmental degradation will promote environmental conservation.

A more practical argument for the use of sustainability screening would be as follows. Many environmental effects are both difficult to measure in physical terms and difficult to value in monetary terms. It is argued that we need some rules of thumb or more tractable selection criteria. We are more sympathetic to this argument, particularly when a large amount of risk and uncertainty is involved. The consequences for project selection may not be very different whether we apply only the ESCBA or also include sustainability screening. The difficulty of defining meaningful and operational criteria obliges us to remain with the problem of when changes in natural resource stocks should be allowed. Introducing more or less well-defined sustainability constraints may only redefine the original problem: finding the optimal use of the environment, that is balancing different services (resources) provided by ecological systems, and balancing short- versus long-term uses.

At the same time, we clearly see that more or less vague definitions of sustainable development may have a role to play at the macro level in setting policy goals. Policy objectives cannot be determined through application of CBA. The shadow prices, distribution weights and discount rates are crucial links between the macro-level goals and the micro-level decisions (project assessment). Whereas many countries have standard parameters to be used in project appraisal, they lack a similar system for *resource pricing* (von Amsberg, 1993). The social costs of using natural resources should be included in project assessments. In this way, the project design and selection would contribute to the accomplishment of primarily policy-determined national environmental targets. This implies a movement towards a system of cost-effective analysis (CEA), where one finds the most efficient (in the true meaning of the word) way to reach the targets.

While we share the concern for environmental degradation and poverty in LDCs with those we have criticized in this chapter, our strategy for addressing this in project appraisal is somewhat different. We have stressed the need for a consistent method and the insufficiency of most alternatives put forward. Moreover, we argue that the main concern in the sustainability debate can be integrated in the CBA framework. The past practice of overlooking environmental effects, applying too high discount rates and giving the same weight to income changes for all groups is *not* in line with basic economic principles. We believe a strategy where one points to the faults of the practice, rather than misdirecting the critique to the underlying theory, has much better chances of success.

NOTES

1. We would like to thank our colleague Odd-Helge Fjeldstad, who worked with us on the report on which this chapter is based. Richard Moorsom, Arne Wiig and M Asaduzzaman made constructive comments on draft versions of the original paper. The usual disclaimer applies. Funding for the project was provided by the Norwegian Research Council.
2. See, for example, Redclift (1987) and Booth (1994) for comparisons of these views.
3. See Hannesson (1993) for a discussion of this point with regard to fisheries management.
4. See Angelsen *et al.* (1994) for a discussion. Lind (1982) gives a comprehensive treatment of these issues based on neoclassical economic theory.
5. The methodology on social CBA (SCBA) for developing countries was developed by Dasgupta *et al.* (1972), Little and Mirrlees (1969, 1974) and Squire and van der Tak (1975). Ray (1984) gives a very good overview of the theoretical foundations of SCBA. Noteworthy presentations of the method also include ODA (1988) and Brent (1990).
6. Table 2.1 draws partly on Bojö *et al.* (1990).
7. See any standard texts on CBA for a further discussion.
8. A complete derivation of such weights is given in the major texts on SCBA; see note 5 above.
9. This would be true if the benefits and environmental costs remained constant over time. If we have increasing environmental costs relative to the benefits, it turns out that raising the discount rate increases the NPV for low levels of the discount rate and reduces the NPV for high levels. See Angelsen (1991, p. 8) and Porter (1982) for details.
10. See Angelsen (1991, ch. 3) for an elaboration of the effect of changing discount rates. Porter (1982) gives a clear presentation of the analysis of projects like hydropower, whereas Farzin (1985) and Stollery (1990) discuss the ambiguous effect of a lower discount rate on resource extraction.
11. Again, Angelsen *et al.* (1994) and most SCBA texts will provide the details.
12. The following exchange between Little and Mirrlees, the authors of the standard *Project Appraisal and Planning for Developing Countries*, illustrates the pragmatic considerations underlying the choice of discount rates. Little explained: 'I said to Professor Mirrlees that we should find a way of producing an interest rate that the World Bank would believe.

They always want 10 per cent or more, and most economists have been talking in terms of a social discount rate of more like 4 or 5 per cent. The World Bank would not find that credible. So the answer was to change the numéraire' (quoted in Berlage and Renard, 1985, p. 691). Little and Mirrlees (1974) and Squire and van der Tak (1975) use uncommitted foreign exchange in the hands of governments as the numéraire in their analysis, not consumption (at the average level), as Dasgupta *et al.* (1972) and others do. In principle, the choice of numéraire should not affect the result of the CBA. In practice, however, it may do because the underlying assumptions often change when the numéraire is changed. See Berlage and Renard (1985) and Brent (1990) for a discussion.

REFERENCES

Angelsen, A. (1991) *Cost-Benefit Analysis, Discounting and the Environmental Critique: Overloading of the Discount Rate?*, Report 1991, 5, Bergen: Chr. Michelsen Institute.

Angelsen, A., Fjeldstad, O.H. and Sumaila, U.R. (1994) *Project Appraisal and Sustainability in Less Developed Countries*, Report 1994, 1, Bergen: Chr. Michelsen Institute.

Baumol, W.J. (1968) 'On the Social Rate of Discount', *American Economic Review*, **58**, (4), September, 788–802.

Berlage, L. and Renard, R. (1985) 'The Discount Rate in Cost–Benefit Analysis and the Choice of Numéraire', *Oxford Economic Papers*, **37**, (4), 691–9.

Bisset, R. (1987) 'Methods for Environmental Impact Assessment: A Selected Survey with Case Studies', in A.K. Biswas and Qu Geping (eds), *Environmental Impact Assessment for Developing Countries*, London: Tycooly International (for UNU).

Biswas, A.K. and Geping, Qu (1987) *Environmental Impact Assessment for Developing Countries*, London: Tycooly International (for UNU).

Bojö, J., Mäler, K.G. and Unemo, L. (1990) *Environment and Development. An Economic Approach*, London: Kluwer Academic Publishers.

Booth, D.E. (1994) 'Ethics and the Limits of Environmental Economics', *Ecological Economics*, **9**, (3), April, 241–52.

Bradford, D.F. (1975) 'Constraints on Government Investment Opportunities and the Choice of Discount Rate', *American Economic Review*, **65**, (5), December, 887–99.

Brent, R.J. (1990) *Project Appraisal for Developing Countries*, New York: Harvester Wheatsheaf.

Buchholz, T.G. (1990) *New Ideas from Dead Economists. An Introduction to Modern Economic Thought*, New York: Penguin (Plume).

Clark, C. (1990) *Mathematic Bioeconomics*, 2nd edn, New York: John Wiley.

Cooper, C. (1981) *Economic Evaluation of the Environment*, London: Hodder & Stoughton.

Dasgupta, P., Marglin, S. and Sen, A. (1972) *Guidelines for Project Evaluation*, Project Formulation and Evaluation series, no. 2, New York: United Nations.

Drepper, F.R. and Månsson, B.Å. (1993) 'Intertemporal Valuation in an Unpredictable Environment', *Ecological Economics*, **7**, (1), February, 43–67.

Farzin, Y.H. (1985) 'The Effect of the Discount Rate on Depletion of Exhaustible Resources', *Journal of Political Economy*, **92**, (5), 841–51.

Hanley, N. (1992) 'Are There Environmental Limits to Cost Benefit Analysis?', *Environmental and Resource Economics*, **2**, 33–59.

Hannesson, R. (1993) *Bioeconomic Analysis of Fisheries*, London: Fishing New Books.

Harberger, A.C. (1971) 'Three Basic Postulates for Applied Welfare Economics: An Interpretive Essay', *Journal of Economic Literature,* **9**, September, 785–97.

Hartwick, J.M. (1977) 'Inter-Generational Equity and the Investing of Rents from Exhaustible Resources', *American Economic Review,* **67**, (5), 972–4.

Leopold, L. (1971) *A Procedure for Evaluating Environmental Impact*, US Geological Survey Circular 645, Washington, DC: US Geological Survey.

Lind, R. (1982) 'A Primer on the Major Issues Relating to the Discount Rate for Evaluating National Energy Options', in R. Lind (ed.), *Discounting for Time and Risk in Energy Policy*, Baltimore and London: Johns Hopkins University Press (for Resources for the Future).

Little, I.M.D. and Mirrlees, J.A. (1969) *Manual of Industrial Project Analysis, vol. II*, Paris: OECD Development Centre.

Little, I.M.D. and Mirrlees, J.A. (1974) *Project Appraisal and Planning for Developing Countries*, New York: Basic Books.

Little, I.M.D. and Mirrlees, J.A. (1991) 'Project Appraisal and Planning Twenty Years on', *Proceedings of the World Bank Annual Conference on Development Economics 1990*, supplement to the *World Bank Economic Review* and the *World Bank Research Observer*, 351–82.

Mähler, K.G. (1990) 'Sustainable Development', in *Sustainable Development, Science and Policy*, Oslo: Norwegian Research Council (NAVF).

Markandya, A. and Pearce, D. (1988) *Environmental Considerations and the Choice of the Discount Rate in Developing Countries*, Environmental Department Working Paper No. 3, Washington, DC: World Bank.

Overseas Development Administration (ODA) (1988) *Appraisal of Projects in Developing Countries. A Guide for Economists*, 3rd edn, London: HMSO.

Pearce, D. (1993) *Economic Values and the Natural World*, London: Earthscan.

Pearce, D. and Nash, C. (1981) *The Social Appraisal of Projects. A Text in Cost–Benefit Analysis*, London: Macmillan.

Pearce, D.W., Barbier, E.B. and Markandya, A. (1990) *Sustainable Development: Economics and Environment in the Third World*, Aldershot: Edward Elgar.

Porter, R.C. (1982) 'The New Approach to Wilderness Preservation through Benefit–Cost Analysis', *Journal of Environmental Economics and Management*, **9**, 59–80.

Ray, A. (1984) *Cost–Benefit Analysis. Issues and Methodologies*, Baltimore and London: Johns Hopkins University Press (for World Bank).

Redclift, M. (1987) *Sustainable Development: Exploring the Contradictions*, London: Methuen.

Ruttan, V. (1994) 'Constraints on the Design of Sustainable Systems of Agricultural Production', *Ecological Economics*, **10**, (3), August, 209–19.

Schulze, P.C. (1994) 'Cost–benefit Analyses and Environmental Policy', *Ecological Economics*, **9**, (3), April, 197–9.

Sen, A.K. (1961) 'On Optimising the Rate of Saving', *Economic Journal*, **71**, (283), September, 479–95.

Sen, A.K. (1982) 'Approaches to the Choice of Discount Rates for Social Benefit–Cost Analysis', in R. Lind (ed.), *Discounting for Time and Risk in Energy Policy*, Baltimore: Johns Hopkins University Press (for Resources for the Future).

Solow, R. (1993) 'Sustainability: An Economist's Perspective', in R. Dorfman and N.S. Dorfman (eds), *Economics of the Environment. Selected Readings*, 3rd edn, New York and London: Norton.

Squire, L. and van der Tak, H.G. (1975) *Economic Analysis of Projects*, Baltimore: Johns Hopkins University Press (for the World Bank).

Stollery, K.R. (1990) 'The Discount Rate and Resource Extraction', *Resources Policy*, March, 47–55.

Strotz, R. (1955/6) 'Myopia and Inconsistency in Dynamic Utility Maximation', *Review of Economic Studies*, **23**, (4), 165–80.

Therivel, R. *et al.* (1992) *Strategic Environmental Assessment*, London: Earthscan.

Tietenberg, T.H. (1984) *Environmental and Natural Resource Economics*, Glenview, Ill.: Scott, Foresman & Co.

van Pelt, M.J.F. (1993) 'Ecologically Sustainable Development and Project Appraisal in Developing Countries', *Ecological Economics*, **7**, (1), February, 19–42.

van Pelt, M.J.F, Kuyvenhoven, A. and Nijkamp, P. (1990) 'Project Appraisal and Sustainability: Methodological Challenges', *Project Appraisal*, **5**, (3), 139–58.

Veeman, T.S. (1989) 'Sustainable Development: Its Economic Meaning and Policy Implications', *Canadian Journal of Agricultural Economics*, **37**, (4), December, 875–86.

von Amsberg, J. (1993) *Project Evaluation and the Depletion of Natural Capital: An Application of the Sustainability Principle*, Environment Working Paper no. 56, Washington, DC: World Bank.

Winpenny, J.T. (1991a) *Values for the Environment. A Guide to Economic Appraisal*, London: HMSO.

Winpenny, J.T. (1991b) 'Environmental Values and Their Implication for Development', *Development Policy Review*, **9**, (4), 381–90.

World Bank (1992) *World Development Report 1992: Development and the Environment*, London and New York: Oxford University Press.

World Commission on Environment and Development (WCED) (1987) *Our Common Future*, Oxford: Oxford University Press.

3. Valuing environmental change: the contingent valuation method and project planning

Dominic Moran

INTRODUCTION

Increasing emphasis on the environmental impacts of projects and the issue of sustainability in general has increased scrutiny of methods which aim to price the environment. Of the methods currently available, the contingent valuation (CV) method is indisputably the most flexible in terms both of the categories of value determined (direct use plus option and existence/passive use values) and of the range of subject goods to which the method can in theory be applied. In bringing non-market costs and benefits into the equation, the development of CV techniques is of direct relevance to project planners preoccupied by the efficiency costs of market failure and the apparent arbitrary nature of environmental impact assessment. Moreover the issue of sustainability – articulated in economic terms as the requirement of non-declining intertemporal welfare – can also be directly addressed, applying the method to goods where elements of existence and other non-use values are thought to be significant.

But the evolution of CV has been somewhat haphazard and there is uncertainty as to how well current methodology translates into developing country contexts. More fundamentally, there is a sense in which the popularity of the technique, in particular the widely held view that anything can be valued, has in fact opened up a Pandora's Box of imminent problems for governments, environmental agencies, project planners and CV practitioners (see Portney, 1994). On the one hand, there is general recognition of the potential advantages for project planning in the possibility of direct enquiry about welfare change. On the other hand, there is growing disquiet over the bounds of survey-based valuation and the efficiency costs arising from imprecise or ill-defined preferences for a whole group of complex or remote goods (in the sense of being difficult to explain or remote from a respondent's transactional experience). Such concerns have given rise to the predictable view in some circles of CV responses representing 'cheap talk' or 'funny money', uncorroborated by real economic commitments.

THE CONTINGENT VALUATION METHOD

The application and sophistication of CV techniques in natural resource valuation has grown considerably in recent years. Carson *et al.* (1994) cite over 1500 applications, ranging from the value of duck hunting permits (Bishop and Heberlein, 1979) to the valuation of non-environmental policies or programmes such as reduced risk of death from respiratory disease (Krupnick and Cropper, 1992). An increasing number of applications in developing countries give cause for optimism that a suitably modified variant may be appropriate in other sociocultural contexts. But the majority of these have been limited to the valuation of direct uses[1] to determine the feasibility of cost recovery in water and sanitation provision. As such, they are simply used to corroborate observed behaviour such as time spent in drawing water from alternative sources and household infrastructural investments.

The major advantage of the technique (over other valuation methods) is that it can be employed to measure non-use values. In other words, the respondent does not have to be a user of the resource in question to provide a valid response to a hypothetical change. The general survey methodology constructs a hypothetical market in which sample respondents reveal their willingness to pay (WTP) to avoid, or willingness to accept (WTA) compensation contingent on a quantitative or qualitative change in the resource of interest. Choice between WTP and WTA questions (the equivalent and compensating surplus) is normally determined by property rights over the resource, but empirical evidence of divergence between the two measures has led many practitioners to recommend a WTP format even if this is theoretically inconsistent with the Pareto principle. Elicited responses are theoretically equivalent to a measure of Hicksian consumer surplus, a theoretically more exact measure than the Marshallian equivalent derived from indirect measures such as travel cost method (see Freeman, 1993). Recent debate concerning the validity of the approach has concentrated on eliminating potential respondent biases (Mitchell and Carson, 1989), respondent cognitive processes (Schkade and Payne, 1994) and choice of elicitation format (Kriström, 1993). Open-ended and dichotomous choice formats have commonly been used. In both cases respondents are presented with a description of the good in question, a market through which its qualitative or quantitative provision might be transacted, followed by a hypothetical change scenario. The open-ended format then prompts respondents to freely state their WTP to avoid the change, while a dichotomous choice approach offers respondents a prespecified sum which they are free to accept or reject. In a bid to increase the statistical power of the dichotomous choice format, more sophisticated designs often follow up initial acceptances (refusals) with amounts which are double the initial bid levels. Issues of design, estimation and the relative merits of single versus double, or even '*n*' bounded dichotomous choice are covered in Hanemann *et al.* (1991).

Empirical research favouring the dichotomous choice approach has emphasized its incentive compatibility (Arrow *et al.*, 1993). In other words, the approach closely approximates a routine market transaction or referendum familiar to respondents and minimizes any incentive strategically to overstate or understate WTP. Both formats involve the calculation of an aggregate welfare measure of surplus derived by multiplying a derived measure of central tendency (mean or median) over a relevant user and/or non-user population. Computationally, this tends to be easier with open-ended responses for which an arithmetic calculation is sufficient. Dichotomous choice responses, on the other hand, are more complex, analysis typically requiring the use of qualitative choice models relating 'yes' or 'no' responses to offer amounts and the computation of an expected mean (Bishop and Heberlein, 1979; Loomis, 1988). Investigators commonly test construct validity of both methods by regression techniques, relating WTP (or probability of a bid acceptance or rejection) responses to relevant socioeconomic and policy-relevant variables.

CV EVOLUTION AND BEST PRACTICE PROCEDURE

Blamey and Common (1993) identify three likely uses for information arising from CV surveys: as an input to cost–benefit analysis, as an input in damage litigation processes and as surrogate referenda. Of the three, litigation has arguably been the catalyst for recent methodological developments, with the whole validity debate influenced by high-profile cases such as the US Department of the Interior versus the state of Ohio and more controversial suits brought by the state of Alaska and the federal government against the Exxon oil company for passive use damages in the wake of the *Valdez* disaster in 1989.[2] High stakes riding on these cases have polarized the debate which is almost entirely concerned with the validity of the approach in a North American context, and the legal admissibility of existence values and the industrial implications for future liabilities and efficiency costs of compliance. In 1993, the dispute culminated in the pronouncement by the National Oceanic and Atmospheric Administration (NOAA) expert panel on suitable protocol for conducting CV (see appendix) which has, rightly or wrongly, been adopted as a point of reference for most subsequent CV applications in the USA and abroad. CV proponents felt vindicated by the qualified endorsement of the method, but the arguments have not stopped.

While this apparently exclusively US affair does not invalidate the use of the emerging 'best practice' elsewhere, in the USA the (lucrative) 'pro' or 'anti' stance of many respected practitioners has been sufficient to stifle open debate on the general applicability of the method in other contexts. This has not dampened the popularity of the technique and applications continue unabated in most OECD countries outside the USA (in the UK, for example, there are well over 50 recorded applications), but in countries where passive damages are not given legal presumption or play an uncertain role in standard cost–benefit procedures, much less attention has been paid to appropriate methodological refinements.[3] Furthermore, much of the CV debate has been outside economics, and it is important to note that many practitioners have been slow to acknowledge, let alone embrace, the contribution of disciplines more attuned to survey research, cognition and processes of value formation. As a result, the science of survey design including the rigorous use of focus groups, content analysis and verbal protocols ('think aloud' analysis) has often been weakly addressed in the process.

Meanwhile, with respect to developing country applications, still fewer (if any) practitioners have been interested in bridging the gap between CV and existing lines of enquiry, such as participatory rural appraisal, which have relied on direct interview and related forms of contingent ranking. In its current guise (for better or worse), CV practice has found its way into the theory and practice of several multilateral agencies such as the World Bank and the Inter-American Development Bank who have access to some of the best, but not necessarily most culturally sensitized practitioners. Such institutions typically want rapid appraisal tools and it is of interest to observe how the drawn-out CV method (which can sometimes require months) can be reconciled with typical project time frames.

PROBLEMS IN CV APPLICATION

Litigation has in some sense soured the debate, but one result is that there are literally volumes of critiques (constructive and destructive, reasonable and unreasonable)[4] of CV practice. While most concentrate on a particular bias,[5] it is pertinent here to refer to two: one fundamental, the scenario problem, and one slightly more esoteric, the statistical derivation of a mean or median willingness to pay value.

The scenario and elicitation problems concern whether or not elicited responses are an accurate representation of consumer surplus corresponding to the change the questioner intends, and not to some sub-set or multiple of the same good. Such embedding or scoping problems are commonplace when scenario descriptions are insufficient and respondents make default assumptions unrelated to the change of interest, or where they are simply not reminded of their budget constraints. Embedding and scoping have been routinely identified by split sample testing, varying the dimensional attributes of the subject good. Insensitivity to scope has been identified as one of the principal invalidating criteria in assessing survey design (see Arrow *et al.*, 1993) and exhaustive scenario testing is recommended.

Incomplete information may also increase existing cognitive difficulties in valuing some categories of goods. Such cognition problems present the more fundamental question of whether preferences are well defined for certain goods, and the related issue of 'admissible motives' in the process of utilitarian value formation. For example, is sympathy an economic value, and what does it mean to say that the 'warm glows' experienced in charitable giving should be disqualified as a manifestation of preferences? There is always some rate of refusal or protest in surveys and one of the difficulties inherent in standard CV approaches is that the investigator must determine whether this results from the respondent having a true zero value or a rejection of the property right implicit in the question format, the credibility of the payment vehicle (the way the good will be paid for) or is the result of inherently non-convex preferences (lexicographic or non-compensatory preferences) for the good in question. In the last case, the limits of CV are truly reached. There are also inevitable cognitive problems in assuming that use and non-use values are conveniently bundled into well-behaved preference ordering in a systematic way, and that the corresponding consumer surplus can be aggregated over the affected population.

The apparently erroneous commoditization of any type of complex good has been most cogently articulated by Vatn and Bromley (1994), who have questioned the validity of valuing anything beyond that with which the respondent has some familiarity. In other words, the use of CV is in question precisely where it is most needed. Increased suspicion also arises from the fact that the vast majority of stated preference surveys are normally not validated by real or experimental evidence. As a result, there is essentially no foolproof way of knowing about the extent of scenario misrepresentation or misinterpretation, but instead a whole area of research on the issue is providing a bridge between economic and other social sciences that may yet lead to an improved theory of preference and choice and possibly alternative consensus and value formation.

The statistical design problem is illustrative of the dichotomy in CV research, for, irrespective of whether the theoretical foundations are stable, a thriving industry has developed around the statistical procedures necessary to analyse data generated by the discrete choice question format. Dichotomous choice models have a longer history in biometrics, engineering and product reliability testing (survival and hazard models) and other areas of economics such as labour and transport (quantal choice and interval censored data). All such models relate a qualitative response (in/out, working/not working, dead/ alive) to a stimulus variable (labour market participation, testing intervals, chemical dose). In CV, such models relate individual binary (1 = yes, 0 = no) willingness to pay responses to the pre-assigned £x amounts and other covariates through the medium of (typically) logit or probit models which combine an assumed distribution for the unobservable random element of the choice and a particular functional form for the link function (see Freeman, 1993). In essence, the choice translates the bid amounts into the probability of acceptance space and allows the computation of an expected mean or a median. Numerous complex issues have arisen in refining the estimation, such as the choice of the distributional and functional forms for the analysis,[6] optimal design of the presented bid vector, treatment of outliers and truncation of the bid range, the choice between the mean and median, problems in asking follow-up questions, and the relative merits of parametric versus nonparametric estimation. The whole area requires a certain level of statistical competence, although fortunately a few algorithms are now available to simplify the task for standard functional forms.[7]

ILLUSTRATIVE CASE STUDIES

Since developing countries represent the next frontier of CV research, the following cases offer a brief illustration of recent applications. A more complete overview of environmental valuation in developing countries can be found in Pearce *et al.* (1994).

Willingness to Pay for Tsetse Fly Control in Ethiopia (Swallow and Woudyalew, 1994)

In sub-Saharan Africa parasitic trypanosomiasis transmitted by the tsetse fly can often result in enormous costs in terms of the impacts on human health and animal productivity. Bated cloth targets had been positively tested for use in tsetse control in the study area, but equipment theft during trials meant that a targeted programme required further local involvement for successful public provision.

With the aid of key informants, livestock-owning and non-owning respondent households were identified and asked about their willingness to contribute to unit provision. Households were asked to contribute in terms of money or labour time, and 59 per cent of 859 households volunteered both money and labour, with an average willingness to contribute labour of 2.2 days per month or 2.1 Birr (5 Birr = US$ 1) in the project's first year. Familiarity with the good on offer (services of the International Livestock Centre for Africa) was an important variable to explain willingness to pay, but the absence of any apparent trade-off between time and money contributions gives some cause for concern. The authors correctly point out that the CV approach is useful for gauging support for public good provision and for setting bounds on payment methods, but that it is less appropriate for evaluating the total benefits of control because of WTP being bounded by income. The authors suggest that the method should be supplemented by more intensive studies of the productivity impacts of the parasite and stress the potential import of less intrusive participatory rural appraisal (PRA) methods.

The Economic Benefits of Surface Water Quality Improvements in Developing Countries: a Case study of Davao, Philippines (Choe *et al.*, 1994)

Is environmental improvement a luxury or a necessary condition for economic development? This study examines the willingness to pay for a seemingly non-vital environmental gain in bathing water quality of a sample of 777 randomly selected households. The scenario was based on a real event involving the closure of an urban beach in Davao as a result of potentially dangerous pollution. Respondents were asked about their willingness to pay to prevent the loss of future recreational possibilities using a surcharge on domestic water charges presented in a double-bounded referendum format followed by an open-ended WTP question. The resulting values indicate that water quality does not appear to be of high value to residents of Davao, giving credence to the argument for development first. The authors are of the opinion that more needs to be done to determine the transition of the income elasticity of demand for environmental improvement, as this has implications for the efficiency of collective provision. The econometric analysis of responses to the CV format is illustrative of the somewhat bewildering array of techniques that may be employed.

Cost and Compensation Issues in Protecting Tropical Rainforests: Case Study of Madagascar (Kramer *et al.*, 1994)

Protected area designation is rarely costless, particularly when restricted areas have historically been traditional common property resources. In such cases there may be pronounced welfare effects arising from the opportunity cost of park resources. This study attempts to forecast land use in the absence of the park and to predict opportunity costs of designation on the basis of current practices and returns. As part of this exercise a study of local household socioeconomic characteristics included a contingent valuation exercise to throw some light on a range of non-marketed products and to see if CV is appropriate alongside non-monetary exchange. The study represents a bold attempt to use CV in a developing country and is sensitive to local sociocultural differences. First, because of local poaching problems, respondents were more sensitive to the coercive implications of a willingness to pay question format. As a result, a willingness to accept question in a dichotomous choice format was considered more appropriate. Second, recognizing the limited use of money, a novel addition to the methodology was the use of an alternative numéraire (rice) to measure preferences. The annual household willingness to pay was determined to be $108.34 per year, which differs significantly from the $91 per year opportunity cost determined from land use forecasting. The authors do not specify whether the two sums should be additive to give total use (marketed and non-marketed value).

IMPLICATIONS FOR PROJECT APPRAISAL

CV methods are likely to grow in importance for project appraisal and, within the expanding literature, practitioners can find applications relevant to the assessment of a variety of external effects. Currently, there is some debate over the need to conduct a full-blown CV study in each and every case. In the first instance, a considerable amount of time, money and controversy can probably be saved by assessing the potential for using alternative market-based valuation methods such as the travel cost method or hedonic pricing (see Johansson, 1990).[9] Secondly, the existence of a diversity of studies may mean that unit values can be borrowed where the conditions between two projects are suitably similar. Clearly, there are potential cost advantages to the practice of benefits transfer (see Brookshire and Neill, 1992; Krupnick, 1993). The area is itself an exciting new (though not uncontroversial) research focus with several environmental agencies contemplating the development of off-the-shelf values libraries.

In extending CV practices to the developing world, the only new questions relate to the suitability of the methodology to alternative cultural contexts and the problems inherent in alternative institutional structures, suspicion of authority and property right rejection, or a suitable payment vehicle. The extent to which the method may be simplified and combined with existing rapid and participatory appraisal methods to deal with these issues is a potential avenue for further research. Similarly, the extension of CV to the largely uncharted area represented by the provision of global public goods, especially as the basis for determining global environmental transfers, is yet another challenge for CV researchers. But the credibility of such studies largely depends on the provision of definitive answers to several methodological problems distinctly closer to home.

NOTES

1. Thereby avoiding the difficulties of non-use valuation encountered with complex and unfamiliar goods.
2. Under the terms of the Comprehensive Environmental Response, Compensation and Liability Act of 1980 (also known as CERCLA or Superfund), US government agencies may sue for damages to resources of which they are trustees. Regulations on compensable damages originally issued by the Department of the Interior were on several occasions challenged in the courts.
3. For example, the NOAA panel recommendations suggest asking about a respondent's willingness to pay as a referendum question. Experience of voting on complex issues involving tax deductions is common in many US states, but may be less appropriate elsewhere.
4. See Hanemann (1994) and Diamond and Hausman (1994) for opposing but balanced assessments.
5. See Mitchell and Carson (1989, p. 236) for a typology of respondent biases.
6. The issue of the appropriate functional form of the analysis is particularly salient for consistency of selected models with neoclassical demand theory (see Hanemann, 1984, 1989).
7. It should be noted that there is essentially no consensus on how to analyse discrete choice data, which in itself is problematic and one reason for preferring the open-ended format in spite of the 'cognitive load' problems of requiring freely stated WTP values.
8. In contrast to CV, such methods are at least associated with some observable market behaviour.

APPENDIX: GUIDELINES FOR CONDUCTING CONTINGENT VALUATION STUDIES

The following guidelines are adapted from the report of the National Oceanic and Atmospheric Administration Panel on the contingent valuation method (Arrow *et al.*, 1993). The NOAA panel's pronouncement including the input of Nobel economists Arrow and Solow came in the wake of bitter and protracted legal and academic dispute over the existence and legal admissibility of passive use damages and the legitimacy of CV to measure them. A comprehensive review of the debate may be found in papers by Hanemann (1994) Portney (1994) and Diamond and Hausman (1994) in a recent issue of the *Journal of Economic Perspectives*.

General Guidelines

1. *Sample type and size*   Probability sampling is essential. The choice of sample-specific design and size is a difficult, technical question that requires the guidance of a professional sampling statistician.
2. *Minimize non-responses*   High non-response rates would make CV survey results unreliable.
3. *Personal interview*   It is unlikely that reliable estimates of values can be elicited with mail surveys. Face-to-face interviews are usually preferable, although telephone interviews have some advantages in terms of cost and centralized supervision.
4. *Pretesting for interviewer effects*   An important respect in which CV surveys differ from actual referenda is the presence of an interviewer (except in the case of mail surveys). It is possible that interviewers contribute to 'social desirability' bias, since preserving the environment is widely viewed as something positive. In order to test this possibility, major CV studies should incorporate experiments that assess interviewer effects.
5. *Reporting*   Every report of a CV study should make clear the definition of the population sampled, the sampling frame used, the sample size, the overall sample non-response rate and its components (such as refusals), and item non-response on all important questions. The report should also reproduce the exact wording and sequence of the questionnaire and of other communications to respondents (such as advance letters). All data from the study should be archived and made available to interested parties.
6. *Careful pretesting of a CV questionnaire*   Respondents in a CV survey are ordinarily presented with a good deal of new and often technical information, well beyond what is typical in most surveys. This requires very careful pilot work and pretesting, plus evidence from the final survey that respondents understood and accepted the description of the good or service offered and the questioning reasonably well.

Guidelines for Value Elicitation Surveys

7. *Conservative design*   When aspects of the survey design and the analysis of the responses are ambiguous, the option that tends to underestimate willingness to pay is generally preferred. A conservative design increases the reliability of the estimate by eliminating extreme responses that can enlarge estimated values wildly and implausibly.
8. *Elicitation format*   The willingness-to-pay format should be used in-

stead of compensation required because the former is the conservative choice.

9. *Referendum format*   The valuation question generally should be posed as a vote on a referendum.

10. *Accurate description of the programme or policy*   Adequate information must be provided to respondents about the environmental programme that is offered.

11. *Pretesting of photographs*   The effects of photographs on subjects must be carefully explored.

12. *Reminder of substitute commodities*   Respondents must be reminded of substitute commodities. This reminder should be introduced forcefully and directly prior to the main valuation to ensure that the respondents have the alternatives clearly in mind.

13. *Temporal averaging*   Time-dependent measurement noise should be reduced by averaging across independently drawn samples taken at different points in time. A clear and substantial time trend in the responses would cast doubt on the 'reliability' of the value information obtained from a CV survey.

14. *'No-answer' option*   A 'no-answer' option should be explicitly allowed in addition to the 'yes' and 'no' vote options on the main valuation (referendum) question. Respondents who choose the 'no-answer' option should be asked to explain their choice.

15. *Yes/no follow-ups*   'Yes' and 'no' responses should be followed up by the open-ended question: 'Why did you vote yes/no?'

16. *Cross-tabulations*   The survey should include a variety of other questions that help interpret the responses to the primary valuation question. The final report should include summaries of willingness to pay broken down by these categories (such as income, education, attitudes toward the environment).

17. *Checks on understanding and acceptance*   The survey instrument should not be so complex that it poses tasks that are beyond the ability or interest level of many participants.

REFERENCES

Arrow, K., Solow, R., Portney, P., Leamer, E., Radner, R. and Schuman, H. (1993) *Report to the National Oceanic and Atmospheric Administration Panel on Contingent Valuation*, Washington, DC: NOAA.

Bishop, R.C. and Heberlein, T.A. (1979) 'Measuring values of extra-market goods: Are indirect measures biased?', *American Journal of Agricultural Economics*, **61**, 926–30.

Blamey, R. and Common, M. (1993) *Stepping back from contingent valuation*, Canberra: Centre for Resource and Environmental Studies, Australian National University.

Brookshire, D.S. and Neill, H.R. (1992) 'Benefit Transfers: Conceptual and Empirical Issues', *Water Resources Research*, **28**, (3), 651–5.

Carson, R.T., Conway, A., Alberini, A., Flores, N., Riggs, K., Vencil, J. and Winsen, A. (1994) *A Bibliography of Contingent Valuation Studies and Papers*, La Jolla, Cal.: Natural Resource Damage Assessment Inc.

Chambers, R. (1992) *Rural Appraisal: Rapid, Relaxed and Participatory*, Discussion Paper 311, Institute of Development Studies, Sussex.

Choe, K., Whittington, D. and Lauria, D. (1994) *The economic benefits of surface water quality improvements in developing countries: A case study of Davao, Philippines*, Washington, DC: World Bank, Environment Department.

Diamond, P.A. and Hausman, J. (1994) 'Contingent valuation: Is some number better than no number?', *Journal of Economic Perspectives*, **8**, (4), 45–64.

Freeman, M.A.I. (1993) *The Measurement of Environmental and Resource Values: Theory and Methods*, Washington, DC: Resources For the Future.

Hanemann, M. (1984) 'Welfare Evaluations in Contingent Valuation: Experiments with Discrete Responses', *American Journal of Agricultural Economics*, **66**, (3), 332–41.

Hanemann, M. (1994) 'Valuing the environment through contingent valuation', *Journal of Economic Perspectives*, **8**, (4), 19–43.

Hanemann, W.M., Loomis, J. and Kanninen, B. (1991) 'Statistical Efficiency of Double-Bounded Dichotomous Choice Contingent Valuation', *American Journal of Agricultural Economics*, **73**, 1255–63.

Johansson, P-O. (1990) 'Valuing environmental damage', *Oxford Review of Economic Policy*, **6**, (1), 34–50.

Kramer, R., Sharma, N., Shyamsundar, P. and Munasinghe, M. (1994) *Cost and Compensation Issues in Protecting Tropical Rainforests: A Case Study in Madagascar*, Environment Working Paper 62, Washington, DC: World Bank.

Kriström, B. (1993) 'Comparing Continuous and Discrete Contingent Valuation Questions', *Environment and Resource Economics*, **3**, (1), 63–71.

Krupnick, A.J. (1993) 'Benefit Transfers and Valuation of Environmental Improvements', *Resources*, No.110, Washington, DC: Resources for the Future.

Krupnick, A.J. and Cropper, M. (1992) 'The Effect of Information on Health Risk Valuation', *Journal of Risk and Uncertainty*, **2**, 29–48

Langford, I.H. and Bateman, I.J. (1993) 'Welfare Measures for Contingent Valuation Studies: Estimation and Reliability', *Global Environmental Change Working Paper Series 93–04*, Centre for Social and Economic Research on the Global Environment, University College London and University of East Anglia.

Loomis, J.B. (1988) 'Contingent Valuation Using Dichotomous Choice Models', *Journal of Leisure Research*, **20**, (1), 46–56.

Mitchell, R.C. and Carson, R.T. (1989) *Using Surveys to Value Public Goods: The Contingent Valuation Method*, Washington, DC: Resources for the Future.

Mitchell, R.C. and Carson, R.T. (1993) *Current issues in the design, administration and analysis of contingent valuation surveys*, Discussion Paper 93-54, Department of Economics, U.C. San Diego.

Moran, D. (1994) 'Contingent valuation and biodiversity: measuring the user surplus of Kenyan protected areas', *Biodiversity and Conservation*, **3**, 663–84.

Pearce, D.W., Whittington, D., Georgiou, S. and Moran, D. (1994) *Economic values and the environment in the developing world*, Nairobi: UNEP.

Portney, P. (1994) 'The contingent valuation debate: Why economists should care', *Journal of Economic Perspectives*, **8**, (4), 3–17.

Schkade, D. and Payne, J.W. (1994) 'How People Respond to Contingent Valuation Questions: A Verbal Protocol Analysis of Willingness to Pay for an Environmental Regulation', *Journal of Environmental Economics and Management*, **26**, 88–109.

Swallow, B.M. and Woudyalew, M. (1994) 'Evaluating willingness to contribute to a local public good: application of contingent valuation to tsetse control in Ethiopia', *Ecological Economics*, **11**, (2), 153–61.

Vatn, A. and Bromley, D.W. (1994) 'Choices without Prices without Apologies', *Journal of Environmental Economics and Management*, **26**, 129–48.

4. Market liberalization and environmental assessment

Colin Kirkpatrick and Norman Lee

INTRODUCTION

There is widespread (nominal) acceptance by governments that the development process should take environmental considerations into account – hence the large number of governments which have, since Rio, 'signed up' for sustainable development. However, the precise means by which environmental considerations are to be integrated within development policies and practices is often unclear.

This chapter explores one aspect of this broad topic in a preliminary way. This is the relationship, in developing countries (LDCs) and countries in transition (CITs), between *market liberalization measures*, proposed to promote development through more efficient resource utilization, and *environmental assessment provisions*, proposed to promote sustainability through the more systematic integration of environmental considerations within the development planning and implementation process. We focus particularly upon two issues: what are the environmental impacts of market liberalization and how should these be addressed; and what are the implications of market

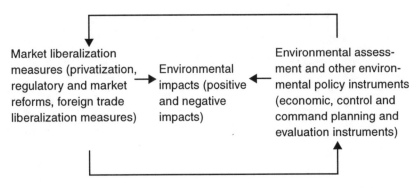

Figure 4.1   Market liberalization and environmental assessment linkages

liberalization for the effectiveness of environmental assessment (EA) policy instruments? Figure 4.1 illustrates the linkages examined in this chapter.

Both issues have received relatively little attention in the research literature and official governmental studies until very recently. Increasingly, during the 1990s, a number of major international bodies have begun to examine market liberalization–environmental quality linkages; these include the World Bank and the International Monetary Fund, United Nations Conference on Trade and Development (UNCTAD) and United Nations Economic Commission for Europe (UNECE), Organization for Economic Cooperation and Development (OECD), European Bank for Reconstruction and Development (EBRD) and certain NGOs such as the Worldwide Fund for Nature (WWF) and International Institute for Environment and Development (IIED) (Munasinghe and Cruz, 1995; ECE/UNEP, 1994; EBRD, 1994a; Reed, 1992; Anderson and Blackhurst, 1992; OECD, 1994a). Nevertheless, the number of completed studies is still relatively small and a number of important empirical and policy questions remain unresolved. In the case of market liberalization–environmental policy (EA) linkages, the topic remains largely unexplored, despite the rapid extension of EA practice since the late 1980s (World Bank, 1994).

THE SCOPE OF MARKET LIBERALIZATION MEASURES

Market liberalization policies and programmes contain a heterogeneous and varied collection of measures whose overall objective is to promote economic growth and development through the more efficient use of resources. This is to be achieved by expanding the role of the private sector and approximating as closely as possible to conditions prevailing in competitive markets.

A variety of domestic market liberalization measures have been promoted in both LDCs and CITs since the late 1970s, often with strong encouragement from the international financial institutions and aid agencies (notably IMF, World Bank and EBRD), who have made financial assistance to these countries, in part at least, conditional upon these measures (and macroeconomic stabilization measures) being adopted. In the case of LDCs, this policy-based conditionality has often been applied through structural adjustment programme lending, where the intention has been to remove various perceived distortions in market prices and incentives, and to ease the regulatory constraints on private sector development. In the CITs, policy-based conditionality has been oriented towards creating the institutional structures and stable macroeconomic environment within which private ownership can be expanded, through the privatization of state-owned assets.

Contemporaneously, there have been policy movements, affecting all types of economies, to liberalize foreign trade both on a regional basis and on an international basis (most notably through the Uruguay Round of the General Agreement on Tariffs and Trade – GATT). These market liberalization measures (combined, in certain cases, with macroeconomic stabilization measures) can be grouped into three broad categories and these are summarized below.

Correction of Domestic Market Disequilibria

The overall purpose of these measures is to correct 'distortions' in factor and product markets. Here, a 'distortion' refers to the deviation between actual prices and opportunity costs to the economy of the items concerned. This divergence can result from 'inappropriate' policy interventions, or from market imperfections; market liberalization measures, however, are, in general, concerned only with the former case (other sources of market imperfections may be assumed to be non-significant or to be corrected by additional but separate policy measures). Policy reforms are designed to create a more competitive domestic market environment through the removal of market interventions and controls. The distortionary impact of both tariff and non-tariff measures on the efficiency with which traded goods are produced has been studied extensively in LDCs, where many countries adopted a strategy of import-substituting industrialization behind high protective barriers. Trade liberalization measures are intended to correct these trade-related distortions in relative price incentives. Similarly, the distortions caused by intervention in separate factor markets – foreign exchange, labour and capital – have been identified as constraints of efficient resource allocation and use. Market controls (for example, price, output, sales controls and controls over market entry and exit) and regulatory burdens on enterprises (licensing and permitting procedures) have also been identified as sources of inefficient, rent-seeking activity and additional resource misallocation costs. The issue of regulatory burdens is particularly important in view of their potential significance in relation to the effects of deregulation on EIA effectiveness.

Privatization of State-owned Enterprises

The term 'privatization' is used to describe a range of policy measures which share the common aim of reducing the state's control over the use of productive assets. These policy measures may initially take the form of a privatization policy, plan or programme covering many enterprises, but, in the most common usage of the term, the majority ownership of individual enterprises is transferred from the public to the private sector. The transfer of ownership can be effected in a variety of ways, including public flotation, private sale, management (and employee) buyout and voucher distribution. The method of privatization will, in turn, have implications for the ownership pattern. Is ownership spread over a large number of local small investors or is there a concentration of ownership, and to what extent is there foreign involvement?

Privatization has been a significant component of the structural adjustment lending (SAL) conditionality applied to LDCs, appearing, for example, in more than two-thirds of all World Bank SALs during the period 1981–91. The pace of privatization in LDCs has accelerated in recent years, with the developing countries' share of world privatization sales increased from less than 10 per cent in 1988 to 40 per cent in 1992 (Cook and Kirkpatrick, 1995a). In the CITs, privatization has been the main means of creating a private market economy. Much of the early privatization activity was concentrated on small-scale enterprises, often in the services sector, but in more recent years there has been a significant level of privatization of large-scale industrial enterprises (Cook and Kirkpatrick, 1995b).

The privatization that has occurred can be classified in a number of different ways: according to the level of aggregation of the privatization measures; according to the nature of the activities which are privatized; according to the scale of the activities which are privatized; according to the form which the privatization takes and the contractual basis upon which it proceeds; according to the extent of private sector development resulting from the changes in enterprise organizational and management practices subsequent to the change in ownership.

International Trade Liberalization

Essentially, this extends the market liberalization strategy to the level of international trade agreements, which include trade liberalization agreements (bilateral, regional or international); international commodity agreements (for example, for cocoa, coffee, lumber, wheat and non-ferrous metals); preferential trade agreements (such as preferential trade treatments for certain developing countries under the Lomé Convention); and bilateral trade agreements (for example, providing temporary protection to certain domestic industries facing strong foreign competition).

With the protracted negotiations over the Uruguay Round, and also the growing importance of the intraregional trade flows, the environmental impact of both multilateral and regional trade agreements has been discussed extensively in recent years (OECD, 1994a, 1994b; Anderson and Blackhurst, 1992).

ENVIRONMENTAL IMPACTS OF MARKET LIBERALIZATION MEASURES

The environmental impacts of market liberalization measures are extremely diverse for two main reasons: the diversity of market liberalization measures themselves and the diversity in the 'country contexts' in which these measures are applied, notably in those variables (such as definition and distribution of property rights, pre-existing environmental controls and their practical efficacy) which may exercise a more fundamental influence, in their own right, on the extent of environmental impacts and on the degree to which these are 'internalized' in decision making within the liberalized markets. In the cases of LDCs and CITs, the second set of factors is likely to be particularly great.

This diversity, both in the market liberalization measures themselves and in the country-specific conditions within which the measures are applied, may account, in part at least, for the limited information which currently exists on the basic questions with which this chapter is concerned: is market liberalization good for the environment or not; and, if not, what are the implications of market liberalization for the effectiveness of environmental assessment? The current literature which addresses this issue comprises a mixture of theoretical reasoning, indirect 'proof by association' evidence and various case studies.

Domestic Market Liberalization and Environmental Impact

Any change in the existing policy framework is likely to have some environmental consequences through the output and resource use effects that follow from changes in economic incentives, following market liberalization. Structural adjustment loans have not normally included specific conditions relating to environmental concerns. The environmental impact of structural adjustment lending, and policy reform lending more generally, has tended to be indirectly assessed, therefore, by identifying conditionality in areas where environmental effects are expected to be significant. The most recent review of environmental effects in adjustment lending simply identifies changes in agricultural output prices (producer prices and export tax adjustments), changes in agricultural input prices (input subsidy changes and reduction in import duties), energy sector policy measures, trade and industry sector reforms (import liberalization and export promotion) and institutional reforms as policy changes which are likely to have significant environmental effects. The frequency with which conditionality in these areas occurs is found to have increased over the period 1988–92, as compared to 1979–88 (Warford *et al.*, 1994).

The failure to conduct a direct environmental assessment of market liberalization reforms has been rationalized by the commentators on the grounds that the liberalization–environmental impact relationship is invariably a 'win–win' situation, a view which was strongly represented in the 1992 *World Development Report* on development and the Environment. A more recent statement of this position is provided by Warford *et al.* (1994): 'Even in the past, where there was limited concern over environment, the resulting neglect was not necessarily bad. On the contrary, good economics, particularly as it emphasises efficient use of resources, is often good for the environment too. There remain, due in large part to government policy failure, many opportunities for "no regrets" policies – i.e. those which satisfy both economic and environmental objectives' (pp. 14–15).

Case study evidence on the impact of market liberalization measures upon the environment is more mixed. Hansen (1990) reviewed almost one hundred World Bank and Asian Development Bank structural adjustment loans up to the late 1980s. His major findings are (a) the environmental impact of cuts in government spending depends on where and how the cuts are made; (b) measures to adjust agricultural input prices towards their economic costs tend to benefit the environment by reducing the use of polluting chemicals like fertilizer and reducing wasteful use of irrigation water; and (c) the environmental impacts of measures to increase output prices to farmers are mixed and depend to a large extent on the chosen cultivation practices and complementary actions.

The study by Munasinghe and Cruz (1995) uses a range of country case studies to identify the environmental impacts of economy-wide reforms. Specific findings of the study include (a) removal of price distortions, promotion of market incentives and relaxation of other constraints generally contribute to both economic and environmental gains; (b) unintended adverse side-effects occur when economy-wide reforms are undertaken while other neglected policy, market or institutional imperfections exist, although such undesirable impacts may be mitigated by new complementary measures that address the specific imperfections underlying the environmental problems; (c) macroeconomic stabilization measures will generally yield environmental benefits but may also have unforeseen adverse short-term impacts on the environment; and (d) economy-wide policy changes will have additional longer-term effects on the environment through employment and income distribution changes.

The case study evidence assembled by other studies, for example, WWF country studies undertaken in 1994, confirm (a) that structural adjustment programmes (SAPs) do have significant adverse environmental impacts where market and policy failures remain and (b) that the overall evidence available at present is fairly limited and conflicting.

Privatization and Environmental Impact

It is common in environmental economic theory to distinguish between two different forms of environmental impact: stocks and flows. Pollution stocks include hazardous waste and other deposits of contaminated materials which pose a potential or real threat to environmental quality or human health. In the privatization context, the issue of liability for environmental costs resulting from existing pollution stocks has been a major content for policy makers although its significance is mainly in terms of environmental auditing, rather than environmental assessment. Who will be responsible for environmental damage which arises after privatization, but is the result of pre-privatization activity (Goldenman, 1995)? The possibility of the new private owners becoming liable for environment damage caused by the earlier activity of the public enterprise has been seen as a major constraint to the inflow of foreign direct investment for privatization sales in the CITs (World Bank, 1994; Environment for Europe, 1994).

The effect of privatization on environmental flows is the relevant relationship for considering incremental environmental impact. Privatization may simply be a change of ownership, with the enterprise continuing to operate under private ownership in the same way as when it was in the public sector. In the earlier privatizations in most CITs, for example, enterprises were transferred to the existing management and workforce, and there was little change in operations, at least in the short run. In this case, the environmental impact of the ongoing operations is unchanged. The more likely outcome, however, will be a significant change in the activity level of the privatized enterprise. Consequently, there will be an incremental environmental flows impact.

As with market liberalization, the environmental impact may be positive or negative: the net effect will be determined by, inter alia, type of activity, degree of competition, existing regulatory requirements and technology choice. Privatization may produce positive environmental effects, such as increased efficiency in the use of national resources and more rapid adoption of cleaner technologies. Where privatization takes the form of liquidation of the enterprise, negative environmental flows may be terminated. The most significant potential negative environmental impacts of privatization are as follows (World Bank, 1994).

- *Stronger incentive to pollute or exhaust natural resources*: without an appropriate regulatory framework, privatization may increase a firm's incentive to maximize profits on existing activity levels, by avoiding the costs of reducing pollution or by overextraction of natural resources.

● *Regulatory relaxation or freeze*: less rigorous environmental standards may be imposed on private firms, whether locally or foreign owned. Or privatization may tend to freeze environmental standards and enforcement at the current level, thereby blocking further strengthening of the environmental regulatory framework.
● *Recapitalization effect*: privatization may revive or recapitalize an enterprise that would otherwise go out of business. It may also lead to an expansion of activity, resulting in intensified pollution flows.

In summary, in response to the basic question, is market liberalization good for the environment or not? – and at the risk of some simplification – we can distinguish three viewpoints: optimistic, pessimistic and pragmatic. The *optimistic* viewpoint is essentially based on two arguments:

1. Market liberalization has a number of consequences which will frequently, if not universally, lead to environmental improvements. For example, it is argued that the correction of price-related distortions (for example, by setting efficient prices for energy or water) and removing taxes or subsidies on particular commodities or factors of production will stimulate the more efficient use of resources (and economic development) and enhance environmental protection and natural resource conservation. Sometimes these improvements are documented; in most other cases the conclusions are derived through simplified analysis.
2. Where unfavourable environmental consequences do occur they are not due to the specific market liberalization measures themselves but to pre-existing sources of market failure (e.g. the absence of a clearly defined system of property rights, absence of satisfactory economic instruments for pollution control). This being so, the remedy does not lie in modifying the market liberalization measures but in ensuring that the other sources of market failure are addressed.

The *pessimistic* viewpoint is also based on two arguments:

1. A number of case studies, supplemented by more anecdotal evidence, are used to illustrate the negative environmental consequences which have followed the implementation of specific market liberalization measures (possibly accompanied by market stabilization measures) in particular countries. For example, where a price rise occurs (for instance, in one form of energy) it may reduce *its* consumption and environmental impacts but lead to substitution effects which are more environmentally damaging (for example, greater use of fuel wood, leading to deforestation, land erosion, river silting and flooding).

2. These increased environmental pressures occur particularly (but not exclusively) in poorer countries (both in LDCs and CITs) and are associated with (a) increased income inequalities (that is, market liberalization may increase the economy's overall growth rate but reduce the standard of living within the poorest section of society, whose response is to engage in environmentally damaging activities, particularly within the informal sector; and (b) changes in trade patterns such that (i) they become more dependent on natural resource abstraction and exporting, and (ii) there is growth of 'dirty' industries including toxic waste disposal. These are countries where property rights are not well-defined, environmental regulations are very weak or non-existent and institutions for regulation enforcement are very defective – and where there is no realistic short- or medium-term prospect of correcting these weaknesses.

The *pragmatic* viewpoint is based upon the following arguments:

1. While the theoretical analysis of the environmental effects of market liberalizing measures is relatively straightforward, where we can safely assume that they will lead to a situation in which all markets are populated by private entrepreneurs, approximate to perfectly competitive markets and environmental externalities are internalized, the analysis of liberalizing measures which move markets in that direction but stop well short of the ideal (and where shifts between public and private ownership occur) is much more complex. Here we have to face up to the uncertain environmental consequences of changes in enterprise objectives, all of the indeterminacies of imperfect markets and all the complexities of second-best solutions. This suggests that it may be more prudent to think of case-specific rather than general theoretic analysis.
2. Good-quality (ex post) empirical studies of the environmental impacts of specific market liberalization measures are still very few in number. The findings of existing studies often conflict, either because they are not strictly comparing like with like, or because of differences in the underlying assumptions built into the analysis, or because of differences in the quality of data used, modelling and other analytical techniques employed. Ex ante empirical studies (that is, studies of the likely environmental impacts of specific market liberalization measures *prior to* their adoption) are very rare indeed.
3. The findings may be very sensitive to the assumptions that are made about the timing of other measures relevant to environmental protection (is it realistic to assume that environmental protection measures are in place *before* market liberalization measures are introduced or should it

be assumed that they will be introduced at some unspecified date *after* the market liberalization measures are in place?).

The provisional conclusions which are drawn in this chapter are that (a) the pragmatic viewpoint is the most tenable at the moment and (b) if this is accepted both for policy and research purposes, new ex ante case studies of the environmental impacts of market liberalization measures will need to be undertaken.

ENVIRONMENTAL POLICY INSTRUMENTS AND MARKET LIBERALIZATION MEASURES

Let us assume that market liberalization measures may have some significant negative environmental impacts, if they are not preceded by (or at least not accompanied by) certain environmental policy measures (the nature of which will vary from one situation to another). In determining what these measures might be, it is helpful to consider first of all what types of environmental policy instruments might be available in the 'shopping basket'. For present purposes these will be grouped into three categories: economic instruments (charges, taxes, subsidies), direct regulations – control and command instruments (permits, licences), and planning and evaluation instruments (EIA, CBA).

Economic instruments are understandably the economists' first-choice method for achieving optimal resource pricing and to internalize environmental pollution externalities. However, we need to be realistic about what can be achieved by this method in the near future, especially in LDCs and countries in transition. The obstacles to their becoming major instruments of environmental policy are formidable: valuation problems (pollution damage for optimal efficiency charging, control costs for cost effective charging and discounted resource values for resource pricing); problems associated with their practical implementation (charging the polluter for a comprehensive array of pollutants – with all the risks of distortions to relative prices if the system is not comprehensive); problems of political acceptance (charges, in particular, are not popular; though double dividend arguments may be, but not with ministries of finance); problems associated with ambiguities over property rights (though this is not peculiar to economic instruments); and problems due to distortions in charges systems when they are captured to serve other purposes (for tax revenue-raising purposes). The net result is that, in all countries, economic instruments are currently applied to a very small proportion of polluting and other environmental activities and in most cases the levels and structures of the charges and subsidies are not consistent with either efficiency or cost-effectiveness criteria.

Direct regulations (control and command instruments) are the predominant instruments of environmental policy in all countries despite their widely acknowledged deficiencies (they are not closely related to efficiency objectives; they are not cost-effective; there are serious problems of non-compliance, especially in LDCs and CITs; and so on). However, at present their practical effects in lowering pollution levels are greater than those resulting from the use of economic instruments. Given that their political acceptability is greater than that of economic instruments it is likely to be more practical *in the short term* to improve the performance of direct regulations rather than economic instruments but unrealistic to assume that entirely satisfactory performance can be achieved by exclusive reliance on these instruments. Also it should be noted that direct regulations often may not be the most appropriate instruments to apply at the strategic policy level.

If all environmental externalities were internalized and all decision makers were rational and perfectly informed, *planning and evaluation instruments* would be unnecessary or, at best, of trivial significance. Given that these conditions do not apply, they have a potentially useful supportive role to play in conjunction with economic and direct regulatory instruments (that is they are not substitutes for these) in achieving environmental policy objectives.

Our concern here is with the means by which environmental considerations are integrated into the preparation, approval and implementation of market liberalization policies, plans and programmes (which eventually translate into the implementation of individual projects). The current thinking (given the imperfections already mentioned, as well as inadequate economic incentives and deficiencies in the coverage, form and implementation of direct regulations) is to use planning and evaluation instruments (a) to encourage the more systematic consideration of environmental impacts in the early stages of preparing policies, plans, programmes and projects; (b) to integrate the resulting environmental evaluation into the approval decision and any conditions which are attached to that decision; and (c) to ensure that the monitoring takes place and remedial action is taken where non-compliance or unexpected environmental impacts occur for other reasons. It is this approach which is elaborated further in the next section.

COST–BENEFIT ANALYSIS, ENVIRONMENTAL ASSESSMENT AND MARKET LIBERALIZATION

Cost–Benefit Analysis

Just as economists understandably turn first to economic instruments as the primary type of instrument of environmental policy, so equally understandably they turn to CBA as the primary tool of investment appraisal at the project level. The underlying logic of taking all social costs and benefits into account across generations is hard to challenge. There are, of course, continuing debates over the detailed methods by which this is achieved. One of these is of primary concern in this chapter: the monetary valuation of environmental benefits and disbenefits. Again, we have to be realistic: despite the advances made over the last 25 years (for example, in contingent valuation/ stated preference techniques), there are many environmental impacts for which the valuation method and the resulting findings are not sufficiently widely accepted for them (for example) to stand up to successful cross-examination in a public inquiry. The state of the art is such that many environmental impacts have to be ignored *or* that they have to be expressed in their physical form. Given that the former is unsatisfactory, acceptance of the latter means logically that the approach of the single-value NPV has to be abandoned and be replaced by some other evaluation framework or approach (multi-criteria, multi-objective analysis) in which the result of the CBA is one (important but not sole) input. Furthermore, in most cases in order to value the environmental impacts in a monetary form it is also necessary to have assessed these impacts beforehand in a physical form for which some kind of environmental assessment (see below) may be necessary.

Additionally, it should be noted, the scope for applying social cost–benefit analysis may be sharply reduced in a privatized market system since private enterprises may only feel obliged to take *private* benefits and costs into account in their project appraisals. Also CBA is primarily a project-level appraisal technique: practical experience in its use at the policy, plan and programme level is much more limited.

Environmental Assessment

This leads on to the consideration of the nature and role of EIA of projects. This is both a *method* of project evaluation and a *process* for integrating environmental considerations into the project cycle. As a method, its purpose is to assess the significant environmental impacts which may result from a proposed project. There is no restriction on the form in which those impacts may be expressed (physical, monetary or both) – the choice is to be determined by the state of knowledge, the use to which the information is to be put and its likely political acceptability for this purpose. The methods used are drawn from different social science and scientific disciplines and there are, at the project level at least, fairly standard methodological steps through which the analysis proceeds: describing the project and highlighting those of its features which may give rise to environmental impacts, describing the baseline environmental conditions, predicting the magnitude of the changes that are expected to occur, evaluating the significance of those changes and integrating these into the overall project appraisal. In order to focus these assessment activities, screening methods are used to help in deciding which projects should be submitted to EIA and scoping methods are used to help in identifying particular types of impacts which are likely to require assessment.

However, EIA is also a *process* whose main components are now typically regulated by law (unlike CBA). All OECD countries now have their own EIA legislation, and virtually all of the major international and bilateral donor agencies and banks have their own EIA procedures which make aid conditional upon conformity with those procedures. A significant and rapidly increasing number of LDCs and CITs also have their own EIA procedures, although many are very recent and some are not yet functioning very effectively. These procedures and regulations contain provisions relating to screening, scope of assessments, responsibilities for their preparation, publication of Environmental Impact Studies (EIS)s, provisions for consultation and public participation, integration of EIS and consultation findings into decision making (for example, with permit approvals), mitigation, monitoring and management plans. Their overall purpose is to try to ensure that EIA is not a 'stand-alone' study which fails to be integrated into the project planning, decision making and implementation cycle.

Strategic Environmental Assessment

A relatively new development, which is at a much earlier stage in its evolution, is the use of a more strategic level environment assessment process and method (SEA) for application at earlier stages in the planning process than the individual project authorization stage (see Figure 4.2, which illustrates the underlying similarities between EIA and SEA processes) (Lee and Walsh, 1992). A UNECE working party recommended in 1992 the adoption of such an approach that might give rise to significant environmental impacts and outlined a set of guiding principles and procedures for such a system. The EC is developing its own proposal for an EU directive on SEA to complement its existing directive on EIA at the project level which was approved in 1985. Wood and Djeddour (1992) have identified a range of different assessment methods that may be used to undertake each of the tasks in the SEA process. These are broadly of two kinds. First, there are those already in use in project-level EIA but which can be adapted for use at more strategic levels of assessment. These include many of the methods used to identify impacts (checklists, matrices, network analyses), for describing baseline conditions, for predicting pollution impacts from multiple sources, and so on. Second, there are those already used in policy analysis and planning studies which can be adapted for use in SEA. These include various forms of scenario and

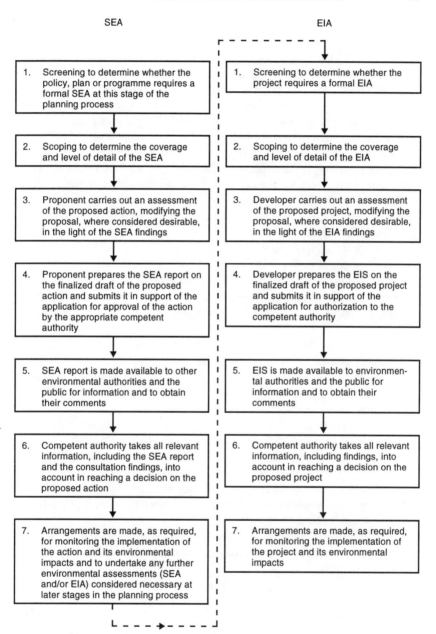

Source: Lee and Walsh (1992).

Figure 4.2 Overview of SEA

simulation analysis, regional forecasting and input–output techniques, site selection and land suitability analysis, geographical information systems (GIS), systems modelling (for instance, for traffic networks, energy systems and water resource systems), policy and programme evaluation techniques (such as multi-criteria analysis, goals achievement analysis, planning balance sheet approaches, cost–benefit analysis, constrained cost minimization analysis, sensitivity analysis and other techniques for handling uncertainty).

A number of individual countries have begun to adopt an embryonic form of SEA and, moving nearer to the theme of this chapter, both the US and Canadian governments have prepared EISs (or their equivalent) for the North American Free Trade Agreement (NAFTA) and the Uruguay Round of the GATT, and the World Bank is already preparing what it calls sectoral EAs and it is expected that they will undertake something similar to an SEA for some future SAPs.

Given the widespread adoption of environmental procedures, EA is a potentially important policy instrument to apply in the planning, approval and implementation of market liberalization measures which may have significant environmental impacts. However, its practical effectiveness is likely to be strongly influenced by two broad considerations:

1. Since most of these measures are initially introduced at the policy, plan or programmes level, it is likely that SEA rather than EIA will be the form of environmental assessment which is more commonly applied. If so, it will be necessary to ensure that the 'state of the art' of SEA is sufficiently developed for this purpose.
2. The process of privatization and deregulation may, in some cases, reduce the effectiveness of SEA and EIA procedures and practices; for example:
    a. in some cases, reducing the regulatory burden may entail simplifying or exempting enterprises from environmental permit requirements (thereby indirectly reducing the effectiveness of any EIA provisions which are integrated into those permitting procedures – Anon, 1994);
    b. in order to speed up the privatization process, EIA procedural requirements may be waived or commenced too late in the approval process;
    c. different regulatory provisions may apply as between public and private enterprises; privatization may therefore diminish (though it could extend) the area of application of EIA and the procedural requirements applicable to different enterprises;
    d. market liberalization measures, combined with macroeconomic stabilization measures, may result in pressures to reduce government expenditure levels, leading to staffing cuts in environmental minis-

tries which reduce their capability to direct and manage effectively the EIA system;

e. if property rights and associated environmental obligations are not clarified as part of the process of land privatization, the responsibilities for inherited and future environmental liabilities will be unclear and this could seriously reduce the potential benefits from using EA instruments.

In principle, these difficulties may be avoided by carefully checking that the form taken by market liberalization measures does not undermine the effectiveness of the EA instruments and other environmental regulations which are in place.

CONCLUSIONS AND IMPLICATIONS FOR FOLLOW-UP

Arising from the above review, three main questions have been raised to which the following provisional answers may be given:

1. *Should market liberalization measures be subject to some form of environmental assessment?* The short answer to this is that, if they are likely to give rise to significant environmental impacts, they should. Since many of these measures will be at the strategic level of policies, plans and programmes, SEA is likely to be the predominant requirement, although EIA (possibly incorporating an environmental audit component to address concerns over environmental liabilities, particularly in CITs) would also be needed for some specific privatization schemes. Among the mitigating measures which EA should highlight are corrections for market imperfections and other policy failures which may be contributing to the occurrence of significant negative environmental impact.
2. *Can environmental assessment procedures be satisfactorily applied in a liberalized market system?* Again, as indicated in the previous section, the answer is a qualified 'yes' – provided the necessary corrective measures are taken to ensure their continued effectiveness and to avoid any weakening of this through the unintended side-consequences of particular forms of privatization and deregulation.
3. *Can SEA be satisfactorily applied (politically, procedurally and methodologically) to market liberalization measures in the LDC/CIT context?* Here also a qualified positive answer is given – provided the following conditions apply or additional actions are taken to secure them:
    a. at the political level: increased awareness and acceptability of the value of SEA as a policy instrument (this will probably require the

demonstration, in the form of real case examples, of how it can work satisfactorily in practice; it may also require effort to overcome any political resistance to a perceived reduction in competencies in key ministries and any concerns over the greater transparency associated with SEA procedures);

b.   at the procedural level: the primary need is to identify the most appropriate ways in which to link SEA procedures to (as far as possible) existing market liberalization policy, plan or programme procedures and to tackle sensitively any concerns over confidentiality which may arise;

c.   at the methodological level: the basic requirement is to identify and develop the most appropriate ways in which to link and analyse the key relationships between two types of system, the economic development/trade system and the environmental system. There is (as previously described) an existing body of scientific and technical knowledge whose usefulness needs to be carefully evaluated for use in the environmental assessment of market liberalization measures with particular regard to: (i) the level of detail at which different types of SEA may need to be undertaken, (ii) the likely availability of data in typical LDC and CIT situations, and (iii) the most appropriate ways in which to handle the substantial uncertainties which will unavoidably arise in this type of assessment work. The follow-up work which may be most urgently needed in these three areas can be deduced from the conclusions already reached above. It should include (i) review of the principal ways in which market liberalization measures may weaken the effectiveness of EA procedures and of the most appropriate actions to address such problems; (ii) review of the principal technical requirements in linking and analysing relationships between economic development/trade systems and environmental systems, and of the extent to which existing knowledge can meet these requirements, followed by an identification of the principal, remaining deficiencies requiring further research; and (iii) ex ante/prospective case studies of specific market liberalization measures in different country (LDC and CIT) contexts focusing both on the SEA/EIA process and procedures which have been followed and on the assessment methods which are used.

REFERENCES

Anderson, K. and Blackhurst, R. (eds) (1992) *The Greening of World Trade Issues*, London: Wheatsheaf.

Anon (1994) 'Deregulation cuts into environmental assessment', *ENDS*, **230**, 34–5.

Cook, P. and Kirkpatrick, C. (eds) (1995a) *Privatization Policy and Performance: International Perspectives*, London: Harvester-Wheatsheaf.

Cook, P. and Kirkpatrick, C. (eds) (1995b) 'Privatisation in transitional economies: East and Central European experience', in F. Burton, M. Yamin and S. Young (eds), *International Business and Europe Transition*, London: Macmillan.

Economic Commission for Europe/United Nations Environment Programme (1994) *Guidelines on Environmental Management in Countries in Transition*, New York: UN.

Environment for Europe (1994) *Environmental Action Programme for Central and Eastern Europe*, abridged version of document endorsed by the Ministerial Conference, Lucerne, Switzerland, 28–30 April 1993, CEC/OECD/World Bank.

European Bank for Reconstruction and Development (1994a) *Transition Report: Economic Transition in Eastern Europe and the Former Soviet Union*, London: EBRD.

Goldenman, G. (1995) *Environmental Liability and Privatisation in Central and Eastern Europe*, a report for the Environmental Action Programme for Central and Eastern Europe, Paris and Washington, DC: OECD/World Bank.

Hansen, S. (1990) 'Macroeconomic policies and sustainable development in the Third World', *Journal of International Development*, **2**, (4), October.

Lee, N. and Walsh, F. (1992) 'Strategic environmental assessment: an overview', *Project Appraisal*, **7**, (3), September, 126–36.

Munasinghe, M. and Cruz, W. (1995) *Economy-wide Policies and the Environment: Lessons from Experience*, World Bank Environmental Paper No. 10, Washington, DC: World Bank.

Nodland, S.I. and Engen, O.A. (1993) 'Privatisation and the Environment: A Survey of the main issues with particular focus on developing countries', paper prepared for the UNCTAD Working Group on Comparative Experiences with Privatisation.

OECD (1994a) *The Environmental Effects of Trade*, Paris: OECD.

OECD (1994b) *Methodologies for Environmental and Trade Reviews*, Paris: OECD.

Reed, D. (1992) *Structural Adjustment and the Environment*, London: Earthscan.

UNCTAD Secretariat (1994) 'Consideration of the country presentations in the light of a cross-country review by the Secretariat of the design, implementation and results of privatisation programmes', paper prepared for UNCTAD Working Group on Comparative Experiences with privatisation.

United Nations Economic Commission for Europe (1992) *Application of Environmental Assessment Principles to Policies, Plans and Programmes*, Geneva: UNECE.

Warford. J., Schwab, A., Cruz, W. and Hansen, S. (1994) *The Evolution of Environmental Concerns in Adjustment Lending*, Environment Working Paper No. 65, Washington, DC: World Bank.

Wood, C. and Djeddour, M. (1992) 'Strategic environmental assessment: EA of policies, plans and programmes', *Impact Assessment Bulletin*, **10**, (1), 3–22.

World Bank (1994) *Environmental Assessment Sourcebook Update: Privatisation and Environmental Assessment: Issues and Approaches*, No. 6, Washington, DC: World Bank.

PART II

Projects, People and Process

5. Human resources, new growth theory and adjustment: implications for human resources projects

Rolph van der Hoeven*

INTRODUCTION

The role of human resources in development planning and the role of the government in human resource development as well as in the broader context of development planning has varied widely over time. Before embarking on a discussion of where we stand at present, we review some of the experiences of the past in the first section of this chapter. This is followed in the second section by a discussion on the recent literature on the so-called 'new growth' theories and the implications of these theories for human resource development. The third section relates the discussion on the new growth theories to the current debate on adjustment policies and serves, furthermore, as an introduction to the last two sections, which discuss the implications of the new growth theory and the recent adjustment experiences for human resource development and projects.

HUMAN RESOURCES AND EMPLOYMENT IN PAST DEVELOPMENT STRATEGIES

A discussion on human resources development can perhaps best be organized by indicating how human resources have been dealt with in various development strategies. Broadly, five types of development strategy can be distinguished which gained prominence between the 1960s and 1990s: a growth strategy, an employment and anti-poverty strategy, a basic needs strategy, a structural adjustment strategy and a human development strategy.

The *growth strategy* emphasized the development of the (capital-intensive) modern sector as a principal vehicle of development and employment creation.

---

* The views expressed here are those of the author and should not be attributed to the International Labour Office.

This modern sector also required a relatively high degree of skill formation on the part of the workforce. Justifications for the growth strategy were based upon a number of premises (van der Hoeven, 1988). One of the most important was perhaps the observation that this strategy had brought earlier industrialized market economies to their present welfare levels. A further justification was that, although employment and poverty alleviation should, of course, be a matter of concern for governments, the best vehicle for poverty alleviation was a redistribution of income increases resulting from growth. It was also thought that in the long run better results could be achieved by growth strategies through rapidly building up capital stock and infrastructure, and that, perhaps not immediately but certainly later on, the poor would benefit more from such strategies. As regards government intervention, the earlier strategies were often informed by the Harrod–Domar growth model which postulated that an increase in savings rates and investment rate would accelerate growth of GDP. The growth strategy was based upon the concept of the labour surplus economy (Lewis, 1954, 1979). The principal characteristic of the labour surplus economy (Fei and Ranis, 1964) was that, given the existence of surplus labour in the rural and artisanal sector, labour would move from rural to urban areas, where slightly above subsistence wages were paid. The urban areas would develop by investing surpluses from the rural areas and from the urban areas themselves. Once sufficient absorption from rural areas had taken place, wages and incomes in the labour surplus sector (which would no longer be a labour surplus sector at that point in time) would rise and a broader interaction between the two sectors of the economy would take place.

For the process to work at a relatively fast rate, however, a number of preconditions would have to be met which were absent in reality (Streeten, 1981). First of all, the differences between urban and rural incomes were much greater than the labour surplus theory presupposed. Colonial heritage, trade union influence and skills related to a higher level of technology often caused higher income differentials and resulted in faster migration than predicted, so preventing rapid absorption of the labour force. Low standards of living in the rural areas acted as a further push factor. Migrants were often among the better educated, thus depriving the rural areas of trained manpower. To what extent this is a positive or negative factor depends on the relationships migrants maintain with their rural hinterland. Return flows of incomes and return of migrants themselves have been shown to have a positive impact on rural development.

Second, the capacity expansion in modern industries often took place with imported, labour-saving technologies. This also prevented absorption of the labour force, while the nature of the technology often tended to create large wage differentials between skilled or managerial workers, on the one hand, and unskilled workers, on the other.

Third, and perhaps most important, the breakthrough in agricultural technology and productivity (through investments and/or through land redistribution) benefiting the entire agricultural sector, which occurred in a number of
developed economies, has been lacking in most countries (Adelman, 1984).
Finally, population growth was more rapid than in any comparative situation
in the development of Western Europe, making the creation of gainful employment for those entering the labour market extremely difficult.

Dissatisfaction with the employment-creating and distributional record of
the growth strategy, together with research findings that showed that many
preconditions for this strategy were in fact lacking, resulted in increasing
attention being paid to other strategies. A first reaction was the so-called
'employment strategy', which emphasized programmes to increase employment in the modern sector and which gained prominence in the early 1970s.
This often involved investigating institutional constraints and biases in the
choice of technologies. However, given the small size of the modern sector,
attention quickly shifted to include problems in the urban informal sectors
and the rural sectors. A major conceptual difficulty arose in analysing the
informal and rural sectors, which is that the concept of employment is unclear or undefined in these sectors. Productivity or income per head proved a
much better yardstick, hence there was a broadening from a restricted employment strategy to a broader *employment and anti-poverty strategy*, which
would affect a much larger part of the population. Such a strategy should, it
was argued, incorporate many more programmes for small-scale rural households, for rural infrastructural works and for redistribution of land, as in
many cases productivity on small plots proved to be higher than on large
holdings. Furthermore, programmes were added to improve incomes in the
urban informal sector. In order to make labour more productive in all sectors,
such programmes also emphasized basic schooling and simple vocational
training. Inequalities in the modern sector were to be tackled through
redistributive fiscal measures (ILO, 1972).

An important element of this broader employment strategy was its attention to incomes. The exclusive emphasis on incomes left out many other
elements of economic well-being, some of which, like education and health,
were regarded not only as elements of well-being but also as inputs to
increase income-earning assets by the poor.

A *basic needs* approach developed which was thus concerned with the
objectives of the development process, and income through employment was
seen as an important means to achieve this. Some important elements of a
basic needs strategy (van der Hoeven, 1988) are the identification of and the
specific attention to target groups in the planning process, the use of corrective measures by the government (through asset or factor reward redistribution) if the development process does not reach the target groups sufficiently,

and the use of the government budget to deliver non-marketable needs to the target and other groups. Another important aspect is the participation of all members of society, not only in formulating targets for themselves but also in finding creative solutions to the problem of reaching these targets. The policy implications of a basic needs strategy rest on the premise that the problem of people not meeting their basic needs should be seen as a structural problem. Because of imbalances in the social and economic systems, certain groups do not receive an equal share of the fruits of development. A basic needs strategy should therefore be regarded more as an organizing concept around which to analyse present and alternative development policies.

The basic needs approach was not readily accepted. Some feared an attention to basic needs would imply a rigid and bureaucratic planning structure, while others thought that, by focusing policies on satisfaction of basic needs, developing countries would accept being unequal partners in the debate on the new international economic order which dominated the development scene at the end of the 1970s. However, before these discussions could come to fruition, developing countries were subjected to a succession of external shocks at the end of the 1970s and in the early 1980s.

The shocks did not all take place simultaneously, but rather overlapped with each other. After the commodity price boom in 1977, the *terms of trade* for most developing countries deteriorated for five consecutive years, improved slightly in 1983 and 1984 and worsened again in 1985. The *growth rate in industrialized countries* fell sharply in 1980, reducing the demand for many developing country products in these important markets. Until 1980, foreign *real interest rates* (adjusted for changes in the export prices of non-fuel exporting developing countries) were low or even negative and many developing countries took advantage of the availability of capital in order to increase external finance for development. After 1980, however, deflationary policies in industrialized countries pushed interest rates up to all-time high levels, making it difficult for many indebted countries already struggling with low export prices of primary commodities and a drop in export volume, to service their debts. This debt service problem (especially the dramatic Mexican crisis) and the growing deficit of the USA led to a sizeable *reduction* in capital flows to developing countries from 1982 on, making it difficult for these countries to finance their current account deficits through additional borrowing. As a consequence, most developing countries were forced to reduce their deficits quickly; that is, to adopt *structural adjustment* policies.

Most developing countries were able to adjust to the effects of these shocks by reducing their current account deficits, albeit with substantial knock-on effects. Capital inflows decreased and the terms of borrowing worsened, which narrowed the margin for a viable balance of payments considerably. This, of course, struck at the roots of growth and employment creation. Furthermore, because stabilization and adjustment were mainly forced upon developing countries by external events, many of them found it difficult to adjust in an orderly manner. Adjustment to changed international circumstances could not be brought about overnight; it involved a restructuring of many aspects of the economic framework through which various policies were implemented, especially those relating to levels of intervention and price control.

Such policies generally need time in order to be fully effective. Furthermore, abrupt changes in government policy met so much resistance that it became extremely difficult to implement them and in some cases they had to be cancelled or reversed The social costs of these shocks and the rapid adjustments have been high (World Bank, 1990; Cornia *et al.*, 1992; van der Hoeven and Stewart, 1993). Especially in sub-Saharan Africa and Latin America, real wages in the modern sector undertakings have fallen considerably and unemployment has risen, the combined effect, of course, being an increase in urban poverty and a decline in the provision for human resources.

This has happened for two sets of reasons: first, because most adjustment and stabilization programmes lacked any form of buffer mechanism to protect the poor. Policies were usually defined with a view to their effect on macroeconomic indicators (levels of government expenditure, exchange rate realignment and credit expansion, for example) with no explicit concern for income distribution and poverty effects. Special schemes to assist the poor were not even considered, for budgetary reasons, (although lately these have become fashionable (van der Hoeven, 1993). Second, because the adjustment and stabilization policies were of a deflationary nature (at least in the short run), most poor people suffered simply as a result of the contraction of economic activity.

As the surge of 'necessary' stabilization and adjustment programmes preoccupied most development thinking and planning, attention to basic needs policies faded away in the early 1980s. Conceptually, the basic needs approach had paid little attention to trade and international policies; in the relatively buoyant climate of the 1970s, a gradual growth of export and international capital inflows was assumed to take place. Admittedly, some elements of the strategy assumed the use of more appropriate and domestically developed technologies and higher consumption levels of locally produced consumer goods, thus reducing the need for foreign exchange. However, this was often not made very explicit in final policy proposals and, when quick savings on foreign resources had to be made, the indirect way of changing demand patterns of consumption and capital goods proved to be too cumbersome and too indirect, and more crude measures of contraction and import restrictions prevailed. A second reason was that basic needs policies assumed a benevolent and efficient state, something that it had in common with most other development strategies.

The combination of a weak underpinning of the external resource link and the fragile political power base, especially in times of great financial uncertainty, often made it difficult to maintain or even introduce a basic needs strategy. In some oil-exporting developing countries windfall gains were often not used to finance more basic needs provisions and in countries facing serious financial crises expenditure on basic needs provision was not only not maintained but was cut, along with most other expenditure items. In most cases it became more difficult for the poor to exercise pressure and to build up more countervailing power (although, as conditions worsened rapidly in some countries, economic and social degradation and the swelling ranks of the poor exerted their own political pressure).

The challenge for human resource development policy rested first on the recognition of the fact that external influences, especially in the present context of globalization, are important and have to inform all policy action on poverty and secondly, on the recognition that an egalitarian development uniquely based upon an elaborated system of public redistribution might be difficult to retain in the future. The lessons from the experience with the basic needs approach are that poverty-focused policies cannot be dissociated from adjustment policies (of which the ultimate aim is to restore external balance on the economy, through internal equilibrium and growth) and secondly that poverty policies should be associated with policies of structural change which give poorer families a greater command over natural, financial and human resources in order to contribute to sustained growth.

A further observation is that one of the premises of the basic needs strategy – that countries could not arrive at growth rates of 8–10 per cent per annum in order to reduce poverty and that therefore redistributive policies were called for – has not been uniformly true. In effect, a small group of countries managed for almost a decade to exhibit such high growth rates. The Republic of Korea's average annual growth rate over the 1980s amounted to 9.7 per cent and China's growth rate over the same period amounted to 9.5 per cent. Growth in these countries was certainly not even, but resulted nevertheless in some recognizable improvements in human resource-related provision.

Against the need to confront human resource policies with structural adjustment (and coping with effects of globalization in general) as well as with the necessity of structural changes, what policy options can be suggested? It is first of all necessary to recognize that causes of setbacks in human resource development strategies have been different in different countries and continents. A temptation for uniform (and often grandiose) policy options should therefore be strongly resisted. Secondly, and related to the discussion above, any discussion on policy options in the 1990s should take into consideration the question whether the adjustment experiences in the 1980s have led to 'new forms' of deprivation of human resource development and whether such new forms need special policy action or not.

Alternatives to orthodox adjustment policies suggest that, in general, adjustment efforts should be spread out over a much longer period and form part of a long-term growth and adjustment policy. Such a policy would call for far more selective economic measures – shaped according to the particular socioeconomic structure of the country – rather than relying solely on blunt macroeconomic instruments such as credit restriction and devaluation. This could also lay the basis for equity-oriented growth and policies aiming at the satisfaction of basic needs.

What would this imply for structural adjustment policies? Emphasis should shift towards activities for stimulating structural change (growth policies, asset redistribution, income-generation activities, sectoral policies). Furthermore, national democratic decision making should be regarded as a means and an end at the same time and concerns for human welfare and employment as a primary, not a secondary, objective in policy making. Such alternatives gained prominence as 'adjustment with a human face' (Jolly and van der Hoeven, 1991). However, despite the political importance given to adjustment it was accepted by many that more prominence should be given to longer-term policy concerns, and the beginning of the 1990s witnessed a resurgence of attention to *human development* issues spearheaded by the annual report of the United Nations Development Programme (UNDP). (For a comparison of the policy implications of the World Bank strategies and the UNDP strategies, see Kanbur, in van der Hoeven and Anker, 1993.)

The main thrust of the *human development strategy* is that human development can progress best in a climate of sustainable and steady economic growth, although economic growth alone will not result automatically in progress in human development. Achieving human and economic development together will imply, for most countries, structural change in the economic and social framework – structural changes in the position in the international economy and in the national formation of incomes and capital. In order to achieve international structural changes, developing countries will need to reduce their dependency on commodity exports. National structural changes will call for a better distribution of ownership and changes in key influences on production such as land tenure and land redistribution, as well as credit facilities and legal structures. A better distribution of factors contributing to human capital formation, such as primary health care, primary education and applied vocational training, will be a vital component of the human development strategy. (For a fuller discussion, see Griffin and McKinley, 1994.)

NEW GROWTH THEORY

In recent years, the process of economic growth has regained new emphasis in the literature. Various authors have recently expressed dissatisfaction with the traditional growth models, in which technical progress is included as a residual to other factors of production and where the level of investment does not affect the growth rate in the long run. In these so-called 'new growth' theories, the discussion on infrastructure and human capital has taken prominence. In essence, the new growth theory relates changes in structural factors – such as education, infrastructure, market access and human resource development – not only to a higher level of income such as in the neoclassical theory, but also to higher growth rates, and therefore provides potentially stronger arguments for growth-enhancing policies. Most of the discussion around the new growth theory either relates to growth experiences in industrialized countries or deals with the question of whether growth rates of developing countries are higher than growth rates in industrialized countries and whether therefore levels of development will converge over the long run. Little attention has been given, however, to specific conditions in developing countries (but see Shaw, 1992; Pio, 1994).

Various authors of the 'new growth school' have tried to endogenize different aspects of what was included in the 'technical progress' residual in the neoclassical growth functions, either through creation of a special production factor labelled 'knowledge industry' (Romer, 1992), through externalities of education and training affecting human capital (Lucas, 1988) or through linking productivity to investment through what earlier analysts called '*learning by doing*' (Kaldor, 1957) and vintage models (Arrow, 1962) or through increased international trade and consequent international capital flows (Grosman and Helpman, 1991).

In the various variants of the new growth theory, human capital formation and technological advancement can be achieved by means of selective government expenditure as well as indirectly through effects of investment, production of new industrial goods, trade and capital inflows. Most models, however, deal with only one aspect and few have dealt with issues which Lall (1992) terms 'capabilities' (and the extent to which firms in countries have such capabilities) enabling them to profit from technical progress spin-offs induced by (foreign) investment and trade. Lall requires firms to have three types of capabilities: *investment capabilities* needed to identify, design, prepare, construct, equip, staff and commission a new facility; *production capabilities*, ranging from basic skills such as quality control and operation and maintenance to adaptation and improvement; and *linkage capabilities* required to acquire and communicate information from outside the firm itself. These capabilities are important for capturing externalities: the more diffuse the externalities, the more sophisticated those capabilities need to be (Latsch, n.d.).

On the basis of the capabilities, some have criticized the trade–productivity link as being two simplistic (Helleiner, 1992; Rodrik, 1992). The importance of outward orientation and the discipline of the international market for a production process to become more productive and being forced to undergo technical progress is accepted by these authors, but they point out that what also is important is government policy of advising and stimulating firms, and of preparing the labour force for new and higher skill-intensive tasks. International competitiveness is usually the outcome rather than a determinant of this process. As Lall (1994) has pointed out, there are various examples of countries which have been outward-oriented and which participated in international trade (as primary exporters) but which have nevertheless exhibited little dynamism.

Hence it remains important to concentrate on which policies directly contribute to increased capabilities to acquire and apply new technical knowledge and thus increase technical progress. Most would argue that widespread education is an important factor, but prospective and actual returns to education are difficult to capture. Some analysts (for example, Colclough, 1993) reject the traditional rate of return analysis in guiding the discussion of the appropriateness of the education system because of the omission of externalities and the influence the supply of graduates from different layers of the educational system has on (future) wage rates (and argue further that these rate of return analyses cannot give an indication as to whether the private returns to education are higher than the social return to education in determining whether education should be privately or publicly financed, a point to which we return later). Dasgupta (1993) also points out the more diversified effects of education and, hailing it as 'encouraging a judicious mix of conscious and trained reflection and experimentation to improve ways of doing things and understanding things' argues that 'ceteris paribus, economies with a larger stock of educated people tend to enjoy faster growth' (1993, p. 99). Pack argues that education enhances productive capabilities: 'Education may lie behind a high elasticity of substitution because of its favourable impact both on the ability to scan and to implement new technologies and the flexibility of the productive mix' (1992, p. 37). Thus it is important, especially for developing countries, to concentrate on policies which increase the capabilities of the labour force, the firm and society at large to cope with technological changes. What lessons do the conclusions of the new growth theory have in this respect?

Many articles on the new growth theory conclude by discussing a relationship between government policies and the acceleration of growth. This relationship is usually confined to the question as to how various elements of fiscal policy enhance either investment or trade and competition and most of the policy recommendations of analysts of the new growth school are consequently recommendations for non-distortionary trade and indirect taxes (and lower direct taxes) in order to enhance investment and trade. Although the role of the government and the public sector in providing the necessary externalities to accelerate growth is acknowledged and sometimes even explicitly modelled, there is little in the way of suggestions as to what its precise role should be.

The observation of distortionary effects of higher taxes on investment and technological advancement usually stems from the observations from a developed country sample. For governments in developing countries, however, taxation and public utility pricing are the major source of revenue since the conditions under which Ricardian equivalence theory puts public borrowing and taxation at par as policy instruments does not hold in developing countries (Burgess and Stern, 1993). General remarks about the distortion of taxes therefore provide little policy guidance. It would appear to be more important to investigate the content of fiscal expenditure and the way taxes are collected in order to assess their effects on equity and growth, which is often absent in the new growth literature because of the highly aggregative nature of the models used.

What other literature has taught us clearly is that fiscal policies have, by definition, an effect on income distribution since taxes determine the net disposable incomes of families. Indeed, one of the potential aims of tax policies is precisely to bring about a redistribution in the economy, although the extent to which this is possible is often called into question (for example, see the discussion in Newbery and Stern, 1987). In many developing countries, tax systems rely heavily upon indirect taxes which make the tax system regressive rather than progressive. For example, in Latin America direct taxes are equal to some 3 per cent of GDP while they are equal to 10 per cent of GDP in Europe (van der Hoeven and Stewart, 1993). A switching of a tax base favouring direct taxes could make income distribution much more equal.

Although public expenditure policy may change income distribution in favour of the poor, it is wrong to assume that higher government expenditure automatically benefits the less advantaged. However, Lipton and Ravallion (1993) in their literature survey provide evidence of various countries where not only current public human resource expenditure patterns but also public expenditure reform benefited the poor more (1993, p. 69).

In the light of the new growth theory, the issue of the distributional aspect of government services becomes more important, since the access to government services is regarded not only as consumption or an imputed income element as in the earlier literature but also as investment in human capital, directly contributing to growth. Whether under such assumptions growth will be more or less equal in the long run cannot be argued a priori. This clearly depends on whether poorer groups through increased access to income-earning assets or high factor rewards can profit from the change in growth rate or not. Evidence of research in the 1970s has shown rather convincingly that insufficient savings as an argument for a trade-off between income equality and growth is often not valid and, were it valid, it is only a weak explanatory variable. Country studies have provided examples of countries which combined high income equality with high growth rates (Adelman, 1984).

These findings for developing country experiences have recently been corroborated by several papers, dealing with industrialized country experiences which combine new growth theory – endogenizing technical progress – with political economic models endogenizing political decisions. The conclusions of these papers are that inequality is harmful to growth. Alesina and Perotti (1994) discuss several causal links which underlay endogenizing political decisions. Links on a more traditional economic footing include the effect of income inequality on the composition of demand and the effect of inequality on factor endowment affecting the supply of human capital. A more equal income distribution leads to increased demand for industrial goods which triggers off innovation and growth, while more equal distribution of capital allows for increased investment in education by low-income groups, allowing them to build up stocks of human capital more rapidly. Among the political explanations, two seem to figure prominently. The first one postulates that inequality leads to voting behaviour to force the government to apply redistributive policies and sanctions higher taxes and larger budget deficits which are growth-destructive. The second explanation is that inequality causes political instability and prevents governments using effective management (Stern, 1991). However Alesina and Perotti (1994) show rather convincingly that the argument that inequality causes higher taxes which consequently harm growth is not finding much support in the data. They explain this mainly on the basis of a weak link between inequality and taxation levels, but one can bring forward as well the weak explanatory power of the level of taxation on economic growth, which Burgess and Stern (1993) have argued. The argument of policy uncertainty in explaining the positive relation between inequality and growth has found some support and is most recently confirmed by the unwillingness of private investors to continue to finance capital flows to Mexico in the wake of the looming conflicts on land redistribution and poverty programmes.

The experiences of the 1980s and some findings of the new growth theory allow us therefore to reconsider the growth and equity debate. The major finding appears to be that, on the one hand, higher taxes and some deficit financing can affect decisions on savings negatively and distort growth while, on the other hand, a higher level of government expenditure (as a result of higher taxes or deficit financing) can increase investment in human resources, support the development of markets and improve infrastructure which, following the new growth theories, contribute to higher levels of growth. The new growth theory thus offers, through the link between distribution of public expenditure on human resources and the generation of future primary incomes, a more dynamic element than hitherto was available.

ADJUSTMENT AND HUMAN RESOURCES

The findings of the new growth theory have underscored the importance of human resources as a major component for growth. However, one of the assumptions which is usually not relaxed in the models of the new growth theory is the full utilization of all factors of production, including labour. The new growth theory models describe a long-run steady-state relationship between investment, human resources and development and, although the process of moving from one set of steady-state growth path to another is expected to be shorter than under the neoclassical growth models, the elapsed time is still rather long: 14–35 years, given a set of plausible parameters, as Villanueva (1994) has recently demonstrated. This raises the question of the relevance of the new growth models in a situation of adjustment, where governments often have to reduce absorption and where the economy is producing below capacity. Do the robust conclusions from studies on technological development and the new growth theory need to be amended in the light of adjustment?

This clearly depends on how one interprets the adjustment process. If adjustment is regarded as a quick process of reducing temporarily the absorption in the economy then there are perhaps reasons to cut back temporarily on non-basic consumption and delay long-term investment, exempting spending on basic consumption and essential social expenditures. However, if adjustment is seen as a continuous process of a country adapting its production structure to changes in world markets and in its comparative advantage, the question of adjustment is directly linked to considerations of growth with strong implications for human resource policies.

It is necessary to distinguish between short-term reductions in absorption and longer-term capacity-building policies, as this will have different consequences for human resource policies. Indeed, it can be safely assumed that skills were not the major impediment to jump-starting growth in some Latin American economies, which can be corroborated by the large decline in real wages for various skill categories (van der Hoeven and Stewart, 1993) and the quick resumption in growth in various countries in the early 1990s.

This emphasis on short-run phenomena should, not, of course, deny those situations where increased skills and education have been associated at the micro level with technology acquisition and productivity increases; neither can the consensus that better health and education is correlated with growth be dismissed. The point to be stressed is that, in looking at elements of a structural adjustment package, human resources development is far from a sufficient condition for growth. It is more an accommodating factor that cannot be absent for a long time and the evidence cited in the second section, that public expenditure on health and education in many developing countries fell in the 1980s, is not a good sign for long-term growth.

The reaction of human resource policies in situations of adjustment needs therefore to differ according to the initial human resource situation a country finds itself in and to the type of adjustment policy needed (a short-term stabilization to rectify some macroeconomic imbalances or a process of longer-term reform to increase productivity and to be more integrated into the world market). If a country is faced with the need for short-term stabilization, as was the Republic of Korea for example in the early 1980s, the major plank of the human resources policy is to minimize the budgetary consequences for human resource policies and not to frustrate the long-term policies of increased capabilities and productivity increase. In applying short-run stabilization policies care should nevertheless be exercised not to alter the fundamentals of the underlying growth policies, assuming that these were sound. Not taking this into account can lead countries to fall into a low-level equilibrium trap, with adverse consequences for the labour market, as Buffie (1994) has shown.

In cases where large structural changes are needed in order for the economy to become more competitive, investment in human resources should be increased and be made more effective at the same time. This would mean emphasizing basic skills through appropriate government interventions and providing incentives for industries to develop vocational training and on-the-job training. However, massive attention to so-called 'social action programmes' clearly needs to be avoided (as we will discuss in the next section). What is called for here is human resource development based upon corrective adjustment (Chowdhury *et al.*, 1986) which implies a focus on higher skills in the workforce and diversification of the production process. This implies appropriate labour market and employment policies.

HUMAN RESOURCES PROGRAMMES AND POLICIES

The rethinking of the adjustment experience in many developing countries, as well as the resurgence of the new growth theory, have led to increased attention to the role of the government in relation to the importance of human resources in development. The new growth theory emphasized the importance of new investment in capital and human resources in order to influence growth rates, thereby providing more arguments for the active role by the government in the development process which had waned as a consequence of the neoclassical growth models in which growth in excess of labour force growth was explained by exogenous technical progress. In effect, one can speak in this respect of a swing back to the growth theories of the 1960s, based on the Harrod–Domar model, which called for active government investment, to increasing savings ratios and investment which guided most developed planning in the 1960s and in turn gave birth to the concept of international development aid. However, in contrast to the newer theories, analysis based on Harrod–Domar models viewed capital as the constraining factor; the implication for human resource programmes and projects was increased attention to high-skilled manpower, with little attention to basic education.

What do the findings of the new growth theory imply for human resources programmes and projects? The models of the new growth theory certainly underscore the need to pay more attention to human resources and the effects of this on technological advancement. However, what the models do not tell us is what would be the right interaction between 'supply' and 'demand' (in a broad sense) of human resources. This is because most models deal with partial problems in which either a government sector is explicitly modelled (as in Barro, 1990) or foreign trade and increased market penetration are seen as making human resources more productive. However, because of these partial attempts it is difficult, if not impossible, at the current stage of techniques to detect to what extent the supply of human resources has become a binding constraint. As Bardhan (1993) has pointed out, the new aggregate growth models underestimate the difficulty of identifying the few sectors and locations where spillover effects may be large. Learning is often highly localized and project-specific and unique gigantic capital projects sometimes do not generate enough of diffuse externalities. Furthermore, the extent of spillover also depends crucially on the nature of competition promoted by the policy environment and of the level of physical and social infrastructure, including the level of education of the general population.

Another limitation which the new growth theories have for practical policy guidance is that in essence they are concerned with long-term development. As argued above, this long-term concern is very much welcomed in the era where policy for many countries is dominated by the urgency of structural change, but the new growth model provides little direct advice on how human resource policies should be approached in situations when the economy is in disequilibrium or moves from one steady-state growth path to another. Most models, however, do indicate that taxes should not be non-distortionary and that foreign trade should not be restricted by special tariffs and trade restrictions, although these conclusions are often based on very specific model assumptions, assessing, inter alia, full equilibrium and full utilization of all production factors (including labour), thus providing little guidance for policy makers overwhelmed by concerns of structural adjustment. What in effect may occur is that, because the recommendations on fiscal and trade policies are easily comprehensible and straightforward, while the recommendations on human resources and technological advancement are more diffuse, fiscal and trade policies will dominate, and guide the partially informed policy maker more than the concern for human resources and technological advancement. Although, as indicated, most authors of the models would not draw these policy conclusions, they may give credence to a continuation of more orthodox adjustment policies, concentrating on fiscal balance and removing trade distortions, which have been found wanting. It remains important to stress the findings of the new growth theory with respect to the importance of investment in human resources and to relate this to the concerns for adjustment and long-term growth, adding to the current debate on human development and poverty (for example, Lipton and Ravallion, 1993).

Again, what are the implications for human resource programmes and projects? A major policy change in the international donor community was a shift from project to programme lending, especially relating to structural adjustment. Kanbur (1993), following Squire (1989), argues that project and programme lending cannot and should not be separated and that, on the one hand, programmes which reduce distortions in an economy also increase the social rate of return of projects, but that, on the other hand, projects often increase supply responsiveness in various sectors, which makes programmes more successful. He further argues that components of programmes should be evaluated as individual projects.

Viewing programmes as 'projects' should lead to the following priorities for human resource programmes and projects. First, for those countries which have not yet achieved it, is the earliest possible achievement of universal primary education, which because of its social rate of return should be free to the user. This should be a fundamental preoccupation of the public sector planner, with universality also extended as quickly as possible to lower secondary education, for the same reasons. Restricting secondary education too severely (for example, on equity grounds or on the basis of rate of return only) has been shown to have perverse effects. An example is seen in the comparison between Tanzania and Kenya. Secondary school access in Tanzania was very much restricted, while secondary school access in Kenya was enhanced by various means, including the popular 'Harambee' movements, in the 1970s and 1980s. The outcome of this is that in Kenya wage differentials for secondary school graduates have been reduced in relation to primary school graduates, while the gap in Tanzania has remained very wide.

Although resources allocated to human resource projects are rarely grossly wasted, the dictates of adjustment programmes and the current slow growth rates in many countries have made it clear that quality of services and relevance to life and labour market needs have to improve considerably (Colclough and Lewis, 1993). In some countries increased efficiency and cost reductions in primary education will not be compatible with providing all children with schooling. In these cases the flow of public and private resources has to be increased in order to achieve universal primary education as quickly as possible.

Although an observation such as this is fairly uncontroversial and accepted by most analysts, much more controversy exists on the issues of higher secondary and post-secondary education, and training and skill acquisition for technological change. Especially in the context of adjustment policies, there seems often to be confusion between the short-term and longer-term effects and implications. In the case of a short-term contraction of the economy, there appears to be little need to alter training programmes. In the case of increased unemployment those directly affected are best helped by public works and nutritional programmes in developing countries where social security programmes are absent or inadequate (van der Hoeven, 1993). The latter have often become part of so-called 'social action programmes' which have included training components. Evaluation of such programmes indicate that the specific training component has often been found wanting. In particular, they tend to be too short and do not contribute to better job prospects for the trainee (Stewart and van der Geest, 1995; Lucas, 1994). Most countries, however, are faced with a much more complicated process of adjustment which necessitates changes in sectoral outputs and productivity as a process of opening up to international markets, often requiring higher skills and more sophisticated technologies – at least if countries do not want to be caught in the low-level equilibrium trap of primary commodity exports (Toye, 1995).

Emphasis put on retraining of the displaced workforce in this process is often advocated but, despite high expectations of these programmes, their effects should not be overestimated and training should be kept fairly general, offering skills which will enhance productivity over a wider range of activities irrespective of what occupation the trainee ultimately takes up (Lucas, 1994). What is more important is that, if the educational system is not able to provide workers with a set of basic skills as a prerequisite for training and undertaking new tasks, a reform of the education and training system is warranted. In this context educational reforms should be carried out in tandem with vocational and skill training and should be integral to a national effort of upgrading technologies (Carnoy *et al.*, 1993) rather than being part of specific social action programmes. Most technology acquisition will be through activities of individual enterprises, but the government has to play an important role in this.

Carnoy *et al.* (1993) list six technology transfer areas which have relevance to developing and transitional economies:

1. importing new technology directly,
2. licensing agreements for the local design or adaptation of technology,
3. sending technical personnel abroad to learn new technological applications,
4. importing foreign experts to teach local personnel how to develop technologies,
5. training local personnel in foreign companies located domestically, and
6. attracting technologically-advanced foreign companies to produce locally and transfer technology through backward linkages to supplies.

Most of these means of technology transfer require some level of public sector involvement and an adequate human resource base. For low-income countries preparing for a more industrialized and/or internationally competitive agricultural future, the least efficient and equitable way to prepare for this is through offering rapidly depreciating industrial skills developed in high-cost vocational institutions. Rather, the way to prepare for the future relatively efficiently and equitably is to increase the quality of primary and secondary education to focus vocational training on immediately applicable skills for self-employment in agriculture, craft, light industrial production and commerce as well as for employment in education and health services. In support of this should be a concentration on investment in infrastructure, agricultural reform and stimulation of small and medium enterprises as part of an overall long-term development strategy.

For more advanced developing economies, training for jobs in fast-growing industries and regions has a higher rate of return than training for slow-growing industries and such needs will be dictated directly by the labour markets themselves (Muqtada and Hildeman, 1993). However, it remains important for the government, as part of an overall human resource development programme, to ascertain both the quantity and quality of primary and secondary schooling as well as to implement an active industrial policy in order to maximize the human potential of the country. Hence, in the light of current adjustment experience, human resource development should emphasize education and basic skills programmes in low-income countries and a combination of education programmes and rather specific industry training projects in more advanced countries in order to allow for rapid technological progress at the different stages of development.

REFERENCES

Adelman, J. (1984) 'Beyond export-led growth', *World Development,* **12**, (9), September.

Alesina, A. and Perotti, R. (1994) 'The political economy of growth: a critical survey of the recent literature', *World Bank Economic Review*, **8**, (3).

Arrow, K.J. (1962) 'The economic implications of learning by doing', *Review of Economic Studies,* **29**, 155–273.

Bardhan, P. (1993) 'Economics of development and the development of economics', *Journal of Economic Perspectives*, **7**, (2).

Barro, R.J. (1990) 'Government spending in a simple model of endogenous growth', *Journal of Political Economy*, **9**, 415.

Buffie, E. (1994) 'The long-run consequences of short-run stabilisation policy', in S. Horton, R. Kanbur and D. Mazumdar (eds), *Labour markets in an era of adjustment*, EDI Development Studies, Washington, DC: World Bank.

Burgess, R. and Stern, N. (1993) 'Taxation and Development', *Journal of Economic Literature*, **31**, June.

Carnoy, M. (1994) 'Efficiency and equity in vocational education and training policies', *International Labour Review*, **133**, (2).

Carnoy, M., Pollock, S. and Wong, P. (1993) *Labour institutions and technological change: A framework for analysis and a review of the literature*, IILS Working paper, Geneva: IILS.

Chowdhury, A., Kirkpatrick, C. and Islam, I. (1986) *Structural adjustment and human resources development in ASEAN*, ARTEP Working Paper, New Delhi: ILO–ARTEP.

Colclough, C. (1993) 'Human development towards an integrated framework for planning in the 1990s', in M. Muqtada and A. Hildeman (eds), *Labour Markets and Human Resource Planning in Asia: Perspective and Evidence*, New Delhi: ILO–ARTEP.

Colclough, C and Lewis. K (1993) *Educating all Children*, Oxford: Oxford University Press.

Cornia, G.A., Jolly, R. and Stewart, F. (1987) *Adjustment with a Human Face*, Oxford: Oxford University Press.

Cornia, G.A., van der Hoeven, R. and Mkandawire, T. (1992) *Africa's Recovery in the 1950s from Stagnation and Adjustment to Human Development*, London: Macmillan.

Dasgupta, P. (1993) *An Inquiry into Well-being and distribution*, Oxford: Oxford University Press.

Fei, J.C.H. and Ranis, G. (1964) *Development of the Labour Surplus Economy*, New Haven, Conn.: Yale University Press.

Fisher, S. (1991) 'Growth, macroeconomics and development', *National Bureau of Economic Research Macroeconomic Annual*, Cambridge, Mass.: MIT Press.

Griffin, K. and McKinley, T. (1994) *Implementing a Human Development Strategy*, London: Macmillan.

Grosman, G. and Helpman, E. (1991) *Innovation and Growth. The Global Economy*, Cambridge, Mass.: MIT Press.

Helleiner, G. (ed.) (1992) *Trade Policy: Industrialisation and Development*, UNV/WIDER, Oxford: Clarendon Press.

Hopkins, M. and van der Hoeven, R. (1983) *Basic Needs in Development Planning*, Aldershot: Gower.

ILO (1972) *Employment incomes and equality: A strategy for increasing productive employment in Kenya*, Geneva: ILO.

Jolly, R. and van der Hoeven, R. (1991) 'Adjustment with a human face. Record and relevance', *World Development*, **19**, (22).

Kaldor, N. (1957) 'A model of economic growth', *Economic Journal*, **67**, December, 591–624.

Kanbur, R. (1993) 'The Human Development Report 1990 and the World Development Report 1990', in R. van der Hoeven and R. Anker (eds), *Poverty Monitoring. An International Concern*, London: Macmillan.

Khan, A. (1993) *Structural Adjustment and Income Distribution: Issues and experiences*, Geneva: ILO.

Killick, T. (ed.) (1994) *The Flexible Economy. Causes, consequences and adaptability of national economies*, London: Routledge.

Lall, S. (1992) 'Technological capabilities and industrialisation', *World Development*, **20** (2), 165–86.

Lall, S. (1994) 'Industrial adaptation and technological capabilities in developing countries', in T. Killick (ed.), *The Flexible Economy. Causes, consequences and adaptability of national economies*, London: Routledge.

Latsch, W. (n.d.) 'Adjustment impact liberalisation and employment in African industry', mimeo, Welford College, Oxford.

Levine, R. (1991) *Cross-country studies of growth and policy: Methodological, conceptual and statistical problems*, World Bank Policy Research Working Paper 608, Washington, DC.

Lewis, W.A. (1954) 'Economic development with unlimited supplies of labour', *Manchester School of Economics and Social Studies*, **22**.

Lewis, W.A. (1979) 'The dual economy revisited', *Manchester School of Economics and Social Studies*, **47**, (3).

Lipton, M. and Ravallion, M. (1993) *Poverty and Policy*, World Bank Policy Research Working Paper 1130, Washington, DC.

Lucas, R.E. (1988) 'On the mechanics of economic development', *Journal of Monetary Economy*, **22**.

Lucas, R.E.B. (1994) 'The Impact of Structural Adjustment on Training Needs', *International Labour Review*, **133**, (5–6), 677–94.

Muqtada, M. and Hildeman, A. (eds) (1993) *Labour Markets and Human Resource Planning in Asia: Perspective and evidence*, New Delhi: ILO-ARTEP.

Newbery, D. and Stern, N. (1987) *The Theory of Taxation for Developing Countries*, New York and Oxford: Oxford University Press.

Pack, H. (1992) 'Learning and productivity change', in G. Helleiner (ed.), *Trade Policy: Industrialisation and Development*, UNV/WIDER, Oxford: Clarendon Press.

Pio, A. (1994) 'New Growth Theory and old development problems', *Development Policy Review*, **12**, (3), 277–300.

Rodrik, D. (1992) 'The limits of trade policy reform in developing countries', *Journal of Economic Prospectives*, **6**, (1).

Romer, P. (1986) 'Increasing returns and long-term growth', *Journal of Political Economy*, **94**, (5).

Romer, P. (1992) 'Two strategies for economic development. Using ideas and producing ideas', *Proceedings of the Annual Conference of Development Economics*, Washington, DC: World Bank.

Shaw, G.K. (1992) 'Policy Implications of Endogenous Growth Theory', *Economic Journal*, **102**, May.

Squire, L. (1989) 'Project evaluation in theory and practice', in H. Chenery and T. Srivastava (eds), *Handbook of Development Economics*, Amsterdam: Anshudon Elsewier.

Stern, N. (1991) 'The determinants of growth', *Economic Journal*, 122–33.

Stewart, F. (1992) 'Short term policies for long term development', in G.A. Cornia, R. van der Hoeven and T. Mkandawire (eds), *Adjustment with a Human Face*, Oxford: Oxford University Press.

Stewart, F. and van der Geest, W. (1995) 'Adjustment and social funds: Panacea in effective poverty reductions', ILO employment working paper.

Streeten, P. (1981) *First Things First. Meeting basic human needs in developing countries*, New York: Oxford University Press.

Summers, L. and Pritchet, L. (1993) 'World Bank World Development Report 1991 The Challenge of Development', *Economic Development and Cultural Change*, January.

Summers, L. and Pritchet, L. (1993) 'The Structural Adjustment Debate', *American Economic Review*, Papers and Proceedings, May.

Toye, J. (1995) *Structural Adjustment and Employment Policy*, Geneva: ILO.

UNDP (1991) *Human Development Report*, New York: UNDP.

van der Hoeven, R. (1988) *Planning for Basic Needs. A soft option on a solid policy*, Aldershot: Gower.

van der Hoeven, R. (1993) 'Can safety nets and compensating programmes be used for poverty alleviation', in R. van der Hoeven and P. Anker (eds), *Poverty Monitoring. An International Concern*, London: Macmillan.

van der Hoeven, R. and Anker, R. (eds) (1993) *Poverty Monitoring. An International Concern*, London: Macmillan.

van der Hoeven, R. and Stewart, F. (1993) *Social policies during periods of adjustment in Latin America*, Occasional Paper 18, Interdepartmental Project on Structural Adjustment, Geneva: ILO.

Villanueva, D. (1994) 'Openness, human development and fiscal policies', *IMF Staff Papers*, **41**, (1).

World Bank (1990) *World Development Report 1990*, Washington, DC: World Bank.

6. 'Folk and pop' in the orchestration of development projects

Alan Rew

THE CONTROL AND APPRECIATION OF SOCIAL FACTORS

Development investment projects are time-bound interventions that use human skills and other types of capital to enhance productive assets. In some cases, they aim to influence productive assets directly through the enhancement of human skills, the stimulation of trade and exchange or the creation of new technologies. In other cases, the intervention stimulates production indirectly through improvements in physical or service infrastructure including research and communications. A major issue in the planning, orchestration and subsequent evaluations of these projects is the degree of actual control over immediately relevant inputs and outputs that is thought desirable and feasible compared to the analysis of the project's context and influence. An understanding of influence and context is an essential part of the project manager's skills: he needs to appreciate the project's setting to better manage it and to influence the impact of hard-to-predict outcomes. The project designers, and then subsequently the project management, attempt to orchestrate the balance of resources and time between direct control and indirect influence and study in order to contextualize their responses. The social is included in these environments of influence and appreciation, together with other non-economic factors such as the ecological and the institutional ones. These non-economic factors are often so conflated that Meier (1994), in an evaluation of UK development research, treats them as a single, residual part of his evaluation.

The analytical contribution of non-economic social scientists working in the development aid agencies has expanded rapidly in the last decade (Rew, 1992). The contribution has focused on two themes that have become increasingly explicit: *cultural identity* and *popular participation*. In the first theme, the social analysts examine the way that the social and cultural dimensions of identity, for example gender, ethnicity, class and childhood, shape development processes. In the second theme, concepts of self-determination and social action, such as for example 'empowerment' and 'participation', are employed and elaborated. In this second aspect of the social development analyst's work, the concepts are used both to restate new development norms and prescriptions – for example, 'decentralized' and 'good government' – and to provide a recognizable vocabulary for the analysis of people as social actors who create localized, complex realities that in turn affect development intentions and outcomes.

In part, this expansion has been the natural outcome of foundations laid in the preceding decade by the pioneering social development specialists in the agencies. But in large measure it has arisen from the changed context for development aid policy created by post-Cold War conditions. In the early 1980s, the focus for strategic analysis was the national government and state institutions. A social analysis was mainly needed to add an extra dimension to investment appraisals that carried through the national government's economic and social policies. In the late 1980s and 1990s, however, there has been an explosion of non-governmental and community-based organizations in both the northern and the southern countries and of their networking and linkages (see Clarke, 1990). This has led to the appreciation that a project's web of stakeholders should include a range of institutions within civic society. At the same time, popular participation has become a necessary part of the agenda and now complements the focus on cultural and social identity that characterized the earlier projects.

Social assessments carried out by the new, NGO-influenced social development professionals, or by consultants managed by them, have proved especially useful to aid agencies when designing projects in the context of 'considerable uncertainty due to a lack of awareness, commitment or capacity' (Norton *et al.*, 1994). In this respect, social assessments have come to occupy a strategic role since they have encouraged and allowed the design of 'process projects' that build on experience and are responsive to change. Yet there are risks in this approach for the professionals and for the expansion of social development expertise. Questions that must be asked about the expansion of social development analysis within the aid agencies concern its sustainable impact on development project operations and aid policy and on the discipline of social anthropology.

Some of the risks concerning the impact on development operations are internal to the aid agencies. They concern the way in which the agencies may wish or need to restrict the impact of social development specialists at policy levels. There are also external factors concerning the changing nature of development aid. Calls for increased foreign development aid to prevent famine, rehabilitate the victims of civil war or to assist in the economic restructuring of formerly central-planned economies increase at the same

time that recognition grows of aid's failures. The argument that more investment funds are needed is countered by the argument that the need for self-
reliance and existing institutional capacities and social contexts limit the
amount of aid that can or should be absorbed. Indeed, there are a series of
moral ambiguities and choices in the relationship between foreign development aid and cultural choice within most third world countries. The demand
from some for more aid – 'because our country is poor' – is countered by
worries about the debt burden and by questions of the kind, 'Can foreign
experts really hope to bring about change in cultures so different from their
own?' And why allow 'experts', whether foreign or local, to be the ones to
decide which aspects of the society need 'developing'? Griffin (1991) has
forcefully restated a long-standing criticism of aid: that long-term foreign
assistance intended to alleviate poverty by promoting economic development
has failed. If it is accepted that foreign development aid is only needed for
short-term emergency assistance then the prospects for all development specialists, including social development specialists, look relatively unsustainable. On the other hand, it could be accepted that post-Cold War changes
have led to a more diverse institutional context for development and for aid
policy, with an increasing stress on civil society local and community-based
organization and NGOs and that, while this has difficulties, it presents, nonetheless, an important professional challenge for social development professionals in particular.

One way of meeting that challenge has come through the development
methodologies and perspectives that are seen as distinctively 'social' and are
largely associated with the analytical and advocacy work of Robert Chambers. His academic background is in development administration and his
contributions on 'farmer first', or 'rapid rural appraisal' (RRA) and now
'participatory rural appraisal' (PRA) are seen as methodological breakthroughs
that address the concerns of the development agencies yet also manage to
espouse grass-roots perspectives and keep 'the voices of the poor and disadvantaged' firmly in the minds of the administrators who might otherwise
prefer to forget them. The combination of grass-roots advocacy and management pragmatics is difficult to capture and place within an intellectual tra-
dition (see Brown, 1994). It might be termed, in keeping with Chambers' own
style of conceptual labelling, 'RPA' – 'radical public administration' – or by
those less favourably disposed, 'SSP – supply-side populism'.

The implications of PRA are not yet clear. The methodological movements
may herald a new progressive stage in the incorporation of social analysis
into development planning. Alternatively, they may, if the supply-side populism
criticism is sustained, lead to a cul-de-sac in aid agency method, with a
general interest in PRA but without its successful incorporation as a central,
guiding principle in agencies' operations. The implications for anthropology

are ambiguous at best. PRA can be regarded as an alternative to classical social anthropology's extractive research methods, or it may be seen (Chambers, 1994, p. 955) as 'an extension and application of social anthropological insights'. It is certainly a suite of methods that social anthropologists should subject to close scrutiny and analysis.

The potential for PRA and of aid agencies' willingness to commit themselves operationally to the empowerment of the disadvantaged and poor is difficult to assess. Advocates have considerable enthusiasm and hope for it. The cases of failure in application are thought to be very few indeed and, anyway, further challenge the enthusiasts towards new methodological achievements in the interests of participation. A perspective on these issues may be gained by assessing the incorporation of sociocultural factors in past development projects, especially those of the late 1970s and the 1980s. Given the importance of basic human needs strategies in the late 1970s, the absorption of a new breed of technical consultant – the social development specialist – should have been relatively easy.

A SURVEY OF AID PROJECT DOCUMENTS AND THEIR CONTEXT

The survey to be reported on here tries to advance the debate by reviewing the state of the operational art at the end of the 1980s through an analysis of key development project texts from a number of aid agencies. The time frame for the investigation, and the fact that the survey period coincides with a change in the development paradigm, was wholly coincidental and not a part of the survey design. The survey concentrated on post-completion evaluation documents accessible in the UK and tried to establish the degree of interest in sociocultural factors within the text. It was undertaken with the encouragement and support of Curtis Roosevelt and T.S. Epstein and was undertaken to advance an understanding of cultural entitlements and human rights.[1] Nonetheless, by the coincidence of its timing the survey does give a picture of the operational art during the 1980s. It allows us to develop a statement of a baseline against which expectations for post-Cold War development activity can be set.

The method for the 'meta-evaluation' was to identify how project planners and evaluation specialists themselves wrote about issues of cultural identity rather than to impose a prior definition of 'social' or 'culture' on the analysis. This inductive way of working would, we felt, allow even poorly articulated views of culture and society to emerge.[2] We accepted that the factors we were interested in might emerge in both implicit as well as explicit ways and that a generous interpretation should be used. Beyond the initial stages of sifting in which broad orders of magnitude can be established, the results are therefore interpretative and qualitative.

Two key questions were asked of a database of 386 project evaluation and appraisal documents, and a sub-sample of 113 reports, from five aid agencies. First, have sociocultural dimensions been recognized, whether explicitly or implicitly, by project preparation and evaluation teams? Second (in the case of the sampled projects only), do they go on to specify a methodology or even a broadly indicated approach that would allow sociocultural factors to be incorporated and integrated with the economic and technical analysis and the recommendations for the project? We have also assumed it might be possible to ask a third question: did the ability to recognize incorporate sociocultural dimensions in design or implementation contribute to the project's degree of success or failure? The results of the survey led us to conclude that it was not appropriate to ask it on this occasion.[3]

A total of 386 database records for project texts were first established from a list of over 1000 documents. The records were entered partly on the basis of availability (of the documents in Swansea or in UK libraries) and partly by an initial judgement about relevance to the survey. Relevance, it was agreed, would be that the sector or type of project would be heavily dependent on many people's behaviour patterns and participation (for example, the adoption of new crops or family planning) or that the project would enforce changes in behaviour patterns (such as resettlement from infrastructure development). Types of project that were only concerned with, say, major highway improvement or the development of trade were not listed. The relevance of the text was established using these criteria through an examination of the tables of content and internal headings. It took a considerable proportion of the total research time of four months to establish the database. It was then decided to take a (random) sample of one in three of these documents and to carry out more detailed investigations. In the event, 113 documents were read in full, giving a 30 per cent sample of the initial population of documents that had been screened. The likely relevant sections of the text were entered in full into an unlimited text database and then successively searched by key words.

The type of projects covered by the eventual database were as shown below:

Natural resources		110
Water and irrigation	72	
Agriculture, rural development and environment	38	
Roads and public infrastructure		93
Education and training		91
Health, population and nutrition		53
Urban, industrial and other		39
Total		386

The survey showed that three-quarters (85) of the 113 reports in the database did refer to sociocultural factors in one way or another. This had not been expected, despite our initial screening for broad relevance. The initial hypothesis had been that a sizeable minority of the documents would evidence notable interest and that the majority would essentially ignore sociocultural considerations. Our view stemmed, in part, from our prior view that probably one-half to two-thirds of investment projects would avoid much reference to social and cultural variables. These factors, we thought from previous project experience, might be treated as marginal in economic and technical design; and in the search for coherence, project design would rely on technical or economic design criteria and treat sociocultural information as largely anecdotal. Only a small but growing proportion of projects would, we hypothesized, have recognized the need for a specialized social science input. We had simply assumed that any evaluation's willingness to address sociocultural factors would reflect either the involvement of specialized consultants on highly specific topics such as resettlement or irrigation management that explicitly prompted a managerial interest in the social and community context of operations.

In fact, we had seen the issue as too polarized and had not counted on the widespread but less specialized awareness of social and cultural context that is evident in the evaluations. Some of this interest may be merely 'lip-service' contractual: to be on the safe side, donors and governments added a 'social' element to collective terms of reference and consultants responded with a 'social' section to meet these requirements. This does not, however, appear to be the key consideration mentions of and there does seem to be a definite awareness of the need to consider them during project planning and implementation. Problems were identified that could not be explained by the technical or microeconomic analyses. The interpretation and use of a sociocultural perspective in design or in implementation strategies, however, is rarely consistent in the documents. Rather, the factors are handled in a largely inconsistent and arbitrary manner.

Social and cultural factors were offered as 'catch-all' factors that could be stated as reasons for difficulty in projects but that are not or cannot be taken further, given the project's design and the state of the operational art. It is clear that an awareness of social context had not permeated the aid agencies' or executive agencies' normal procedures to any extent. Cultural and social considerations are generally viewed as 'outside' the agency and as about 'the customs of the locals', rather than as an essential aspect of technical assistance work and design. For example:

> The understanding of Indian village life has always been influenced by a romantic notion according to which the Indian village community is basically harmonious

with a unified leadership that is capable of managing the village resources [whereas the current conception] stresses its incipient class, caste and factional conflicts. It also recognises the deficiencies of local political institutions. Local leaders are often biased in terms of class, caste and faction and they have little capability of managing the joint property resources. (Swedish International Development Authority (SIDA) Evaluation Report, 1987/8)

The extract shows that sociocultural factors are thought to influence development programmes. The evaluation's overall conclusion is that the project benefits failed to trickle down to 'the target groups' – poor and marginal farmers, landless labourers, scheduled castes and women – who were 'on the whole left outside the project'. The document concludes: 'The only possible conclusions from this failure to reach the target groups are (1) that the goal of reaching them was unrealistic from the start or (2) that the project has failed to work out or implement institutional mechanisms to attain this goal.' We are left, then, with questions, not answers. Does the failure to develop any local institutional mechanism in the project imply a chauvinistic dismissal of the local leadership and its incompetence; or does it mean that the project was misconceived from the start; or that it would have succeeded, had there been no target groups?

The inclusion of a non-economic social scientist in the project implementation and evaluation teams was one clear indication that the agencies were explicitly aware of social and cultural factors and could deal with them on an established institutional basis. It was, however, difficult to establish the extent of these specialists' impact on design or implementation. In some 5–10 per cent of the projects, it was apparent that separate sociocultural studies had been commissioned and were usually attached as annexes. Surprisingly, there was no direct indication in the main texts of how these studies has been utilized.

It is necessary to present another result of the survey in order to understand this combination of the consciousness of culture and society with an arbitrary treatment of it. With relatively few exceptions, it is the projects that are seen as the fundamental entities. The projects are not viewed as an explicit set of objectives and aims, planning processes and resource flows with respect to the recipient society. They are most often seen in quite mechanistic terms, as discrete economic and even physical entities or as containers of development that have been placed in the local society and economy for its members to open. With rare exceptions, the agency starts from an engineering or economistic discourse that makes issues of social agency and cultural identity only incidental to the project design and implementation.

It is this discursive hiatus and the lack of an apparent methodology to incorporate the sociocultural factors that may explain the inconsistency and dual tendency within the data. On the one hand, there is an evident wish to include culture as an explanation for project outcomes and processes. On the other hand, culture and society are seen as obstacles to the project or, largely implicitly, as factors to be managed reactively if the project is to succeed.

In some 90 per cent of all reports, management is cited as either a problem, a shortcoming or as inefficient. In fact, these mentions occur so frequently with all agencies and sectors that we felt it may not be sufficient to treat the findings at face value but that is also necessary to examine whether 'management' was being use as an oblique way of referring to something else. Closer examination of the texts does reveal that the 'management' problems often reveal concerns about 'the management capacity' of local officials and entre-preneurs, breakdowns in cross-cultural communication, a subsequent intoler-ance, a mismatch between local leadership and cultural values and the management structures of the projects, and conflicts between the develop-ment community's interests and those of the local staff and beneficiaries. We concluded that 'management difficulties' can often be a proxy indicator of social conflict that invited a fuller, less internalized and coded analysis. What might otherwise appear to be a rather straightforward middle-level manage-ment function can in the context of an externally funded development project become a point of friction between project personnel and within local com-munity relations, ultimately frustrating top-level management in its attempt to resolve it. An evaluation of the effectiveness of technical assistance per-sonnel observed:

> seemingly trivial issues play a role within the organisational climate ... vehicles are a particular problem. The use and abuse causes frequent problems and mis-trust. Both sides perceive the other as using the cars for illegitimate purposes! Expatriates are using it for vacations and locking it when they go on home leave and local staff for private transport and family purposes. (Norwegian Agency for Development (NORAD), 1988, p. 120)

Another proxy indicator of sociocultural awareness may be gender aware-ness. In 35 per cent of the texts, discussion of social and cultural traditions was intertwined with discussion of customary gender relations. To some extent, this conflation arose through the stereotyped lumping together of two 'difficult' social development areas for the ease of implementation and evalu-ation management purposes. In other cases, it arose because 'gender rela-tions' were validly seen as a sub-component of a social and cultural assessment and therefore included without special comment or separation; perhaps in other cases heightened awareness of one had led to a heightened awareness of the other.

Underlying the original survey design was a hypothesis that there would be variation according to donor practice and according to the nature of specific sectors. Because of the small numbers involved, the results cannot be thought conclusive. Nonetheless, there were a number of results that challenged our initial guesses about what we would find and in some cases appeared counterintuitive and suggestive of further research.

There was considerable variation in the styles of each agency's evaluation reports, emphasizing the differing origins and charters of organization and accountability of the aid agencies, the scale of the projects they tended to organize, and the dominant intellectual traditions of the countries concerned. In keeping with these contrasts, our preliminary expectations had been that the World Bank was probably less ready to recognize sociocultural factors than the (mainly European) bilateral agencies.[4] The Bank's known emphasis on the necessary economic efficiencies of the markets for labour, land and capital when dealing with welfare issues was assumed to be inimical to the development of social action methodologies. Equally, it had been assumed that the more collective and state welfare traditions of post-World War II Europe would encourage the planning of projects that were more sensitive to social and cultural factors. However, to judge from the texts, the World Bank appeared as sensitive to sociocultural factors as any of the bilaterals and in some cases was even more so. The one agency that had most thoroughly incorporated sociocultural factors was SIDA. This is not always consistent, but the evaluation reports did show a tendency towards greater use of social, cultural and historical interpretations of development. On the whole, however, the variations in agency style and traditions were not thought to be especially important as an explanation of sociocultural awareness.

There are also contrasts by project type or sector. Of the five major classifications into which the data falls – natural resources and irrigation, roads and infrastructure, education, health and population, and urban and industrial development – the educational and training projects were distinctive in their relative lack of recognition of social and cultural factors. Over 30 per cent of these project documents appeared to take no account of these factors. By contrast, the health and population projects all made some mention of these factors and in some cases had the fullest accounts and acceptance of behavioural aspects. It is difficult to see that it is the nature of the sector's context that could produce these contrasts. Rather, it is that there is relatively little search for the attitudinal and social backgrounds influencing educational outcomes, whereas there is concern to trace beliefs and behaviours related to health care and disease prevention. Two other unexpected sub-sectoral findings concern small-scale industry and environmental conservation. 'Environmental conservation' projects, with 11 projects in the database, and 'small-scale industries', also with 11 projects in the database, had no mentions of sociocultural factors. The result was unexpected for small-scale industries since these projects need to explore the relevance or not of the cultural context for small businessmen and their behaviour. It is also surprising in the case of

environmental conservation since in many cases questions of resource conservation will involve the enforcement of state rights over the tenures, liveli-
hoods and customary uses of minority and/or resource poor groups.

CURRENT SOCIAL DEVELOPMENT PRACTICE

Although the survey was carried out at a time that allowed an account of the
projects of the 1980s, many of the issues raised in the results are of continuing importance today. The survey revealed that there was a diffuse interest in
social and cultural factors but also lack of impact through failure to develop a
methodology. The relative lack of impact continues to worry social development specialists working in international aid organizations even though recent methodological developments promise a greater medium-term prospect
of sustainability, effectiveness and recognition than there was in the early
1980s. The survey results showed that there had been a variable impact on
sectors. Variable impact continues to be a tactical and strategic issue and has
considerable importance for the careers of social development professionals.
Some are unfortunate in having to work with divisions that are suspicious or
antagonistic to the growth of social development expertise, while cognate
professionals forge alliances of mutual benefit. For example, the education
development and human resources specialism continues to be dominated by
economists whose analysis is economistic rather than sociological.

The long-term role of social development specialists is also somewhat
unclear. There is, for example, considerable variation between aid agencies in
the way they incorporate social development expertise. In some cases, the
critical social development mass is dispersed into a range of geographical and
technical functions. In others, it is concentrated, and possibly contained, in a
single division. Sociocultural assessment is now very much part of the project's
'furniture', but its practitioners worry about their impact and effectiveness.

The survey does raise the question of whether or not the analytical paradigm used by the social development analysts could be improved or was even
minimally satisfactory for its dual purpose of both capturing local knowledge
and realities and allowing for summary and synthesis for use by project
planners. The texts we surveyed indicate evidence of a static external analysis. It was dependent on the professional expertise of the analysts who should
provide a social engineering expertise comparable to the core irrigation engineering specialisms with whom they had to work: they provide the 'people
side' of the design. The social experts were largely dependent on their personal and academic authority when trying to convince other technical specialists. The emphasis on a special 'folk' or 'indigenous' knowledge that was
to be uncovered, analysed and then made manageable was both an asset and a

handicap. It gave social analysts a distinctive field of enquiry and technical authority but it expected them to provide a method for controlling the cultural or indigenous elements, and thus gave rise to in-built disappointment. The disappointment was not, however, radical. It was widely accepted that human behaviour is difficult to predict and that the other technical specialisms have comparable problems in predicting risk and uncertainty. All project planners accept that there can be both expected and unexpected results from an intervention. These results can, in turn, be either desirable or undesirable. On the whole, the effect of sociocultural factors was seen, in the project documents, to lead to results that were unexpected and undesirable. Those results that were both expected and desirable were attributed to the design of the project, good luck, skill in implementation management and so on. The aim in employing a sociocultural specialist was to anticipate more of the previously unexpected results and to design out the undesirable factors. These are not easy tasks to accomplish for a lone specialist acting in a technical and outsider's role.

Lessons are learnt over time and organizations may need years rather than months to change practices and procedures. It is not at all clear what time period is needed for aid agencies to distil new methods from cumulative experience and to adopt recruitment aims, training and procedures that ensure project staff have a better understanding of the influence of sociocultural factors. Nonetheless, the growing acceptance of the need to incorporate sociocultural analysis has been especially marked in certain technical fields in the last ten years. There has been, in particular, a marked acceptance of non-economic social science contributions in the field of irrigation management, in the design and implementation of water supply improvement schemes and in farming systems research. The field-based research publications of Korten (1980) Korten and Alfonso (1981) and Uphoff (1992) on irrigation management have demonstrated the need for more contextual and experiential accounts of policy implementation and scheme management. At the same time, social anthropologists may have grown more rather than less sceptical about anthropology's terms of engagement in development work and this has made the incorporation of its insights even more difficult to realize. To take just one well researched example, Porter *et al.* (1991) have evaluated the history of an Australian assisted aid project in Kenya from technical, economic, cultural and political perspectives. They concluded that the designers' and managers' continuing wish to control the project impacts and to create a scheme that mirrored the interests of the Kenyan state, Australian bilateral aid and the Australian design consultants also led to widespread disappointment, an unsustainable scheme and a project management system that further obscured the local population's response and their knowledge systems.

Chambers (1992, p. 48) blames a tyranny of professionals and outsiders for the failure to appreciate the need for new lessons:

> ...we, the professional outsiders, had a monopoly of powers of analysis. Most outsiders have then either lectured, holding sticks and wagging fingers, or have interviewed, machine-gunning with rapid fire questions, interrupting, and not listening beyond immediate replies. ... Our beliefs, demeanour, behaviour and our attitudes have been self-validating. Treated as incapable, rural people have behaved as incapable, hiding their capabilities from us, and even from themselves. Nor have we known how to enable them to express, share and extend their knowledge. The ignorance and inabilities of rural people have been not only an illusion, but an artefact of our own arrogance and ignorance.

To move beyond this impasse, the assimilation of lessons based on the new professionalism of the NGOs and a recognition of past errors and inadequacies is needed. Chambers has done much to undermine the tyranny of the outside professionals with their reliance on technical and questionnaire surveys administered, usually, with insufficient regard for local realities and contexts. After a period of experimentation with quick-and-dirty rapid rural appraisal methods, the emphasis in alternative appraisal techniques is now on relaxed and participative methods (PRA). Chambers argues (1992, p. 45) that there is need for a movement away from extractive methods of data gathering and analysis to methods that reduce external dominance and that start a process of empowerment. He writes: 'Both the traditional questionnaire survey, and the classical social anthropological investigation are extractive even though their means of extraction differ' (ibid., p. 44). The need is for participatory data gathering and analysis through which the initiative is passed to the people. 'The time of PRA may have come.'

What is PRA? It is a set of techniques and methods 'intended to enable local people to conduct their own analysis, and often to plan and take action' and there has been a major growth in this activity in recent years. Chambers (1994) describes it in some detail. It is 'a growing family of approaches and methods to enable local people to share, enhance and analyse their knowledge of life and conditions, to plan and to act'. It flows from and owes much to 'activist participatory research', 'applied anthropology', field research on farming systems, agroecosystem analysis and its parent 'rapid rural appraisal'. Chambers acknowledges that the problem with rapid rural appraisal is that, while having the virtues of simplicity of data collection, cost efficiency and on-site (even if hurried) investigation, it also has the vices of no quality control and the ever-present danger of an extractive learning by outsiders. It facilitated the rapid production of plans and reports but did not contribute to sustainable local action and institutional development.

Chambers traces the introduction of participation into the standard planning practice of rural development to the 1980s or even before. By 1985, it was a recurrent theme in Michael Cernea's edited volume, *Putting People First*, that drew on experience from earlier years. Around 1988, participatory RRAs were listed as one of a number of 'RA' methodologies. Subsequently, there was an explosion of innovation in India, especially in the NGO sector. By 1992, Chambers was in a position to take stock and review the developments in techniques and methodology.

The effectiveness of location-specific projects depends on good-quality information about local interests and effective communication between outsiders and community members. PRA has gained popularity as a method of information collection that is held to be more reliable than conventional social research because 'the objective is less to gather data, and much more to start a process ... the outsider is less extractor and more convenor and catalyst'. The approach has gained considerable popularity in natural resource project planning, especially in forestry and farming systems research and in programmes designed to achieve equity for women and in health and nutrition projects. It is used by a variety of agencies, especially NGOs, at project and programme level.

A major recognition of its potential is the adoption of PRA approaches in poverty assessments by the World Bank. Norton and Stephens (1994) show how the incorporation of participatory research techniques to discern local-level perceptions of poverty is able to 'give a voice to the poor' while also enriching the World Bank's technical poverty profile and filling lacunae in that institution's understanding of the dimensions of poverty. The use of participatory research methods was found to have an important policy relevance and not just anecdotal or illustrative utility. The data collected showed the variation in the attributes of poverty and led to more meaningful internal discussion within the Bank itself. There were also gains identified, from the Bank's point of view, in the link between governments' poverty strategy documents, the Bank's lending strategy and the involvement of institutional 'stakeholders' within the country concerned. The forging of these links was thought most promising in the case of Morocco and Peru, although 'to be sure, both countries represent examples where the participatory involvement entailed a strong 'carrot and stick' approach to Bank government dialogue' (ibid., p. 223).

This apparently ready acceptance of PRA (and its in-house advisors and managers) by the aid agencies contrasts with the far more cautious incorporation of individual social analysts by the aid agencies in the 1980s. The contrast may stem from the cumulative results of incremental lessons learnt from operational experience. It can be argued that the initial experience of the 1980s has led to the replication, a decade later and on a larger scale, of the earlier lessons. Alternatively, it can be argued that the main difference is conceptual. The projects of the 1980s stressed cultural and social identity considerations; the newer projects have stressed process, social action and empowerment.

Norton and Stephens (1994), reviewing the use of PRA within poverty assessments in Africa, note trade-offs between the immediate duties of the Bank's task managers and the need to address the institutions of civil society in poverty alleviation programmes. They show that the principal analytical tension within PRA centres on the relationship between the participation of 'primary' and of 'institutional' stakeholders. It is worth noting, in this regard, that anthropological analysis may be being advanced by anthropologists working within the aid agencies in a way that the discipline of social anthropology does not fully appreciate – partly because it does not find it easy to review the relevant literature sources. Nonetheless, with this and a few other exceptions (Mosse, 1994; Rew, 1994) little has been written by anthropologists about the local-level and theoretical context of rapid and participatory appraisals within major aid agencies.

A very important contribution to the theoretical and critical literature of development planning research methods has been made by my colleague David Mosse (1994). Mosse has been in a position to see both sides of the picture through involvement in the PRAs but was also able to maintain a critical stance to the development and use of the methods within the community. It is especially interesting that each of the cases he reports is perceived by PRA advocates as the *one* case in which it was rejected. This is not, however, true even for southern India, where it has been pioneered. I am aware of cases in which rural elites have declared their lack of interest in the exercise or in which it is apparent that the exercise misfired somewhat and that groups within the rural population could not voice their disquiet or wishes.

Mosse's contribution is to show, not that a PRA failed, but that some of the information from PRAs is likely to be problematic. The information is elicited in a social context where the influence of power, authority and gender inequalities is great and highly likely to bias the PRA exercise and results. In particular, it is the public (and self-consciously so) nature of PRAs that makes the production of local knowledge an outcome of what Mosse calls 'officializing strategies' and 'muting': the interaction of insiders with outsiders in a public forum turns the information into action within an 'officializing' context and also mutes and silences the voices of women. Furthermore, there is a heavy bias towards *verbalized* information and certain kinds of practical knowledge are encoded in the culture in ways that make it difficult if not impossible to gain access to them by PRA means. The knowledge remains encoded in technical routines and practical experience and cannot easily be elicited verbally. Public and private participation and observation are needed over time, and not just intensive interrogation in the context of reversals and visual techniques.

Poor, low-status people want to combine security with self-determination and so will resist, from time to time, the call to voice their needs. Issues of cultural identity and indigenous knowledge remain: the 'incapacities' or mutedness that Chambers and Mosse both note are not reached simply by a change in the role and behaviour of outsiders within a framework of supply-side populism. Chambers himself notes five dangers in the use of the method. These can be compressed into potential dangers of ritualism and insincerity, amateurish overenthusiasms and hostility from the participating specialisms and disciplines. Perhaps the biggest challenge, he writes, is in the establishment of PRA as a way of operating in large-scale organizations. So far, there has been an acceptance on the part of NGOs, government field organizations and some universities and training institutions. Its incorporation into the major agencies and the degree to which anthropologists analyse the institutions of civil society from within the agencies still need more detailed examination. The results from the survey of documents are one contribution to the continuing analysis that is needed.

NOTES

1. The survey originated from an idea of Scarlett Epstein. It was sponsored and funded by Curtis Roosevelt and the Roosevelt Institute. I am especially indebted to them both for their personal interest and support and for the extended discussions that led to the research reported on here. I was ably assisted by Ikaweba Bunting and Damian Rew, both of whom searched for and then entered the relevant documentary texts. Ikaweba Bunting was responsible for the textual analysis and the draft final report; Damian Rew was responsible for the initial design and maintenance of the database. The responsibility for the overall design and analysis is mine alone.

2. The key words used to identify actual or potential cultural factors were the following: culture, cultural, sociocultural, socioeconomic, sociopolitical, traditional, local, indigenous, institutional, ethnic social considerations, ethnic patterns, institutional setting, land tenure, customs, social structures, indigenous structures, traditional practices, historical settings, farm structure, impact on women, social organization, community-based, historical patterns.

3. The investigation had aimed initially to research the precise relationship between cultural sensitivity and project success and to do so with a combination of wide multilateral and bilateral coverage and selected detailed investigations of particular projects. As the research began, it became clear that these aims were too ambitious. The coverage had to be considerably reduced because documents were unobtainable from certain selected multilaterals and the aim of surveying the contribution of cultural factors to project success had to be amended accordingly.

4. The bilateral agencies were the United States Agency for International Development; the United Kingdom Overseas Development Administration; the Swedish International Development Agency; and the Danish International Development Agency. The one multilateral agency was the World Bank. The United Nations Development Programme (UNDP) and

the Food and Agriculture Organization (FAO) were not able to release evaluation documents.

REFERENCES

Brown, D. (1994) 'Seeking the consensus: populist tendencies at the interface between consultancy and research', in A. Rew (ed.), *From Consultancy to Research? The interface between consultancy and research*, proceedings of a conference held at the Centre for Development Studies, University of Wales, Swansea, March.

Cernea, M. (1991 *Putting People First: sociological variables in rural development*, 2nd edn, Oxford: Oxford University Press for World Bank

Chambers, R. (1992) 'Rural appraisal: rapid, relaxed and participatory', IDS Discussion Papers 311, 1–90.

Chambers, R. (1994) 'The Origins and Practice of Participatory Rural Appraisal', *World Development*, **22**, (7), 953–69.

Clarke, J. (1991) *Democratising Development: the role of voluntary organisations*, London: Earthscan.

Eyben, R. and Ladbury, S. (1994) 'Popular participation in aid-assisted projects: why more in theory than practice?', in S. Wright and N. Nelson (eds), *Power and Participatory Development: theory and practice*, London: IT Publications, pp. 192–200.

Griffin, K. (1991) 'Foreign Aid after the Cold War', *Development and Change*, **22**, (4), 645–85.

Hann, C. (ed.) (1994) *When History Accelerates: essays on rapid social change, complexity and creativity*, London: Athlone.

Hobart, M. (ed.) (1993) *An Anthropoligical Critique of Development: the growth of ignorance*, London: Routledge.

Korton, D.C. and Alfonso, F.B. (eds) (1983) *Bureaucracy and the Poor: Closing the Gap*, West Hartford, Conn.: Kumarian Press.

Meier, G.M. (1994) 'Review of Development Research in the UK: report to the Development Studies Association', *Journal of International Development*, **6**, (5), 465–512.

Mosse, D. (1994) 'Authority, gender and knowledge: theoretical reflections on the practice of participatory rural appraisal', *Development and Change*, **25**, (3), 497–526.

NORAD (1988) Evaluation of Technical Assistance.

Norton, A. and Stephens, T. (1994) *Participation in Poverty Assessments Workshop on Participatory Development*, Washington, DC: World Bank.

Norton, A., Owen, D. and Milimo, J. (1994) *Zambia Poverty Assessment: Volume 4: Participatory Poverty Assessment*, Washington, DC: Southern Africa Department, World Bank.

Porter, D., Allen, B. and Thompson, G. (1991) *Development in Practice: paved with good intentions*, London: Routledge.

Rew, A. (1992) 'The consolidation of British development anthropology', *Development Anthropology Network*, **10**, (1), 23–6.

Rew, Alan (1994) 'Social Standards and Social Theory', in C. Hann (ed.), *When History Accelerates: essays on rapid social change, complexity and creativity*, London: Athlone.

SIDA (1988) Evaluation Report India Assistance Programme.

Uphoff, N. (1992) *Learning from Gal Oya: possibilities for participatory development and post-Newtonian social science*, Ithaca, NY: Cornell University Press.

Wright, S. and Nelson, N. (eds) (1994) *Power and Participatory Development: theory and practice*, London: IT Publications.

7. The ODA's process approach to projects: experience in India and lessons for project management

Ita O'Donovan

INTRODUCTION

The history of *evaluation* in the Overseas Development Administration (ODA) has tended to be one of post-evaluation (Higginbottom, 1990). A broad overview from several studies in a range of countries highlights some of the concerns derived from ODA evaluations:

- a concern that project appraisals have been too optimistic in relation to project costs;
- a concern that the desire to engage in a policy area rushed the sectoral analysis and project preparation period;
- a concern that projects were schedule-driven, thereby impeding the learning process;
- a concern that consultants sometimes get too involved in project development;
- a concern that evaluation has tended to be an internal process which excludes some major stakeholders;
- a view that improved project procedures could deal with most of the above concerns.

These concerns raise issues about general project processes and particular evaluation processes. In 1991, the ODA adopted a wide strategy aimed at achieving qualitative improvements in the delivery of aid. A contributing factor here was increased pressure by governments to demonstrate value for money. Part of this strategy involves the introduction of a process approach to projects. This new approach to project preparation and management encourages a team-based analysis of project requirements, a participative approach to working partners overseas and a clear definition of the project's purpose and structure. The introduction of a process approach has been linked with a system of project management developed by TeamUP Technologies Inc. This America-based company has worked closely in the field with ODA to develop and enhance their methodology. The TeamUP approach is a participative tool used to develop a project-logical framework.

The views expressed in this chapter are based on a review of a sample of projects in India for the ODA (O'Donovan, 1994a). The sample included projects for which a process approach had been adopted and others which were not so clearly categorized in terms of process. The purpose of this chapter is to focus on key concepts and issues that arise for the ODA in implementing a process approach to projects. The chapter first examines the ideal model of a 'blueprint approach' at one end of a continuum with the ideal model of a process project at the opposite end. The validity of this dichotomy is questioned. It will be suggested that it is probably more fruitful to consider the complexity of all projects and the need to maintain a balance between the classical contract elements of projects and the relational contracts of projects.

The point is made that certain internal and external management factors need to be addressed by the ODA in developing an effective process approach to projects. Emphasis is placed on the dynamism of the project cycle and key factors are identified within the total cycle for improved project management. Links are made between the management of change and project management and certain critical success factors are identified which increase the possibility of impact and sustainability. Finally, the chapter considers project management in terms of decision making, networking, autonomy, clarity of relationships and evaluation.

THE BLUEPRINT PROJECT APPROACH

Let us first look at a blueprint model which has a long operational history within the ODA and other major aid agencies. The model of a blueprint can be characterized as a project which is designed and delivered to a set time frame from which there should be no deviation. Classically, this is often represented as an engineering project such as bridge building or road construction. There are clear known objectives, inputs, activities, outputs, costs and time frames. While it is recognized that the blueprint project will be located in the wider environment, there is confidence that the schedule of activities can be adhered to.

In essence, the blueprint approach places great faith in the following elements: a donor-dominated planning process; donor-driven technological expertise to include knowledge and skills; donor ability to maintain the time schedule of project activities to completion; the recipients' willingness to facilitate and participate in the project at designated points, and the recipients' ability to absorb the direct transfer package. The blueprint model in its purist form involves ownership and control by the donor. One suggested imperative for this approach is the need to be accountable to one's own government for efficient expenditure of the public purse. In psychological terms, the blueprint project framework becomes a classical contract between the donor and recipient. It is analogous to a job description where one's duties and responsibilities are itemized. The danger is that a job description is what people work to when they work to rule. What is omitted in such a contract are the relationship elements, such as ownership and commitment, willingness to collaborate, share information and cooperate in the outcomes. Kay (1993) in his analysis of successful enterprises demonstrated clearly that these relationship elements contribute to distinctive capability and competitive advantage in the delivery of public or private goods and services.

THE PROCESS PROJECT APPROACH

In contrast, the process approach to projects suggests very much the idea of an open system, which is so permeated by influences that it is extremely difficult to state precisely what it will contain, especially in terms of exact costs, time frames and activities. In its purist form, it is possible to state objectives in terms of goal and purpose; then project personnel are requested to devise outputs and activities for the first year of the project. Subsequent activities and outputs need then to be defined on the basis of project learning and their ability to contribute to goal and purpose. The model recognizes that change in one part of the system is likely to have ripple effects on other sub-systems. The process approach to projects emphasizes the following elements: a project is a set of activities within a boundary which is permeable, ownership and commitment from stakeholders is essential to project success and therefore all known stakeholders should be involved from inception; the project process must be a joint learning process between stakeholders; the learning process is expected to build capacity and contribute to sustainability; learning implies the ability to reflect on current practice within a project and, if necessary, or change procedures and approaches.

The process approach emphasizes the relationship aspects of the project. It seeks to include stakeholders in collaboration, cooperation and the sharing of project-related information to increase the possibility of successful planning and implementation (Korten, 1980). The emphasis is on ownership and commitment right from inception. In contractual terms, there is a reliance for success on the implicit relationship side and the project appears to struggle to produce the classical contract model of the blueprint variety.

The question arises, is this concept of two distinct types ('blueprint' and 'process') really valid, with the secondary question as to whether particular kinds of projects lend themselves more easily to one or other approach: for example, civil engineering projects point to blueprint and institutional development to process. Both questions are easily challenged and what we are really looking for is a balance within projects of classical and relationship contracts. To clarify, the process approach recognizes more clearly that a project is an open system and that success in terms of impact and sustainability requires projects to be interactive learning processes. It is also a question of knowing where and when (and how) we should emphasize key contractual relationships; it is essentially about clarity of roles and relationships.

A PRELIMINARY BREAKDOWN OF THE PROBLEM

Table 7.1 shows a simple relationship between known and unknown tasks, the environment and design. Complexity of design increases with unknown tasks and instability and unpredictability in environment. The process approach to projects is seeking to recognize the complexity involved in managing the project process by highlighting the importance of the task and environment relationship for the project cycle. Practical experience and evaluation reports confirm that this is generally the case. The project is ultimately striving to be in balance with its environment, meaning the economic, social, historical and political contexts in which it takes place.

Table 7.1   Project task, environment and design

Project tasks	Environment	Design of project cycle
Known	Stable and predictable	Simple
Unknown	Stable and predictable	Less simple
Known	Unstable and unpredictable	Complex
Unknown	Unstable and unpredictable	More complex

A STRATEGIC SHIFT FOR THE ODA

In developing a process approach to projects, the ODA is seeking to establish a distinctive capability in this area. To succeed it is necessary for potential partners/stakeholders in ODA activities both to understand what is meant by the process approach and to want to work in that way in relation to projects. The question then is, how can ODA convey to potential collaborators the benefits of adopting the process approach? There are four essential requirements for the process approach to projects:

1. the requirement to have a clear specification of the totality of projects: this is often represented in a project framework;
2. the need to gain participation, commitment, ownership and learning among and between project stakeholders, as encapsulated in the process approach to projects;
3. the requirement to get things done: this requires action on the ground as well as flexible responses from ODA internal procedures;
4. to manage the project efficiently and effectively.

The skill, therefore, is to find ways of maintaining a balance between the desire to have specificity within project documentation and the need to demonstrate the ability of ODA to respond to the needs and learning experiences that arise within projects from the moment of conception, coupled with the desire for projects to maintain visibility on the ground.

The next section looks first at the concepts of specification and ownership and then at the need to achieve project outcomes while managing the project efficiently and effectively.

ESSENTIAL REQUIREMENTS WITHIN THE PROCESS APPROACH TO PROJECTS: EXPLICIT AND IMPLICIT CONTRACTS

In all organizational processes there are different kinds of exchange relationships. This is true of project processes. Some exchange relationships are implicit and others are explicit. The most common are *spot contract* relationships where there is an agreed immediate exchange of a good or service. In many cases, this is insufficient protection for the parties to the exchange. In such cases, people use a second kind of contract, often called *classical contracts* to make the details explicit, especially where there is a long-term relationship envisaged in the exchange. A project framework is a good example of a classical contract. The essence of a classical contract is that it contains detailed provision as to how transaction between parties will evolve as time unfolds. The desire is to clarify what will occur between the parties to the exchange. Implicit in the notion of classical contracts is the idea of accountability and performance management. If you specify requirements, it implies that you intend to hold some party accountable for achievement or non-achievement. Therefore it is essential for successful implementation of classical contracts that performance is tightly managed. People must be accountable for performance at the individual and collective level. The idea here is that the creation of classical contracts, as in a project framework, will outline the expected behaviours of involved stakeholders and prove sufficient in regulating inconsistencies. The blueprint approach to project management is very much based on this premise.

There is, however, a third kind of contract, which is also long-term and is called a *relational contract*. Its provisions are often only partly specified and enforcement is through the need the parties have to continue in exchange relationships with one another. Relational contracts are often best suited to situations where there is a need for commitment but where specification in terms of material outcomes is difficult. Relational contracts are often concerned with commitment to cooperate and coordinate when circumstances cannot be fully anticipated. The process approach to projects, with its strong emphasis on participation and ownership, demonstrates these requirements frequently. Relational contracts are associated with words like 'trust' and 'honesty' between parties and have a degree of informality attached to them, in the sense that they are unwritten. Relational contracts are often most advantageous when the outcomes to the parties in the contract are more sensitive to the size of the cake than to its division. This is often true in projects.

All organizations are defined by contracts and relationships. Distinctive capability is created by putting classical contracts and relationships together in a balance of forces which complement one another. A key point here is that, if you can write the contract down, so can another organization. Relational contracts go far beyond the written word. Through them the organization seeks to demonstrate support and commitment by creating a climate where the whole is the dominant consideration. In the case of projects, project purpose would be the dominant whole. Relational contracts imply that parties to them cannot always hope to get the best deal for themselves. In fact, the scenario is that parties explore the 'win–win' situation in all cases. It is in situations where we need to bring the combined strengths of more than one specialism together to achieve an outcome that we can best demonstrate our distinctive capability. This is a permanent requirement within a process approach to projects and, in reality, within all projects. Relational contracts are most important when we need people to work on behalf of the whole. In simple terms, this requires stakeholders to trust one another, to share information, to support each other in sensitive ways, to be flexible in response, to step outside their own specialisms. These requirements apply within the ODA and its agencies, to cross-governmental institutional working relationships and to stakeholder working relationships.

INTERNAL AND EXTERNAL FACTORS WHICH NEED TO BE CONSIDERED IN DEVELOPING DISTINCTIVE CAPABILITY IN A PROCESS APPROACH TO PROJECTS

A recent review by the writer of a sample of projects in India clearly demonstrated the importance of effective internal and external working relationships for the successful outcomes of a process approach to projects and the development of distinctive capability. The following internal and external factors were identified as needing to be addressed by the ODA to facilitate the development of the process approach.

Internal Factors

- The development and/or further enhancement of core skills such as the management of change; political sensitivity; negotiation skills.
- Recognition that, as projects are accountable to donor, project partners, their environment and beneficiaries, project management must manage these accountabilities.
- There is a need for greater clarity in the roles and responsibilities shared between ODA and its agencies so that delegated authority is linked directly to lines of accountability.
- The issue of managing risk assessment.
- How the process approach is conveyed/presented to the projects evaluation committee.
- Fuller exploration of the contribution that the TeamUP approach can make to the development of project frameworks that reflect a process approach.
- New ways of monitoring and evaluating which support a process approach and demonstrate accountability.
- A way of expressing what are the core processes within a process approach.
- The importance of clarity of purpose to be recognized as a means of judging the appropriateness and validity of project activities and outcomes.

External Factors

- The importance of communicating the process approach to ODA external partners and wider stakeholders and demonstrating commitment to them and the approach, by investing time and effort in developing an understanding of its requirements.
- The importance to successful project outcomes of wide-ranging networks and an understanding of how these networks operate.

- Recognition that the beginning of a project starts with a shared objective, thus forming the basis for a relationship ,with project partners. From then on, ODA should seek to build on the common ground, thus widening functional convergence.
- The need for a clear understanding of the political context of decision choices
- A need to manage the internal and external interface while acting as catalyst, facilitator and provider.
- A need to maintain a balance between classical contracts and relational contracts while pursuing ODA's purpose with partners and stakeholders.
- A need to establish reputation with ODA partners and stakeholders. Reputation is the way the ODA can communicate commitment to its approach and stakeholders. Such a reputation could include: (1) honesty and integrity in disclosure of information relevant to project outcomes; (2) use of language in project negotiations concerning time frames, and (3) flexibility in budget commitments and recognition of the need for visibility in projects in the sense of maintaining action on the ground.

IMPLICATIONS FOR A PROCESS APPROACH TO PROJECTS

The evidence gathered from the Indian sample clearly demonstrated that a process approach to projects requires a recognition that projects are open systems. This means that change in one part of the system is likely to have ripple effects on other sub-systems. For example, a change in project personnel can mean an increase in project performance, or conversely a decrease according to the disposition of the individual(s) towards the project objectives. A process approach implies a firm belief in a partnership between donor, recipient governments, their institutions and primary stakeholders. In terms of managing the process approach to projects, it is important for ODA to consider the inequalities that exist between the different stakeholders. Can all the stakeholders participate and, if not, would this have direct effects in terms of achieving globally defined targets?

The process approach seeks, through participation and learning, to encourage project stakeholders to feel a sense of ownership and commitment, which will facilitate the building of capacity and the sustainability of project outcomes. This objective has to be balanced against the contextual realities of many bureaucracies where frequently there is no formal incentive for personnel to adopt new ways of operating. In terms of project management, ways need to be found to support people in adopting new practices. This has traditionally been addressed by offering training and development opportunities for individual stakeholders. More recently their have been more innovative practices in offering support to projects. These include the TeamUp approach to designing the project framework; finding ways of disseminating good practice from similar projects within the region; and offering collaborating professionals the opportunity to seek independent expert advice and information on project-related developments that is one step removed from project personnel.

A process approach to project management demands the ability to demonstrate how progress is being achieved at the different levels of activities and outputs within a project. *Hence the importance of clarity of project purpose as a means of judging the effectiveness and validity of project activities and outcomes.* Thus the management of the process approach to projects should be approached in a holistic manner. This requires a long-term and wide perspective of the total resource commitment to a project, in terms of people, material, financial and contextual management. This means that the dynamism implicit in the term 'project cycle' must be reactivated. The total review process of projects in India built up a picture of important elements which need to be present within the project cycle.

IMPORTANT ELEMENTS FOR ODA WITHIN THE PROJECT CYCLE

The project cycle describes the main stages in a project from identification to preparation, appraisal, implementation and final evaluation. Under these headings, the following factors were identified from the total range of evidence as important to a successful process approach to projects.

Identification

a. Following identification of need, it is important from the time of initial contact for ODA to have clear boundaries about what the recipients want from a particular project. This needs to be widely understood and agreed by all involved on ODA's behalf from initial discussions to the end of project involvement.
b. The importance of a good research and intelligence function in relation to institutional analysis, project analysis, problem analysis and risk analysis.
c. The importance of early identification of key stakeholders in the partner institutions who will promote the project purpose and ideals.

Preparation

d. Comprehensive assessment of sectoral and institutional capacity jointly shared.
e. The importance of building and managing the relationship with potential stakeholders to achieve sufficient agreement on the means to tackle the problem. This is linked to the value placed on good personal relationships and how this operates to facilitate action/outcomes within the Indian bureaucracy.
f. The sensitivity to be aware when it is strategic to indicate the nodal agency for a project, coupled with the appreciation of the professionalism that exists among potential partners in developing project proposals.
g. Consideration of the mechanisms that are used and/or available to create common commitment among stakeholders, in terms of roles and responsibilities. Equally, an appreciation of the need to negotiate and clarify common ground on issues where stakeholder interpretations will differ, the aim being to achieve mutual understanding and design of any support project or main project.
h. The need for a Logical Framework to reflect clearly the learning process within a process approach to projects.

Appraisal

i. The importance of presenting the broad concept of a project in terms of both the content of the project and the process by which it will be achieved.
j. The importance of clarity of project purpose to the appraisal process.
k. The importance of finding the correct balance between acceptable risk management and the need to have a degree of budget flexibility to stimulate and facilitate project progress.
l. The importance of finding appraisal mechanisms which are sensitive to the need for responsive time frames in terms of maintaining credibility with future partners and stakeholders.
m. The importance of ODA considering on each occasion whether their project-related personnel have the requisite process-related skills and knowledge to facilitate the achievement of a particular project purpose.
n. At appraisal it should be clear that the Department is responsible for project purpose, with the Field Management Offices (FMOs) having clearly delegated roles and responsibilities in relation to activities and outputs.
o. At appraisal it should be clear in terms of roles and responsibilities where accountabilities lie.

Implementation

p.   The project as a process which ensures joint learning takes place, and
     where the results of learning are incorporated into project activities.
q.   The need to consider the resource implications of implementation in
     terms of people, material, financial and contextual management.
r.   The need for projects to maintain activity levels during implementation.
s.   The need for more diversity in methods of evaluation; during implemen-
     tation, progress reports should demonstrate clarity of purpose and how
     the process approach is achieving value for money in terms of sustain-
     ability and other ODA policy priorities.
t.   The requirement within a process approach to manage a whole set of
     iterative processes; this requires boundary management at all stages of a
     process approach to projects.

Evaluation

u.   The importance of the Logical Framework reflecting at any given time
     the current focus of a project.
v.   The need to clarify the capability of the TeamUp approach to reflect the
     complexities of a process approach to projects.
w.   The importance to project success of a sensitive and frequent perform-
     ance review process which feeds back into project plans.
x.   A project's ability to demonstrate measurable impact.
y.   Monitoring and evaluation should include donor and recipient stake-
     holders.

Ultimately, a project is seeking to be in balance with its environment. In
trying to achieve such a balance, there is need for ODA to recognize more
clearly the link between a process approach to projects and the management
of change.

MANAGEMENT OF CHANGE AND PROJECT MANAGEMENT

One of the most important weaknesses in models of change is the idea that
change occurs in a series of stages (O'Donovan, 1994b). This is paralleled
within the project cycle and within the project framework. What one needs to
remember is that change and project management occur in an environment

which is constantly moving. Both models provide a framework of discrete steps/stages. In reality, at any one time a project is being pulled in various directions. Internal or external forces do not exert their pressure in a unitary manner on project plans, activities or stakeholders; they are themselves in motion. Organizations and projects comprised multiple 'clusters of activity sets', multiple stakeholders whose own membership, ownership and goals are constantly changing and as a result are constantly influencing organizational and project life through various routes (Nadler, 1981).

Projects are a coalition of interests and a network of activities. Changes are not always guided by the project leaders or principal stakeholders. Political interests also come into play in the identification and labelling of project or change activities. Change processes or project processes can no longer be classified simply as moving from one state to another. Change occurs at different paces and places within a project. Projects need to look innovatively for clusters of activity where the implementation of ideas will find fruitful soil.

Once we consciously recognize the clear links between project management and management of change, there are some *critical success factors* which project planners and managers have to respect:

1. While it is true that a project must be planned, it is necessary also to conceive of it as a dynamic integrative collaborative process which seeks to engage people in clusters of activity moving in a common strategic direction (project purpose).
2. Project planners and managers must recognize the realities of organizational power, control and resistance and, in particular, the fact that change will not happen unless the political dynamics of projects are addressed.
3. Project planners and managers must clearly identify those who will gain from the proposed changes in a variety of ways and thus support the project.
4. Projects must always be questioned in relation to the strength of the 'why do it' question, against the strength of 'why not'.
5. Projects must get people involved, but in the right things; continuous communication is vital.
6. Projects must not cause the organization as a system to be out of balance; people must be supported in understanding and operating in their changing working environment.
7. Projects are about learning and reviewing and allowing the review process to influence future action.

The above list recognizes what we know to be true, that a project is a continuous dynamic process that affects culture, norms and values of organizations and systems. To be successful a project has to be a learning process for both the top and bottom of structures. Any person engaged in a project has to be conscious at all times that it operates dynamically and simultaneously at two levels: the *content level*, which is the 'what' of the plan and at the *process level*, which is the 'how' of the plan.

It is useful to consider project management in terms of decision-making zones (Jacobs, 1995). If we recognize three zones of decision making for a project, at the centre in zone 1 are factors which are controlled by managers within the project itself. These include the setting of objectives, deployment of staff, time scales and allocation of resources. Surrounding these in zone 2 are elements over which the project can exert some influence, but which it does not control: for example the objectives and actions of other project stakeholders. At the outer limits, in zone 3 are factors over which the project can exert no influence but which affect performance. These factors include national policies, cultural practices, political stability, cost and prices.

In the past, when projects were seen predominantly from a blueprint perspective, there was a strong tendency to believe that high levels of control within the project (zone 1) would bring deserved success. The review process of projects in India showed clearly that success depends on the ability of the project to operate in all three zones. This has immediate implications for project management. Projects must demonstrate strong capacity to 'network' successfully if they are to enhance the prospect of project impact. All the evidence from successful networks shows the importance of sharing knowledge, flexibility in response, sharing capacity and making spare capacity available to one another, and explicitly monitoring the quality of what each member of the network is producing. In addition, project partners' and stakeholders' confidence in ODA decision making is crucial to this process.

REFERENCES

Higginbottom, A. (1990) *Training Synthesis Evaluation Study,* Report EV 525, London: ODA.

Jacobs, C. (1995) 'Strengthening Educational Institutions in Sub-Saharan Africa: Evaluating the Role of Technical Assistance', unpublished PhD thesis, University of Birmingham.

Kay, J. (1993) *Foundations of Corporate Success,* London: Oxford University Press.

Korten, D. (1980) 'Community Organisation and Rural Development: A Learning Process Approach', *Public Administration Review,* **40**, (5), 480–511.

Nadler, D.A. (1981) 'Managing Organisational Change: An Integrative Perspective', *The Journal of Applied Behavioural Science,* **17**, (2), 191–211.

O'Donovan, I. (1994a) *Report on the issues that arose from the review for ODA of a sample of process projects in India.*

O'Donovan, I. (1994b) *Organisational Behaviour in Local Government,* London: Longman.

8. Process and blueprint in water resources development

Tom Franks and Ian Tod

INTRODUCTION

In the 'blueprint' approach to project planning, planners request information from the field, process the information into projections, diagnose emerging problems where output is falling below what is needed and establish projects or activities to rectify the shortfall within the context of an overall strategy (Moris, 1981). The blueprint approach often results in insufficient understanding of the capacities and capabilities of the people affected by the project and the resulting projects frequently perform poorly because the supposed beneficiaries are unwilling or unable to make use of the resources provided by the project.

The blueprint approach was a product of the development projects of the 1960s and 1970s. These were typically for the construction of large-scale infrastructural or industrial facilities, implemented in the public sector. They were characterized by their large engineering content, their high cost and the consequent need for careful planning and strict accountability. They came to be called 'blueprint' projects' because of their relationship with the blueprints of engineering drawings. Such projects were appropriate to their times and requirements, and have been well summarized by Gittinger: 'a project is a specific activity, with a specific starting point and a specific ending point, intended to accomplish specific objectives' (Gittinger, 1982, p. 5).

As experience and evaluation through the 1980s showed that many of these projects were failing to deliver benefits as intended, it was realized that a change in approach was required. Part of the strength of the blueprint approach lay in its detailed planning and clear focus on well-defined objectives. However, this came to be seen as inappropriate to the newer type of projects which required a more flexible, participative approach to planning and implementation. This was a reflection both of the increasing complexity of development involving people as actors and beneficiaries, and of the increasing democratization of development made possible through improved communications and growing political awareness. The need for a new approach was particularly apparent in the water sector, where many projects were perceived to be failing the intended beneficiaries. The answer is seen to lie in the 'process' approach, which focuses on development through learning, participation and bargaining between all the stakeholders with a legitimate interest. An early rationale for this was provided by Rondinelli: 'one way ... is to recognise that all development projects are policy experiments, and to plan them incrementally and adaptively by disaggregating problems and formulating responses through a process of decision-making that joins learning with action' (Rondinelli, 1983, p. 89).

The process approach is widely promoted as a way of addressing the shortcomings of the blueprint approach because local people participate in all planning stages. They are motivated to identify the constraints to their own development, and to develop their own strategies to improve their situation in a form of action learning. Project activities are designed to assist people to implement their strategies. An assumption underlying the process approach is that people know what they need but do not have the technical or institutional knowledge to implement their goals. Process planning has been mainly focused on groups or communities (Uphoff, 1987), but it is interesting to note that it is being taken up by major international lending agencies such as the World Bank. Although such agencies have traditionally been very closely identified with large-scale blueprint projects, designed to facilitate the delivery of large tranches of investment finance quickly and efficiently, it is now recognized that such projects are often neither successful nor sustainable and elements of the process approach are needed (Picciottu and Weaving, 1994).

Discussions of process projects tend to focus on methods of collecting information and facilitating discussions within communities. Ways of incorporating the views of communities and other information gathered during participatory meetings into overall project plans are not so well documented because communities are rarely, if ever, allowed to be the sole arbiter of their own development plans, as broader technical and institutional factors have to be taken into account to define what is possible (Dudley, 1993). For example, the availability of finance is usually subject to some conditions such as restrictions on the type of activity, or the maximum investment allowed per capita or per area. Some of the limitations can be defined at the start of the planning process, while others may only become apparent during implementation. A key factor in successful process projects is the project's ability to adjust to these limitations throughout the project cycle.

The consequence of imposing limitations on process planning can be illustrated by considering the planning of water resources. Communities rarely have complete control of their own water resources. Possible interventions to improve the utilization of water resources will affect neighbouring communities or be affected by the interventions of other communities. In addition, there are usually multiple demands on water resources and not all of these demands may be complementary. Additional planning at higher levels (such as district, regional or national) is required to integrate the plans of different communities and resolve competing demands. Both of these activities will limit what is possible within a project designed by process planning.

Unfortunately, higher-level planning methods for water resources have inherent characteristics of the blueprint approach, in that key decisions can be made without reference to the groups or communities affected and the needs of one community can be overlooked because of the overall needs of other communities. The agencies responsible for higher-level planning of water resources are often large bureaucracies with hierarchical structures and a tendency towards centralized decision making and blueprint planning. Such organizations are not usually sympathetic to the process-planning approach.

In recent years, process planning has been applied to the planning of water resources projects, mainly for irrigation projects where there are clear groups of beneficiaries, and the benefits of process planning are appreciated by all those involved. It has also come to be seen as a necessary part of planning flood control facilities and for domestic water supplies, particularly in rural areas where community management is seen as vital to success. Indeed, process planning is now seen as an essential element in the overall planning of water resources development, where the emphasis is on integrated river basin management which takes into account the needs of all the users in the basin (see, for example, Acreman, 1994; Adams, 1992). This theme, and the need to combine key features of blueprint and process planning, are taken up in the two case studies described below.

PLANNING FLOOD CONTROL AND DRAINAGE FACILITIES

The first case study concerns the planning for the Flood Action Plan (FAP) in Bangladesh, which was set up in response to the disastrous floods of 1987 and 1988. As originally conceived, this was predominantly an engineering plan established on a traditional blueprint approach. It was considered that the severe flooding problems experienced by the country were best tackled by the construction of lines of embankments along the major rivers, together with a number of major structures for controlling or diverting the floodwaters. These embankments and structures, which would be very expensive, would be put in place following the traditional project cycle approach of identification, formulation, appraisal and construction which has been applied to many donor-funded infrastructural projects in the past.

As the plan progressed, however, it underwent a series of significant changes which affected both its process and its output. At the start, the underlying paradigm was an autocratic/technocratic approach which favoured a top-down style of planning and relied on finding technical solutions to flooding problems. This gradually changed to a democratic/environmental paradigm, which emphasized a more participatory approach to planning and stressed the need to find a variety of structural and non-structural solutions to flooding. The planning processes then changed to reflect this change in paradigms: public consultation became a major exercise within the plan, with much greater emphasis being put on beneficiary involvement. Environmental issues also became more important, so that the plans had to take account of factors besides those of human safety and agricultural production which had been assumed to be of paramount importance in the early stages of the plan. Finally, flexibility in the range of options being considered was increasingly stressed.

The changes in planning paradigms for the Flood Action Plan could be seen to be operating at all levels, at the micro level within the project planning teams, at the meso level for individual projects, and at the macro level in relation to water resources planning for the whole country. A feature of the planning was that it was generally the responsibility of large, international, multidisciplinary teams. In the case of one particular part of FAP, the North West Regional Study, the overall team comprised some 45 professionals from Bangladesh, the UK and Japan. Process planning needed to begin within these teams and involved a major series of discussions, team meetings and group working, as well as a regular series of meetings with the client institutions and donors, in order to develop an approach which was truly interdisciplinary and flexible, and yet worked within the overall constraints and framework of the plan.

At the project level, there was an intensive exercise in public consultation. Previous surveys which had asked questions about flood problems and solutions had experienced difficulty, for two major reasons. First, communities were unused to serious participation in such an exercise and were reticent about getting involved with complete strangers. Second, there was a lack of context for the consultation since the project team had no prior knowledge of what problems the community was facing. In order to overcome these difficulties, a structured series of meetings was held throughout the project area with groups of local people. The sequence involved an initial meeting between the local people and selected members of the project team, in a particular locality, which would start with a discussion of the overall problems of the area. The discussion was eventually directed towards flooding problems, but a major feature of the initial meeting was that it involved listening only, on the part of the project team, rather than the presentation of possible 'solutions'. This, in itself, was part of the process approach for the project team because many of them were not accustomed to the idea of a responsive rather than proactive relationship with local people. After the initial meeting, the ideas discussed were reviewed by the project team and incorporated in the planning framework. These were then taken back to the local community at a second meeting when possible approaches and solutions to the flooding problems could be discussed. If necessary, an iterative pattern was adopted, with further discussion and suggestion of new ideas to modify the plans being prepared, though there were clear limits to the extent to which villagers would give up their time for discussions on what seemed to them to be hypothetical situations.

One interesting effect of the change in the planning paradigms was a gradual shift in the government institutions involved and in particular the executive agency of the Bangladesh Water Development Board (BWDB) which had overall responsibility for the plan. BWDB has many of the characteristics of land and water development agencies in South and South-east Asia; these have traditionally enjoyed a high status and access to plentiful resources through the large budgets that they control for the construction of new and expensive water schemes. They are staffed by a well-educated elite of engineers, who enjoy a status in society on a par with doctors and lawyers. Several generations of access to education, status and resources have led to an organizational culture of well-intentioned autocracy, with a preference for involvement in new blueprint construction schemes because they are both more interesting professionally and better resourced. The changes seen in the planning processes of the Flood Action Plan are, however, gradually being reflected within the BWDB in the emergence of younger engineers with an interest in the processes of community participation in water development and a knowledge of operation and maintenance practices, to balance other, more traditional, skills in new construction.

Another important stage in the process was to institutionalize this form of public participation at the political level. Hitherto, both local and national government services have been run on a 'service delivery model', usually determined by experts who traditionally have not consulted communities. One of the ways to proceed towards institutionalization of public participation is to involve members of parliament in the process. This was done through a systematic process of meetings with politicians in particular regions and also by a series of large-scale conferences, on an annual basis, to publicize as fully as possible the work being done on the Flood Action Plan and to invite comments. Although there was some initial suspicion of the involvement of politicians, particularly from members of the project team, this was a necessary and integral part of the process approach, and the political involvement must be encouraged – only in this way will attitudes to public participation change at the highest levels so that the process may take root and become a part of an overall approach to development.

The present situation is that the technical planning stage for the first phase of the Flood Action Plan is complete and the political process is now paramount in deciding which way to proceed. The eventual outcome of the process approach to the plan was very fruitful. However, it perhaps took longer than necessary because no formal stakeholder analysis was carried out initially, so that it took some time to identify the interested parties and the range of potential solutions which should be considered. In the end, elements of a blueprint approach will be required to put flood control structures in place, whether these are physical, in the form of embankments, or institutional, in the form of floodproofing, flood warnings and the like. A key factor contributing to the overall success of the plan will be the way in which appropriate elements of the blueprint and process approaches are combined.

PLANNING IRRIGATION FACILITIES

The second case study describes the planning of small-scale irrigation facilities in villages in Western India. The facilities are being planned as one component of a natural resources development project. Project planning is based on a process approach in which villagers were motivated by project staff, through meetings with individual households, groups or the whole village, to identify their own development problems, set goals and priorities and develop strategies for achieving them. Project activities are designed and implemented to support villagers in the implementation of their own strategies. Wealth ranking of village households was undertaken to ensure that poorer households were participating and benefiting from project activities.

During the planning process, villagers identified shortage of water as a major development problem because of the variability in the amount and the timing of rainfall during the monsoon, and unreliability of rainfall during other seasons. Self-sufficiency in food grain production is one of their major goals and improved crop production through the provision of irrigation is part of their development strategy.

During the planning of irrigation schemes in project villages, the process approach needed to accommodate some aspects of the blueprint approach to ensure that irrigation was sustainable and that the project could meet its objectives. Some of the issues where aspects of the two approaches were required are discussed below.

Equity

To maintain equity in the distribution of project benefits and to ensure that socioeconomic differences between households were not exacerbated, project staff encouraged villagers to allow poorer households or those households not benefiting from irrigation to improve their income by means of priority access to other village resources such as common land. Water is a common resource and, by providing water for irrigation, beneficiaries have been given preferential rights over the resource. In return, households receiving water will give up some of their rights to other common resources.

It was also hoped that poorer households would take over some responsibility for management of the irrigation scheme, in return for an income from 'profit' made from selling water to farmers. In this way, farmers receiving irrigation water would share a portion of their increased incomes with the non-benefiting households. However, it is interesting to note that villagers have rejected this approach so far, and it may prove unrealistic.

Development Costs

The benefits of irrigation are proportional to the quality and area of land owned. Not surprisingly, the poorest households own only small areas of poorer-quality land located in more remote parts of villages, and better-off households owning good-quality land receive most of the benefits. Schemes were extended to provide irrigation water to the more remote land of poorer households even though the overall cost was increased, and the resulting scheme was not technically and economically the most efficient use of water.

Impact on Women

The impact of irrigation on women is not well understood, but, as women are major participants in agricultural production, the effects of irrigation development on women were considered. As men usually dominate village-based forums, separate meetings were held with women to ensure that their needs were taken into account during the planning and design of schemes.

Phasing of Project Activities

The project area has hilly terrain and vegetative ground cover is sparse. Rainfall runs off quickly and soil erosion is severe. Soil and water conservation measures and reforestation are being financed as separate activities by the project. Irrigation can exacerbate soil erosion as flows of irrigation water are difficult to manage on the steep slopes found in many places throughout the project area. Farmers tend to take advantage of the short-term gains from irrigation rather than consider the long-term losses arising from erosion of the soil. They are often unwilling or unable to invest in soil conservation measures prior to irrigation water being available because of the expense or the time required to construct the measures, but, for irrigation development to be sustainable, the project has had to develop ways of ensuring that necessary soil conservation measures are undertaken prior to irrigation water becoming available.

Scale of Planning

Villages are the basic unit for planning project activities, but most villages cover only part of hydrological catchments, and the availability of water for irrigation in a particular village is dependent on water resource developments upstream. The development of whole catchments is needed to avoid villages constructing schemes that use the same water, and the blueprint approach is required to assess the needs of different villages and evaluate different development scenarios.

The process approach is focused on developing village-based institutions, but solutions to fully utilize the water resources within a catchment can require cooperation between villages which will require different higher-level institutional arrangements. For example, a large water control structure may be required to provide water for several villages. The villages benefiting need to cooperate to operate and maintain the structure and to collect charges to cover the repayment of capital costs and operation and maintenance costs. The complexity of the institutional arrangements will increase when the villages or irrigation groups do not receive the same benefits from the structure. A blueprint approach to institutional development may be required to ensure the structure's sustainability.

CONCLUSIONS

The process approach to project planning has been developed because of the poor performance of projects planned following the 'blueprint' approach. Greater participation by stakeholders in the planning process has helped to improve the performance of projects, including utilization and returns from project investments, equity in distribution of project benefits and maintenance of project facilities.

The process approach can improve project planning significantly, but its limitations should be recognized to ensure that unrealistic expectations are not placed on it. Some activities will need to be planned using aspects of the blueprint approach, and the restrictions that this imposes on process planning should be recognized from the outset. This includes definition of the ways to include the information gathered during process planning into an overall development plan, and the ways to deliver the facilities, services or institutions defined by that plan.

Future progress seems to lie in striking a fruitful balance between the process and blueprint approaches. There is clearly a need for a flexible, participative approach to development, whose outcome will usually be a plan of action and an agreed objective to be achieved. There then comes a need to adopt the plan and to deliver new facilities or institutions to achieve the objectives. This will need some element of the blueprint approach, including a carefully considered plan of action with an accompanying budget and defined organizational responsibilities. Within the public sector, in addition, there will always be a need for accountability because of the involvement of public money.

Alongside this will be a continuing need to foster and support cultural changes within the organizations responsible for water resources management, so that process and blueprint approaches to development can be successfully managed. Perhaps the best documented example of this is the Philippines, where the National Irrigation Agency underwent a significant change in organizational culture as a result of a number of similar factors (Korten and Siy, 1989). More flexible institutions seem to be slowly emerging as blueprint planning of new water schemes gives way to a people-oriented flexible process of integrated water development.

Various attempts are being tried to combine the best elements of the blueprint and process approaches. Examples include the emphasis of the UK's Overseas Development Agency on the 'logical framework' approach which combines such concepts as problem analysis, hierarchies of objectives and stakeholder analysis with basic elements of scheduling and programming based on critical path analysis. However, some interesting research remains to be done on the most fruitful ways ahead. If successful, these could be important components of overall moves towards more open, flexible and accountable approaches to development which meet real needs.

REFERENCES

Acreman, M.C. (1994) 'The role of artificial flooding in the integrated development of river basins in Africa', in C. Kirby and W.R. White (eds), *Integrated River Basin Development*, Chichester: Wiley.
Adams, W.M. (1992) *Wasting the Rain: Rivers, People and Planning in Africa*, London: Earthscan.

Dudley, E. (1993) *The Critical Villager – Beyond Community Participation*, London: Routledge.

Gittinger, J.P (1982) *Economic Analysis of Agricultural Projects*, Baltimore: Johns Hopkins Press.

Korten, D. and Siy, R. (1989) *Transforming a Bureaucracy: the Experience of the Philippines National Irrigation Administration*, West Hartford, Conn.: Kumarian Press.

Moris, J.R. (1981) *Managing Induced Rural Development*, International Development Institute, Indiana University.

Picciottu, R. and Weaving, R. (1994) 'A New Project Cycle for the World Bank', *Finance and Development*, December, 42–4.

Rondinelli, D.A. (1993) *Development Projects as Policy Experiments*, London: Routledge.

Uphoff, N. (1987) 'Activating community capacity for water management in Sri Lanka', in Korten, D., *Community Management: Asian Experience*, West Hartford: Kumarian Press.

9. Managerial skills and managerial effectiveness: an alternative to functionalism

Farhad Analoui

INTRODUCTION

During the last two decades, there has been growing concern about the effectiveness of senior managers (Margerison, 1982; Kakabadse *et al.*, 1984; Analoui, 1990) and officials and executives in the public sector (Analoui, 1993; Willcocks, 1992). Despite this increasing interest, the topic of managerial effectiveness has suffered much neglect 'in comparison with the other areas of management literature such as managerial roles and function' (Willcocks, 1992, p. 4). The problem is mostly attributed to the presence of a great deal of confusion and ambiguity which surrounds the questions of 'what is effectiveness' and 'who is an effective manager' (Brodie and Bennett, 1979). The most commonly held view is that 'an effective manager is one who gets results' (Dunnette, 1970, p. 43). However, what is regarded as valuable in one organization or company may not be the same in other work-related settings (Morse and Wagner, 1978).

Basically, the major perspectives from which the study of managerial effectiveness has hitherto been attempted can be divided into two: those theorists and researchers who have adopted a traditional positivist approach (Langford, 1979) who show concern for *objectivity* and *order* by operating within the intellectual realm of functionalism, as opposed to more recent writers such as Willcocks (1992) who have attempted to understand effectiveness from an alternative perspective. The later scholars and theorists subscribe to the intellectual paradigm which places emphasis on the *actors* as social agents and the need for understanding and considering their (managers') own viewpoints, motivation and self-awareness. This perspective is concerned with values which are subject to interpretation and the operation of 'social agreements' including the subjective analysis and understanding of the individual managers involved. These views are best represented by those who subscribe to the social action theory (Silverman, 1970; Bowey, 1976; Burrel and Morgan, 1979).

This chapter concentrates on an analysis of the effectiveness of the senior officials involved in the management of projects and programmes in the public sector. It attempts to view effectiveness from a social action theory perspective by identifying the awareness amongst senior managers of categories of managerial skills and knowledge which, if acquired, would (they believe) result in an increase in their performance and effectiveness at work. The results of two separate research projects which have been carried out in a number of public sector organizations in Zimbabwe and India are used as a basis for supporting the general hypothesis that the awareness shown by managers of their own management needs is an indication of their potential contribution to increased effectiveness at work. After the introduction of a variety of points of view, definitions and perceptions which have been adopted towards studying the topic, a model of senior management's awareness of the kind of skills and knowledge required for enhanced effectiveness will be introduced and relevant conclusions will be reached.

MANAGERIAL EFFECTIVENESS: SOME DEFINITIONS

Langford aptly argues that, 'in common with many of the concepts in the social sciences, managerial effectiveness does not lend itself easily to the often expected, clear-cut and non-ambiguous definitions found in the physical sciences and can be open to accusations that there are as many opinions as there are experts' (1979, p. 33). As a general rule a definition not only offers a point of view but also tends to reveal the underlying ontological, epistemological and other assumptions concerning human nature held by the researcher or theorists involved. Most definitions cited seem to be of a prescriptive nature, with emphasis placed on what should be done rather than on defining what effectiveness really is.

A standard (dictionary) definition refers to effectiveness in terms of 'results and consequences, bringing about effects, in relation to purpose, giving validity to particular activities' (Brodie and Bennett, 1979, p. 14). Drucker (1974) demonstrates the importance of effectiveness, suggesting that it is the foundation of success: that it is concerned with the achievement of results, whatever the results may be, for whatever purpose, for whatever persons. Campbell *et al.* (1970) define effective managerial behaviour as any set of managerial actions believed to be optimal for identifying, assimilating and utilizing both internal and external resources towards sustaining (over the long term) the functioning of an organization unit for which a manager has some degree of responsibility. These (and similar) attempts at definition seem to place considerable emphasis on 'managerial behaviour'.

Reddin (1971), on the other hand, stresses the 'achievement of output'and suggests that effectiveness is the extent to which a manager achieves the output requirements of his or her position. Burgoyne (1976) has adopted a more philosophical approach to effectiveness which questions the very purpose and functions of management. He believes that confusion arises because the term 'management' does not indicate a clearly defined function; it can mean either an activity or an organizational function, in either an occupational or social classification.

Some writers hold a holistic, even simplistic view. For example, Kirchoff (1977) argues that effectiveness is the satisfying of many goals rather than the optimizing of one. Drucker (1974), too, attempts an all-embracing definition by stating that 'effectiveness is doing the right thing'. These definitions cross the border into considerations of managerial competence and, in this sense, the term 'competence' is extended to cover the qualities, innate abilities or personality strengths which are found in an effective manager.

Brodie and Bennett (1979) aptly summarize these views by concluding that most definitions revolve around the individual, what he or she does and how he or she achieves goals, targets and objectives. In fact, most definitions reflect a system frame of reference with emphasis being placed on the interrelatedness and causal nature of managerial input and outputs.

The very few attempts that have been made to view effectiveness from the social action approach include the works of writers such as Bowey (1976) who is concerned with 'meaningful actions', arguing that meanings or intentions are reaffirmed in action which may lead to change. One of the most interesting views on effectiveness, as offered by Morse and Wagner (1978), stresses the 'degree of awareness' of the rights and opportunities to choose actions appropriate to the environment, the management job, the situation and his or her own preferences. This definition is in line with what Bowey (1976) terms a 'Combined Useful Theory', whereby the interrelationship and interaction with the environment are combined with the perception, choices and preferences displayed by the individual managers concerned.

Langford (1979) skilfully draws the conclusion that effectiveness is a multidetermined entity depending on the manager, her or his position, the organization and the socioeconomic environment. The attributes of these component parts will all interact to determine effectiveness, or the lack of it. Langford goes on to suggest that effectiveness is determined by a set of relationships, as defined above, established within the constraints imposed by the manager, the organizations and the socioeconomic environment (p. 34).

MAJOR PERSPECTIVES ON EFFECTIVENESS

While some attempts have been made to measure managerial effectiveness, the perspectives adopted concerning its nature tend to reflect the theorists' and writers' underlying assumptions concerning ontology, epistemology and human nature (Burrel and Morgan, 1979; Ackroyd and Hughes, 1981). However, it is important to recognize that approaches to the study and measurement of effectiveness each illuminate particular aspects and thus provide a 'way of seeing' (Meanen, 1979).

Traditional Positivism and Functionalism

The writers who subscribe to the values of traditional positivism approach effectiveness from a view which has in mind a world of rationality and need for order. This point of view suggests that there are basically two criteria which need to be considered when dealing with the issue of increasing managers' effectiveness at work: result (or output) and input (managerial activity). Langford (1979) proposes a contingency model of effectiveness and identifies four categories, together with an overall general criterion necessary for effectiveness to take place: (1) the manager's work, (2) the manager her or himself, (3) relationships with staff, and (4) the manager as part of the organization. The 'input' embraces the above four criteria. The overall criteria, the 'output', is concerned with allocation of resources and achieving purposes and goals. Willcocks states that 'there is a difficulty in identifying indicators or measures which lead to empirically observable examples of the concept of effectiveness' (1992, p. 4). Moreover, from his point of view, the conversion of input to output in a given system would prescribe a congruence or fit between managerial input and output which may not necessarily be true.

Campbell *et al.* (1970) propose a person–process–product model of managerial effectiveness. The 'person' refers to the individual manager's characteristics, traits and abilities, while 'product' is viewed in terms of organizational results such as profit maximization and productivity. The 'process' signifies on-the-job behaviour and activities. Morse and Wagner (1978) argue that, in attempting to measure and evaluate managerial effectiveness, organizations have placed emphasis on either the person or the product and that the process has received little attention. This, they say, is due to the unclear nature of 'what constitutes effective managerial behaviour' (p. 23).

Mintzberg (1973) places emphasis on managerial roles and how they are carried out, rather than on measurement of the organizational output. There is also another cluster of theorists and writers on effectiveness who subscribe to the presence of multiple contingencies, both internal and external to the organization, as influential factors which directly affect managers' effectiveness (Child, 1977). While this way of approaching effectiveness is plausible, as Brodie and Bennett (1979) remark, 'it says too little and what it does say is at a mundane level' (p. 27).

Social Action Theory: An Alternative Approach

There are a group of theorists and researchers who put forward an alternative perspective, which places the individual managers, as the social actors, in the centre of the construct. Consequently, the reality is regarded as being socially constructed and socially maintained (Silverman, 1970). This view is in contrast with the views of those writers who subscribe to underlying assumptions of positivism and therefore tend not to view the organization and management as 'part of an objective and concrete reality' (Willcocks, 1992, p. 6). The social action approach is based on the premise of an interpretative paradigm which places emphasis on pluralism and goes as far as to suggest that the form and content of managerial work are shaped by political forces within the organization (Willmott, 1984).

What may complicate the matter within developing countries is the presence of 'cultural' forces of different kinds which are often taken for granted when effectiveness has been looked at in the Western world. Culture in this sense of the word is the values and beliefs in which the actor is immersed and by which his or her behaviour is influenced, if not totally determined.

Considering the complexities involved, the writer shares the concerns and emphases of the social action theorists when attempting to examine the effectiveness of senior officials in the public sector. For our purposes here, the input–process–output approach is too mechanical and cannot accommodate 'awareness' of the managers of the nature of the factors which will contribute to their effectiveness. Furthermore, research both in Western and in less developed countries suggests that managers, in particular senior managers and officials, are aware of the degree of their own and their organization's acceptable standard of effectiveness.

The managerial skills and preferences analysis which has been adopted here does not exclude the realities of demands, constraints and opportunities which limit or expand the manager's choices. It is the writer's belief that managers who are aware of what will make them effective are also aware of limitations and obstacles to their own effectiveness at work.

MANAGERIAL SKILLS AND INCREASED EFFECTIVENESS: PERCEPTIONS AND PREFERENCES

There is a growing belief that the acquisition of the right managerial skills, knowledge, values and thoughts will enable managers to deal with the demands and constraints which they face (Joyce, 1979). Mintzberg (1973), when observing executives doing their jobs, discovered an entirely different picture from that which was suggested by classical writers on management. He suggested that an effective manager is one who can competently perform the prescribed information, interpersonal and decisional roles, and apply skills and 'know-how' which play an important part in gaining managerial competencies at work.

Stewart (1982) contends that, by restructuring their jobs, senior managers manage their time and thus are enabled to do what they choose to do. This is done unconsciously as well as deliberately. Drucker (1974) also firmly believes that effective skills such as time management related to prioritization and systematic decision making within specific contexts can be taught. Langford, too, when arguing for the situational influences upon effectiveness, concludes that 'effectiveness is related to situation and is determined by the skills related to three different kinds of learning: learning skills, learning new forms of responses and learning to abstract and conceptualise' (1979, p. 41). Reddin (1974) also refers to 'volunteerism' and 'choice' by stating that managers are change agents who are conscious of what makes them more effective. He further contends that effectiveness depends on using the appropriate behaviour which matches the situation, and effective managers possess skills of situational sensitivity: that is, being able to read situations and successfully match the right behaviour or knowledge to those situations. There are indeed a host of management writers and theorists, such as Kirchoff (1977), Kakabadse *et al.* (1987); Willmott (1984); Jones (1988) and Peters (1989), who support the view that the acquisition of the right managerial skills (appropriate to the situational factors) will contribute to the effectiveness of managers.

What is deduced from the review of the literature concerning the importance of managerial skills and knowledge for managers' effectiveness is that an alternative to the functional approach for understanding what makes managers more effective may have some validity. This may be summarized as follows:

1. Managers are aware of their own effectiveness.
2. Managers can learn from their own experiences and the experiences of others with whom they interact.
3. Managers can become more effective by acquiring managerial skills

which enable them to deal with the task in hand, people and the situational demands and constraints.

4. Managers' perceptions of the range of skills which they require to realize their aim of increased effectiveness reveal the aspects of their job believed to play a significant part in their effectiveness.
5. The range of skills which managers perceive as necessary for their increased effectiveness includes those which will consequently enable them to cope with the demands, constraints, choices and situations at work.

Traditionally, the managerial skills which were recommended for increased effectiveness were often 'prescribed' and based on the notion of 'generalization'. What managers, in particular senior managers/officials, perceived as necessary for them to achieve greater effectiveness has only recently become the focus of attention. This is particularly evident in the writings of management specialists who are concerned with the increased effectiveness of managers and officials within developing countries. Much of what has been written in this field is comprised of 'shopping lists' of the skills and knowledge which are assumed to be essential for the growth and development of the managers and their institutions. Indeed, it may well be true that senior managers and officials do have to perform most or even all the roles that Mintzberg suggested (or that even they may feel, regardless of their differing cultures and organizational characteristics, that they need to deal with the constraints and demands of any situation) but one should remember that what senior managers view as criteria for effectiveness in one setting may not be as effective in another. To remedy this apparent neglect, the author believes that, since managers' perceptions are influenced, if not formed, by their organizational as well as other socioeconomic and cultural forces, a true assessment of what makes them effective at work should include their views, preferences and expressed needs which have been systematically and empirically discovered and determined.

SENIOR MANAGERS' EFFECTIVENESS IN THE PUBLIC SECTOR: A COMPARATIVE ANALYSIS

Recently, two separate studies have been carried out within developing countries: one in the Zimbabwean public sector and the other in the Indian Railways Organization. These studies were concerned with the identification of the range of managerial skills and knowledge which were perceived as necessary for the increased effectiveness of the senior officials.

Zimbabwean Public Sector

The first study involved 16 organizations. These included ministries, parastatal organizations, research and other national centres. A total of 41 senior officials were surveyed and interviewed. The respondents were responsible for the management of projects as well as general administration. The senior officials benefited from formal education at graduate level and beyond. Of the whole group 41.5 per cent were graduates, 12.2 per cent had postgraduate diplomas, nearly one-third (29.3 per cent) possessed masters degrees and some (9.2 per cent) were educated at PhD level. Their work experience in their previous position varied from one to 11 years. This study will be referred to below as the Zimbabwe study.

Indian Railways Organization

The second study was concerned with understanding the level of awareness of the senior officials within the Indian Railways Organization of their own management development needs. The study commenced in 1994 and took place over three years. It consisted of a survey questionnaire, semi-structured interviews and the use of participant observations. In order to ensure the reliability of the data and also to maximize the return response rate, the self-administered method for the survey questionnaire was employed. From 110 senior officials taking part, 74 were either individually or collectively interviewed. It was decided, in order to increase the reliability of the data and to maintain the quality of the information generated, that only the views and data available from respondents who were also interviewed should be included in the final analysis. These included directors of the railways institutions, management advisors, divisional heads, divisional advisors, general managers and chief officials.

A total of 21 respondents (31 per cent) had less than 10 years' service experience while 15 respondents (20 per cent) had between ten and 20 years of service with the IRO. The majority of the respondents (approximately 60 per cent) had more than 20 years' experience. Most managers who took part in this survey were also responsible for implementing projects of one kind or another which invariably involved tasks which were carried out in the field.

THE PERCEIVED NATURE OF MANAGERIAL ROLES

What do senior managers/officials perceive as the main component of their job? In categorizing managerial roles, Mintzberg (1973) refers to the roles that managers play at work to get the job done. However, what is not clear is whether the emphasis is on the task or the people aspects of the job. In both studies, in order to see the extent to which senior respondents were aware of the nature of their work and how far they identified with it, they were asked, 'In your position, do you consider your role as being responsible for supervising (managing) (a) people, (b) operations or (c) both?'

The majority of the senior managers in the Zimbabwe study (despite the differences in terms of their backgrounds, organizations and managerial positions in the hierarchy of the public sector) had similar views concerning the work and their main roles. Interestingly, while three respondents (7.3 per cent) categorically viewed their roles as managing people, more than twice as many (17.1 per cent) viewed their role in terms of managing operations. All the respondents in the latter category were asked, 'What do you mean by managing operations?' They all referred to the task in hand, for example projects of one kind or another for which they were held totally responsible and accountable. A large proportion of the participants (63.4 per cent) described their main role as being responsible for both people and operations. As one senior official explained, 'Of course, when you think about it, you cannot separate people from operations.'

The senior officials in the Indian railways also had similar views. As shown in Table 9.1, five respondents (6.8 per cent) viewed their main managerial role as that of managing people and an even smaller proportion described their role as that of managing the task. Almost all respondents found it easy to make a distinction between people and the operations but it was not surprising to see that 86.5 per cent of the respondents described their role as being responsible for both. The senior officials in the Indian Railway study also commented on the importance of managing people at work. They made

Table 9.1   Perceived nature of managerial work

Q: In your position, do you consider your role as being responsible for supervising (managing) (a) people, (b) operations or (c) both?

Category	Zimbabwe study frequency	%	Indian study frequency	%
People	3	7.3	5	6.8
Operations	7	17.1	3	4.1
Both	26	63.4	64	86.5
No response	5	12.2	2	2.6
Total	41	100	74	100

comments such as, 'How can a manager manage operations without managing people? People are an indispensable ingredient of the operations.'

It was interesting to discover that, in both studies, both the quantitative and qualitative information suggested the presence of a high degree of awareness amongst senior staff about the importance of the role which managing people played towards increasing their own effectiveness and that of their organization.

The overall impression given was that senior managers generally believed that the technical and social skills which they needed to acquire for their effectiveness were not necessarily mutually exclusive but that, by and large, they attached greater importance to the managerial skills necessary for handling people at work. In other words, despite the differences in the nature of their managerial work, effectiveness at work was largely viewed as being correlated with awareness of the need, and ability, to manage people.

PERCEIVED MANAGEMENT DEVELOPMENT NEEDS

What categories of skills and knowledge did the senior managers perceive to be essential for their increased effectiveness at work? Were they the skills, knowledge, behaviour and attitudes which are necessary to get the task-related aspects of the job done, or were they the skills which enable the managers to deal with the people at work? More importantly, how aware were the senior officials of their own needs for self-assessment and the development of their own potential for achieving increased effectiveness? In order to determine the answers to these questions, the managers in both studies were asked (see Table 9.2): 'If you were provided with an opportunity to participate in a short management training and development course, how much do you prefer its content to cater for (a) the technical aspects of your job, (b) the people-related (such as communication) and (c) the assessment and development of your own potential in order to become even more effective than you currently are in your job?'

The range of responses was from 'little', 'a moderate amount' to 'a great deal'. These were given the factors 1, 2 and 3, respectively, which represented the degree of perceived importance which the respondents placed on their responses. As shown, on the whole respondents from both studies clearly confirmed that the perceived importance which they attached to 'people', 'task' and 'analytical and self-related aspects of the job' were not mutually exclusive. In the Zimbabwe responses, marginally greater importance was placed on the people-related aspects, whereas in the study in India marginally greater importance was placed on the task-related aspects: 'If the train does not run on time, the organization is not doing what it is supposed to do.'

Table 9.2   Perceived importance of the managerial skills, knowledge and the job-related aspects for increased effectiveness at work

Response	Factor (allocated)	Category	Zimbabwe		India	
			Resp.	%	Resp.	%
Little	1 x R	Task-related	96	29	197	34.02
Moderate	2 x R	People-related	111	34	192	33
A great deal	3 x R	Analytical and self-related	119	37	190	32.81
Total			326	100	579	100

These small variations appear to be related to the differences in the nature of the work within the organizations. In particular, there is a more inherently technical area of work involved in the Indian railway organization.

It was interesting to see that many respondents were of the view that, while effectiveness could be managed at an individual level, the discovery of one's own managerial potential, orientation and attitudes required special expertise. As for increased effectiveness, the following conclusions could be drawn from both studies.

1. Senior managers reveal awareness of their own ability and need to improve their effectiveness through systematic assessment and development of their own management potential in their job.
2. In order to be an effective senior manager, there is a need for the skills and abilities to manage people.
3. The ability to manage the purely task-related aspects of the job is also important for the overall effectiveness of the managers at work.

Senior managers viewed their effectiveness at work as being related to getting the job done (task) through people and to being aware of the need to improve their own skills and potential. Although in both studies the organizations involved placed emphasis on 'task', the senior officials involved showed a dual awareness of organizational objectives and their self-related interests and aims.

CURRENT AND PREFERRED MANAGERIAL SKILLS

In both studies the senior officials were given a list of managerial skills relevant to their management development needs and were asked to indicate their responses on the scale of 'a little', 'a moderate amount' and 'a great deal'. The respondents were also asked to choose four of those skills which they thought would result in their increased effectiveness in their managerial positions.

The respondents in both studies clearly showed a preference for the people-related aspects of the job and the need to increase awareness and knowledge of self-related potential for getting the job done effectively. As shown (see Tables 9.3 and 9.4) the skills for managing and motivating people and effective communication were found to be of the first and second order of importance to them. The respondents in the India study referred to the training and development of their employees and decision-making skills as the remaining two categories of skills which they thought were required for their increased effectiveness. The senior managers in the Zimbabwe study showed interest in managing their overall performance

Table 9.3   Preferred managerial skills for increased effectiveness of senior officials in Zimbabwean public sector

Order of priority	Managerial skills	Mean score
1	Managing people and understanding their needs	5.4
2	Managing effective communication	4.5
3	Improving overall effectiveness	4.3
4	Managing finance	3.7

Table 9.4   Preferred managerial skills for increased effectiveness of senior officials in Indian railways

Order of priority	Managerial skills	Mean points
1	Managing and motivating people at work	32.4
2	Managing effective communication	24.3
3	Training and development of the employees	20.3
4	Decision making	14.0

and also managing finance as important aspects of their increased effectiveness.

In both studies, it was evident that the senior managers, on the whole, showed awareness of the importance of being effective, though it was apparent that they found it much easier to discuss operational efficiency in personal terms than in organizational terms, perhaps simply because public sector organizations were seen to be by nature relatively 'inefficient'. This suggests that within public sector organizations it is often overall effectiveness which counts rather than operational efficiency.

CONCLUSION

Effectiveness at work is difficult, if not impossible, to measure. At a personal level, effectiveness may mean different things to different people in different organizations. The input–process–output model suggests that one of the most important ingredients is the skill and knowledge of the individual manager. It is evident from the findings of the two studies discussed above that the adoption of a social action approach which places the individual manager in the centre of the analysis provides the researchers with valuable insights as to how effectiveness is perceived from the point of view of the actors who wish to be effective at work.

A pluralistic view which considers the subjective views, personal interests and objectives allows for greater realization and understanding of what the managerial job is all about and how it could be carried out more effectively. It is clear that interaction with others and awareness of the importance of the specific areas within which effectiveness might be improved is a key requirement for the improvement of both project and programme management. It is also apparent that not only awareness of individual and organizational constraints and demands but also the views of the key stakeholders will have direct implications for how well the job is being done and how effective managers are.

Because of their position within the organization, senior managers gain considerable awareness of the organization's objectives, activities and relationships within its wider political and financial environment. It is apparent that the extent of effectiveness as it has been examined here, is also determined in part by an awareness of the skills and knowledge needed to satisfy wider social needs. Specifically, in the light of the studies discussed here:

- senior programme and project managers are aware of the need for increased effectiveness and of what is perceived by their organizations as an appropriate level of managerial effectiveness;

- senior managers recognize a need to acquire skills and knowledge in all three areas of task, people and self-development, with particular emphasis on the last two areas;
- there is a direct relationship between increased awareness of self and the potential for development, managing people at work and overall increased effectiveness;
- there is an individual (unshared) view of effectiveness which increasingly and intentionally becomes congruent with the organizational (shared) view and with measures for improvement on the part of senior managers;
- effective senior managers show a well developed awareness of their own needs, the needs of their colleagues and organizational needs which are instrumental not only in getting the job done but also in contributing to the achievement of objectives from a broader perspective.

REFERENCES

Ackroyd, S. and Hughes, J.A. (1981) *Data Collection in Context*, London: Longman.

Analoui, F. (1990) 'An Investigation into Management Training Development Needs of Senior Officials in Zimbabwe', Research Monograph No 2, August, Development and Project Planning Centre, University of Bradford.

Analoui, F. (1993) 'A Study of the Management Development Training Needs of Senior Officials Within the Indian Railways', a Research Report, June, Development and Project Planning Centre, University of Bradford.

Bowey, A.M. (1976) *The Organisation*, London: Hodder & Stoughton.

Brodie, M. and Bennett, R. (eds) (1979) *Managerial Effectiveness*, Thames Valley Regional Management Centre, Thorne and Stace Ltd.

Burgoyne, J.G. (1976) 'Managerial Effectiveness Revised', discussion paper, University of Bradford.

Burrel, G. and Morgan, G. (1979) *Sociological Paradigms and Organisational Analysis*, London: Heinemann.

Campbell, J., Dunnette, M., Lawler, E. and Weick, K. (1970) *Managerial Behaviour, Performance and Effectiveness*, New York: McGraw-Hill.

Child, J. (1977) *Organisation – A Guide to Problems and Practices*, New York: Harper & Row.

Drucker, P.F. (1977) *Management*, London: Pan Books.

Dunnette, E. (1970) 'Assessing Managerial Performance', proceedings of a one-day seminar, London: Independent Assessment and Research.

Jones, M.L. (1988) 'Management Development: An African Perspective', *Management Education and Development*, **17**, (3), 702.

Joyce, L. (1979) 'Management Training: Developments and Trends', *Journal of European Industrial Training*, **3**, (6).

Kakabadse, A., Ludlom, R. and Vinnicombe, S. (1987) *Working in Organization*, Aldershot: Gower.

Kirchoff, B.A. (1977) 'Organisational Effectiveness and Policy Research', *Academy of Management Review*, **2**, (3), July, 347–55.

Langford, V. (1979) 'Managerial Effectiveness – A review of the literature', in M. Brodie and R. Bennett (eds), *Perspectives of Managerial Effectiveness*, Thames Valley Regional Management Centre.

Lorsch, J.W. and Morse, J.J. (1974) *Organisations and Their Members: A Contingency Approach*, New York: Harper & Row.

Maanen, V. (1979) 'The Fact of Faction in Organizational Ethnography', *Administrative Quarterly*, **24**, 539–50.

Margerison, C. (1984) 'Where is Management Development Going?', in A. Kakabadse and A. Mukhi (eds), *The Future of Management Education*, Aldershot: Gower.

Mintzberg, H. (1973) *The Nature of the Managerial Work*, New York: Harper & Row.

Morse, J.J. and Wagner, F.R. (1978) 'Measuring the Process of Managerial Effectiveness', *Academy of Management Journal*, **21**, (1), 23–35.

Peters T.J. (1989) *Thriving on Chaos*, New York: Harper & Row.

Reddin, W. (1974) *Effective MBO*, Management Publications.

Silverman, D. (1970) *The Theory of Organisations*, London: Heinemann.

Stewart, R. (1982) *Choices for a Manager: A Guide to Managerial Work*, New York: McGraw-Hill.

Willcocks, S.G. (1992) 'Managerial Effectiveness and the Public Sector: A Health Service Example', *International Journal of Public Sector Management*, **5**, (5), 4–10.

Willmott, H.C. (1984) 'Images and Ideals of Managerial Work: A Critical Examination of Conceptual and Empirical Accounts', *Journal of Management Studies*, **21**, (3), 349–68.

PART III

Towards Sustainable Development: Perspectives
and Practice

10. Rural development via community participation: issues and lessons in project planning from the Sierra Leone experience

George Ola Williams

INTRODUCTION

This chapter examines the economic and social influences on participatory development efforts at village level within rural Sierra Leone. It uses case studies selected from the Bo and Pujehun districts, and examines the experience of the Bo/Pujehun Integrated Rural Development Project (B/PRDP) which attempts to promote a participatory development pattern among village communities. The research was conducted in case study villages in Southern Sierra Leone. The villages represent a balance between those which received support from B/PRDP and completed their self-help projects (Mbundorbu, Senehun Ngola, Komende) and those which did not (Kpumbu, Gumahun).

Although the contribution of village communities' human and financial resources to address their common problems at village level pre-dates colonialism, as a core donor agency strategy for support to community projects, it was a novelty in Sierra Leone prior to 1982. The aim of the approach was to involve village communities in the identification of development problems and the planning, implementation and funding of self-help projects at village level, as a means of ensuring the adoption and continuity of such development efforts at village level when external support ceased.

Although this represents an attractive sustainability focused development model, implementing it within the context of rural development was not without problems. This chapter attempts to examine the major community-related and external factors which impinge on efforts aimed at promoting a participatory development strategy at village level, and suggests the implications for rural development planning in the 1990s.

THE BO/PUJEHUN RURAL DEVELOPMENT PROJECT AND THE CONCEPT OF COMMUNITY PARTICIPATION

The project represents an attempt at technical cooperation between the governments of the Federal Republic of Germany and the Republic of Sierra Leone, and was established in 1982. It is aimed at improving the standard of living of the rural population (360 000) within the Bo and Pujehun districts in southern Sierra Leone on a sustainable basis. Sector programmes were established in the spheres of agriculture, fisheries, primary health care, rural roads and community infrastructure development (which was funded through the Community Action Fund, CAF). The project's activities were coordinated by the Ministry of National Development and Economic Planning and implemented via existing government ministries/institutions, thereby making maximum use of available government personnel. Each of the sector programmes had a large team of front-line field staff who were in direct contact with farmers, fishermen, traditional birth attendants and other village leaders.

Lele (1975) perceives participation as aiming to 'sensitise people and, thus, to increase the receptivity and ability of rural people to respond to development programmes as well as to encourage local initiatives'. Uphoff and Cohen (1979) encapsulate participation as 'the active involvement of people in the decision-making process in so far as it affects them'. Pearce and Stiefel (1979) similarly described participation as being concerned with 'the organised effort to increase control over resources, and regulate institutions, in given social situations, on the part of groups and movements of those hitherto excluded from such control'.

Within the context of the Bo/Pujehun Rural Development Project, participation was perceived as a process involving a demonstrated commitment of resources by the village community in the form of materials, cash, labour and time, an involvement of the target group in the decision-making process as it relates to the planning or coordination of their own efforts, an equitable sharing of benefits generated by the projects, a sense of self-direction by the target group, wherein the role of the field agent would be reduced to one of awareness creation or motivation, and an involvement by the target group in the monitoring and evaluation of the project (Karimu, 1987).

An attempt will now be made to examine the major influences on people's capacity at village level to be involved in the planning, financing and implementation of self-help projects. These are influences within the control of the community such as the nature and type of leadership, the availability and organization of household labour, the existence of income-generating self-help organizations and the perception of project benefits by the village communities.

THE INFLUENCE OF LOCAL LEADERSHIP STRUCTURE

The importance of local leadership in the successful implementation of community-based projects has been recognized by other researchers (Adebayo, 1985, p. 24; Rashidduzzaman, 1982; Lisk, 1985; Voh, 1982, p. 17). Askew (1982, p. 105) also observes that the source of power of a leader is a crucial factor determining their control and function over those they lead.

It was observed in the case studies that some villages, notably Mbundorbu, Senehun, Ngola and Komende, were able to organize themselves to plan and successfully implement self-help projects including those partly funded by the Bo/Pujehun Project. These were mainly schools, village community halls and bridge-building projects. Other villages, such as Kpumbu and Gumahun, were not able to implement or complete similar CAF-supported construction projects.

Evidence from the survey seems to suggest that, among the crucial factors responsible for the successful completion of such projects, is the influence of leadership. Respondents were asked to assess the role of their leaders in the implementation of CAF-funded projects. While over 90 per cent of the respondents in Senehun, and 83 per cent of the respondents in Mbundorbu concluded that their leaders were helpful and instrumental in achieving the completion of the self-help projects at village level, in Gumahun and Kpumbu, over 60 per cent and almost 45 per cent of the responses, respectively, concluded that their leaders' influence was either insignificant or detrimental to the projects.

But who are these influential leaders? Among the 'absolutely helpful' key leaders identified by the respondents were the paramount chief, the section chief, the town chief, the town speaker, the *marweh* heads (a marweh comprises from two to five family households bound together by strong kinship ties, with common right to the same land) and the village 'Mammy Queen' (head of women's organization). Within these broad patterns there were inter-village variations.

A series of arguments have been advanced to explain the influence of traditional village leaders in Sierra Leone. Richards (1989, p. 8) suggests it may be linked to the particular 'moral economy' within Mende tribal society, wherein the poorer members of the village community depend on their kin and brethren such as *marweh* heads for economic and social protection. Such family members would look to such leaders to assist with social obligations such as court cases, or to loan them seed-rice at planting time or consumption rice during the hungry season between July and August. This bond of dependence consolidates the position of traditional village leaders.

Clapham (1978, p. 78), on the other hand, explains the influence of chiefs in rural Sierra Leone as being due to weaknesses in the conventional constraints and obligations on chieftaincy, such as chiefdom councillors and court chairmen. The village imam is also an important figure at village level, which is due to the fact that, in most villages, he may be the only member of the village decision-making body literate in Arabic, which is useful for record-keeping purposes. Evidence was adduced in the case studies to support the views of Little (1967) and Seligman, C.G. (1966, p. 33) that in some villages real power lies in the hands of 'traditional secret societies' which they use to influence decisions at village level. For instance, there was a long-standing conflict between two of the *marweh* leaders in Gumahun, which had a nega-tive impact on the school project, and the matter had to be referred to the secret society 'kangaroo court', where it was resolved.

For effective community participation to occur, it appears that it then becomes an issue of the extent to which these influential leaders at village level are prepared to use their influence to (a) broaden the decision-making process, (b) mobilize local human and financial resources for development efforts at village level (this may sometimes involve the threat of financial penalties for non-cooperation), (c) acquire outside resources to complement local resources, and (d) willingly use these to bring broad-based benefits to the community.

THE AVAILABILITY AND ORGANIZATION OF LABOUR AT VILLAGE LEVEL

The unavailability of labour at village level represents one of the most serious constraints faced by farmers in Sierra Leone (Richards, 1986, p. 67; Spencer, 1975). The agricultural labour problem in West Africa has been accentuated by low population densities and selective rural–urban migration of the most active cohort of the rural population (Dennis, 1988, p. 132). Analyses of the 1985 Population Census of Sierra Leone reveal that only 59 per cent of the country's 3.5 million people were resident in the rural areas (Atkins, 1988, p. 10).

Labour peaks in the farming calendar occur mainly during bush clearing, cultivation, planting and harvesting. In between these tasks, weeding, bird scaring and the construction of fences against rodents take place. There are also gender labour tasks distinctions, with weeding and harvesting being mainly done by women. These farming-related tasks are normally performed between the end of March and early November. Given this scenario, the months of relatively low labour demand are December to March, correspond-ing to the dry season. In some villages, however, December to January marks the beginning of preparations for a series of social events at village level, such as initiation rites into male and female secret societies. At times, a large section of the village population may be encamped in the (secret society) bush for a period of four to six weeks. December and January are also usually reserved for repairing the wattle mud and thatch roof houses typical of villages within rural Sierra Leone. For some villages, therefore, the relatively 'free' period that they have to implement such community projects is between mid-January and February.

It appears, however, that the crucial element is the capacity to organize the available labour to synchronize with the farming calendar. In Senehun, for instance, the village carpenter who constructed the furniture items for the school had his farm cultivated by labour from within the village community free of charge. Similarly, to ensure a minimum distortion to their farming tasks, *marweh* heads alternately sent one or two representatives each week to assist the skilled workers during the construction phase of the project (see Williams, 1990).

THE INFLUENCE OF INCOME AND EXPENDITURE PATTERNS

The influence of local resources in promoting participation at village level still remains a subject of debate. The comparative value of the income and expenditure data collected during the survey is limited by the fact that they represent cash profiles within selected households income in three of the villages. The average annual net household income (1989/90) in these villages of Le1975 (Mbundorbu), Le1728 (Komende) and Le1688 (Senehun) cannot be considered different enough to warrant firm conclusions. This seems consistent with the observation of Buscher (1985) that there is a high degree of income equality in rural southern Sierra Leone, with a gini ratio of 0.24, which he attributed mainly to the land tenure system which provides access to land to almost 'everybody' in the rural areas.

Despite the limitations imposed by the available data, the study did reveal a consistent seasonal pattern of income, expenditure and net income. July, August and sometimes September were consistently portrayed as months in which resource levels were generally low, while the period November to December, as well as April, were generally observed to be months with high income levels and a general surplus of financial resources. These observations underscore the need to coordinate the implementation of self-help projects with the agricultural calendar at village level, to correspond with periods when it would be easier to raise cash contributions from the village community.

EXISTENCE OF FUNCTIONAL INCOME-GENERATING SELF-HELP INSTITUTIONS AT VILLAGE LEVEL

It was observed that attempts at promoting community participation were far more productive in villages with existing income-generating 'functional' self-help organizations than in those without. Participation involves costs in financial and human terms which need to be sustained on a continuous basis. In Komende, for instance, members of the Co-operative Society used the Fishing Society's funds to pay their community cash contributions in respect of the bridge project which the village implemented. The Fishing Society also provides fishermen with credit facilities, which has made it possible for some people to own fishing gear at village level. The Senehun Ngola Youth Organization also gives out interest-free loans to members who wish to use those loans for the purpose of paying community cash contributions for self-help projects.

VILLAGE COMMUNITIES' PERCEPTION OF BENEFITS

The issue of incentives and motivation has long been the subject of sociological theories wherein it has been argued that people are more willing to be positively involved in an activity if they feel their action is likely to benefit them directly (Blau, 1964; Etzioni, 1975). When that perception of the village communities comes to nothing in the direction of benefits, it has a negative effect on their willingness to continue with that activity (Lele, 1975).

During the survey an attempt was made to ascertain the origin of CAF-funded self-help projects in the study villages. In addition, respondents were asked to indicate the most serious problem they felt their village had experienced prior to the implementation of the CAF Project. In Gumahun, most respondents, understandably, responded that the most serious problem the village had prior to the implementation of the school project (which was not completed) was that of road communication, as its 11-mile access road to Ngalu had always been in a terrible state of disrepair, impeding road communication during the rains. On the other hand, the need for a new school building in Senehun could not have been more urgent as the former school was becoming too small to accommodate over 200 pupils, drawn from almost every household in the village.

FACTORS AT THE LEVEL OF THE BO/PUJEHUN PROJECT

Since the establishment of CAF, over 500 small-scale infrastructure projects (water wells, public toilets, culverts/bridges, schools and community centres) have been funded in over 300 villages. It appears to have been a popular package which, among other factors, is owing to its technical simplicity, involving mainly mud bricks, sticks, stones combined with cement and corrugated iron sheets, and also including training in masonry and carpentry for two people selected by the village community. The community cash contribution represented only 10 per cent of the cost of the important materials and the village provided the labour for the project.

Similarly, the fisheries programme used, as a medium for training and extension at village level, youngsters between the ages of 11 and 17 (as well as a few adults), who were trained in the art of handling, constructing and repairing fishing nets. They now pass on their skills to other members of the village community. This has been a very popular package as well and has considerably reduced the need for imported nets.

The agriculture programme has also consistently emphasized small farmers' involvement in the implementation of the crop packages via the village nursery concept, as well as the use of the knowledge and skills of farmers. However, there is evidence to suggest that the low uptake of some of the programme's crop packages may be due to poor project design. The programme's experience with its seed-rice package is a case in point. Its low input approach did not incorporate the use of fertilizers and other essentials which were required for its improved seed-rice varieties to perform better than local traditional varieties. Not surprisingly, there was no significant difference in yields (820kg/ha for improved, and 734kg/ha for the untreated traditional varieties). Most farmers, therefore, reverted to their traditional varieties and used the improved subsidized variety as consumption rice. The programme had to be scaled down as it did not achieve its twofold objective of increasing productivity and multiplying improved seeds in the project area.

THE NEED FOR NGO COORDINATION

The implementation of a participation strategy promoting community labour and cash contributions could be counterproductive if conflicting policies are pursued by other development agencies within the same region. The experience in one of the study villages, Komende, is a case in point; here its development inputs in the form of fishing nets, tree crop seedlings and seed-rice, from the Catholic Development Agency, were free grants-in-aid with no cash contributions from the village community, unlike the Bo/Pujehun Project's approach of promoting the use of the community's financial, labour and material resources in partnership with donor support to promote sustainability when outside help ceases. Such conflicting policies created confusion for the village communities.

THE SIERRA LEONE GOVERNMENT'S DIFFICULTIES IN MEETING ITS FINANCIAL COMMITMENTS

As a result of the unique structure of the Bo/Pujehun Project which is implemented via existing government ministries, the national economic trends experienced by the government have also had an impact on the project. When the project was established, an agreement was reached with the then Federal Republic of Germany that, apart from providing almost all the local staff for the project, the Sierra Leone government would also contribute 10 per cent of the total local cost of operating the project each year, and that this figure was to be gradually increased annually. The bulk of this contribution was used to fund part of the operation and maintenance costs of the project vehicles, as well as to pay performance incentives and overnight allowances to field staff. This was necessary, not least because it augmented the meagre wages and salaries of such extension staff.

As a result of the government's cash flow problems in the late 1980s and early 1990s, there was a serious delay (sometimes lasting three months) in the payment of government salaries, as well as the government's development contribution to the project. Not surprisingly, this seriously affected staff morale.

IMPLICATIONS FOR PARTICIPATORY RURAL DEVELOPMENT PLANNING IN THE 1990s

The foregoing details have revealed some of the major strengths and weaknesses in the implementation of a participatory approach in rural development programmes. Notwithstanding this observation, attempts aimed at generating community cash and labour contributions, as well as enhancing the technical and organizational skills of village communities to identify and articulate problems to be acted upon, still represent an attractive option in the planning of rural development programmes. Given this scenario, what are the crucial issues on which we should concentrate to ensure an effective mobilization of the target communities as evidenced from the case studies? It appears that five main areas are worthy of consideration.

The Development of Human Resources at Village Level

It is clear that the use of members of the village community to perform some tasks that would have otherwise been performed by outside agencies has manifold advantages if benefits at village level are to be sustained after the termination of donor support. Evidence from the case studies suggests that members of the village community had been trained and used as trainers in the techniques of mending and repairing fishing nets, the maintenance of village hand pumps, establishing tree crop nurseries and the training of traditional birth attendants in clean-delivery practices or administering oral rehydration therapy. This is not without problems, amongst them the intensive supervision and training required.

The Need for Viable Income-generating Projects to Sustain the Enthusiasm for Community Contributions

Community participation involves costs in human and financial terms. Even when donor support is present, village communities still have to make financial contributions to the project, sometimes against the wishes of members of the community. Sustaining a participatory development programme in some communities that are financially hard-pressed and can hardly produce enough food crops for themselves to last for a 12-month period, with little surplus, if any, left to be sold in the market, will not be easy. Even the drugs for the primary health care programme, as well as the fishing nets, were paid for at cost value to enable the revolving funds used to replenish supplies to operate effectively.

The continuity of these schemes will therefore require a broad-based circulation of benefits, generating surplus financial resources at individual family level. Without such income-generating schemes to complement and support the implementation of community projects, the strategy is unlikely to be sustainable.

The Recognition that Labour is in Short Supply and the Need to Design Participatory Rural Development Programmes to Meet this Problem

In view of the fact that labour problems in most parts of Africa have been accentuated by age-selective rural–urban migration, the design of participatory development programmes will need to circumvent this problem. One of the options, for instance, would be a synchronization of the low-labour demand period in the farming calendar with the implementation of village infrastructure projects. This is in view of the fact that farming is the most important economic activity at village level and determines to a great extent operations in the other sectors of the village economy.

A Genuine Attempt to Learn from Target Beneficiaries

An immense transfer value could be derived by examining how the problems to be addressed were handled in the past by the target group, as the basis on which the programme is designed. The inclination should not always be to introduce 'new methods' that may not be appropriate to the economic and social framework of the local environment. The crucial issue will be in engaging with the village communities, in a way that will recognize and extract the knowledge they have already, to address the given problems they face. Richards (1986, p. 13), for instance, cites an instance in which some farmers in Sierra Leone delay weeding on the grounds that it will hold back the growth of rice and produce a more abundant harvest.

The Need for Commitment to the Concept of Community Participation at National Level

In instances where there are various NGOs operating in the same areas, the implementation of a participatory strategy can only be effective if the principle of community cash and labour contribution, and involvement in the decision-making process is taken seriously by all. Conflicting messages by different agencies can only produce chaos and confusion among the village communities. This can only be avoided if there is a firm rural development policy at national level, which specifies the government's implementation guidelines, as well as a serious financial commitment to rural development programmes. The long-term effectiveness of a participatory rural development strategy will invariably involve the strengthening of local government structures, such as district and chiefdom councils, to play their natural liaison roles between national governments and local communities.

CONCLUSIONS

The foregoing details have highlighted some of the potential influences on a participatory rural development strategy at village level. Despite its attractiveness in promoting self-help and the sustainability of development programmes, its successful implementation is contingent upon community-related and external influences, some of which emerge at national government level.

Within village communities, the leadership structure and the prevailing sociocultural norms governing the decision-making process are amongst the significant elements determining the degree of community involvement in the implementation of rural development projects. The crucial issue is the extent to which such leaders will be prepared to broaden the decision-making process, to acquire outside resources and mobilize local human resources in bringing broad-based sustainable benefits to their villages. There is a need to enhance the skills of these leaders via a massive training programme in a way that will make maximum use of their knowledge and experience.

Similarly, in view of the observation that community participation involves costs, in financial and human terms, its long-term sustainability will greatly depend on whether the communities will continue to afford their cash contributions. In an area where financial resources are scarce, there is need for a participatory strategy to incorporate economic projects that can generate widespread financial resources on a long-term basis at individual family level. Among the other considerations is the need for the design of programmes which are appropriate to the sociocultural framework within which they are being implemented.

Attractive though the ideals of community participation and self-help may seem, transforming its theory to a sustainable long-term reality is not a modest task, and will require serious intent and commitment at community, donor agency and national government levels.

REFERENCES

Adebayo, A. (1985) 'The Implications of Community Leadership for Rural Development Planning in Nigeria', *Journal of Community Development*, **20**, (1), 24–31.

Askew, I. (1982) 'Community Participation in Health and Education Programmes: An Organizational Perspective', unpublished PhD thesis, University of Exeter.

Atkins, W.S. (1988) *Preparation of a Rural Development Programme: An Assessment of Policy and Institutional Development in Sierra Leone*, Brussels: European Economic Commission Delegation (unpublished document).

Blau, P. (1964) *Exchange and Power in Social Life*, Chichester: John Wiley.

Buscher, L. (1985) 'Main Findings of the Sierra Leone Country Report', in *Integrated Rural Development – Research Results and Programme Implementation*, proceedings of Bonn conference.

Clapham, G. (1978) *Liberia and Sierra Leone: An Essay in Comparative Politics*, Cambridge: Cambridge University Press.

Clayton, E. and Petry, F. (1981) *Monitoring Systems for Agriculture and Rural Development Projects*, Rome: FAO.

Dennis, C. (1988) 'Women in African Labour History', *Journal of Asian and African Studies*, **xxiii**, (1–2), 125–40.

Etzioni, A. (1975) *A Comparative Analysis of Complex Organisations*, New York: Free Press.

Karimu, J.A. (1981) 'Strategies for Peasant Farmer Development: An Evaluation of a Rural Development Project in Northern Sierra Leone', unpublished PhD thesis, University of London.

Karimu, J.A. (1987) *Clientele Participation Approach: Notes and Annexes to Main Report*, Ministry of National Development and Economic Planning, Sierra Leone.

Lele, U. (1975) *The Design of Rural Development: Lessons from Africa*, World Bank Research Publications, Baltimore: Johns Hopkins Press.

Lisk, F. (1985) *Popular Participation in Planning for Basic Needs*, Aldershot: Gower for ILO.

Little, K.L. (1967) *The Mende of Sierra Leone*, 2nd edn, London: Routledge & Kegan Paul.

Pearce, A. and Stiefel, F. (1979) *Inquiry into Participation: A Research Approach*, Geneva: UNRISD.

Rashidduzzaman, M. (1982) *Rural Leadership and Popular Control in Bangladesh.* Washington, DC: University Press of America.

Richards, P. (1986) *Coping with Hunger: Hazard and Experiment in an African Farming System*, London: Allen & Unwin.

Richards, P. (1989) 'Progress in Hunger: Participatory Action Research and Extension for the Bo/Pujehun Project', Dept. of Anthropology, University College London.

Seligman, C.G. (1966) *Races of Africa*, Oxford: Oxford University Press.

Spencer, D.S.C. (1975) 'The Economics of Rice Production in Sierra Leone, (Upland Rice)', Department of Agricultural Economics and Extension, Njala University.

Uphoff, N.T. and Cohen, J. (1979) 'Feasibility and Application of Rural Development Participation', A State of the Art paper, Cornell University.

Voh, J.P. (1982) 'A study of factors associated with the adoption of recommended farm practices in a Nigerian village', *Agricultural Administration*, **9**, 17–27.

Williams, G.O. (1990) 'Community Participation, Self-Help and Local-Level Institutions at Village Level: An Analysis of the Bo/Pujehun Rural Development Project in Southern Sierra Leone', unpublished PhD thesis, Development and Project Planning Centre, University of Bradford.

11. Learning big things from small countries: tales from the South Pacific with lessons for programme and project planners and managers elsewhere

Frank A. Wilson, M.T. Wilson and John Launder

INTRODUCTION

The South Pacific traditionally conjures up a picture of a relaxed, untroubled way of life in an enviable environment. There is some justification for the persistence of this image; absolute poverty, while not unknown, is rare and, in spite of a incidence of cyclones in the region, food security does not feature high on the list of key problems for planners and managers in the agricultural sector. In economic and social terms, however, options are severely restricted: employment and enterprise promotion opportunities are limited and there are growing threats to the environment (Kakazu, 1994, pp. 1–36). Dependence on aid flows, and in some cases remittances, has become built into the planning framework of the countries of the region (Wilson, F.A., 1994).

This chapter draws on recent experience in two South Pacific countries, Western Samoa and the Solomon Islands, and, referring to specific projects and programmes, suggests that there are a number of lessons for planners and managers in other (larger) countries. The first section paints a broad picture of the economic development trends and prospects for the region, with particular emphasis on planning at national, sector and project level. The following two sections examine some relevant aspects of two European Union (EU) programmes of assistance to the two countries, drawing from recent analyses of the Rural Development Programme in Western Samoa and Stabex support in the Solomon Islands. A final section points to some of the wider implications for planners and managers elsewhere.

ECONOMIC DEVELOPMENT IN THE SOUTH PACIFIC REGION

For our purposes here, the region can most sensibly and realistically be said to comprise the independent island states members of the South Pacific Forum (which was established in 1971). The membership is currently made up of the Cook Islands, Federated States of Micronesia, Fiji, Kiribati, Nauru, Niue, Papua New Guinea, the Republic of the Marshal Islands, Solomon Islands, Tonga, Tuvalu, Vanuatu and Western Samoa. In a geographical sense, the region also includes foreign territories of metropolitan countries such as New Caledonia, French Polynesia, Wallis and Futuna and American Samoa. The 13 independent states shown above occupy a land area of 525 948 sq. km and a vast sea area of over 17 million sq. km. The total population of these countries in 1990/91 was 5 459 400, with an average density of 10.3 per sq. km. Papua New Guinea dominates the region in many respects but particularly in size, containing 68 per cent of the population and a massive 88 per cent of the land area. Of the 'smaller' island states, Solomon Islands, Fiji, Vanuatu and Western Samoa make up the major portion of the remaining land (95.7 per cent) and population (79.0 per cent).

A well respected writer on South Pacific Island affairs has recently described the economic policies of the island states in the South Pacific as

> diametrically opposite to what is now widely recognised as being the set of policies ... needed to provide the basis for sound economic development, namely development of comprehensive property rights, high savings and investment rates, low trade barriers, low levels of state activity in production and marketing and, above all, stable macro and microeconomic policies. (Duncan, 1994)

The island states of the region have been characterized by low savings and investment rates and a high level of public sector involvement in production and marketing of goods and services; property rights have been inadequately developed, especially with regard to crop production and forested land; trade barriers have been at a high level and economic policies have been variable in consistency and subject to change.

Although from the mid-1960s and through the 1970s most of the countries discussed here enjoyed better average incomes than the majority of LDCs – and (see below) significantly higher external assistance per capita – the high levels of aid-assisted public investment have not been translated into growth. Economic growth during the 1980s was sluggish and particularly so in comparison to growth of population, with some countries experiencing falls in GNP per capita. For most Polynesian countries (including Western Samoa), opportunities for outmigration have mitigated the effects of population pressures and allowed substantial remittances. For most Melanesian states (including the Solomon Islands) outmigration has not been a safety valve and population pressures on land and more widely on the environment are a growing problem.

Successive budgets have been dominated by wages and salaries and the maintenance of these appears to be a priority which has contributed significantly to the difficulties encountered in attempting to apply the processes necessary for effective structural adjustment policies (Smith, 1987). In this regard, Hughes (1992) has argued persuasively that governments of South Pacific Island states have for too long shied away from establishing what he terms the 'basic machinery of collaboration and mutual confidence needed for coherent policy making'. He suggests that only in times of crisis (such as post-coup Fiji, the Bouganville mine closure or the devastation of cyclones in the Solomons and Western Samoa) have governments and people really got to grips with adjustment and reconstruction in a collaborative manner.

Natural resources are the basis of economic development in the region and agriculture, forestry and fishing make up the bulk of GDP and exports for most countries. Agricultural production levels, export earnings and foreign exchange-saving local food production earnings have been disappointing and resulted in rapidly growing food imports contributing adversely to trade and payment imbalances. Overexploitation of forests and fish stocks by foreign companies are a major concern. While regional actions against abuse of offshore fishing rights have been very successful, doubts remain about the future of inshore fisheries and bait stocks. The very high levels of felling and of log exports (particularly in the Solomon Islands) have been largely unchecked as landowners and governments have been attracted by the high revenues available.

The public sectors have been highly aid-dependent, with much of the capital expenditure being donor-financed. Overall aid per capita is high compared to that of other developing countries. Total official aid to island states members of the South Pacific Forum was US$ 788 million in 1992. Disregarding the aid to Papua New Guinea, which took up 56 per cent of the total amount, the balance to the other states was equivalent to US$ 198 per head. However, the era of high aid flows may be coming to a close. The ending of the Cold War has reduced the geopolitical importance of the region and in this regard the response of governments which have been given notice that less aid should be expected (especially from key bilateral donors, Australia and New Zealand) is critical. Meetings of Forum heads of state and finance ministers in 1994 and 1995 addressed the overall theme of developing more self-reliant and sustainable economies. Statements in the Forum meeting's official communiqué included the importance of 'managing our own resources' and 'special measures to achieve rational development objectives and to finance them in a sustainable manner'. This reflects coded and at times more direct messages from donors that island states governments should do more to manage and fund their own development programmes. The most recent meeting of finance ministers referred specifically to the 'changing international environment' and in this context concluded as follows:

> We agreed that we needed to examine expenditure and budgetary processes and direct resources to the highest priorities. This means that governments need to examine themselves, matching the size and skills of their public sectors to the individual needs of their countries. We noted that in general this would lead to smaller public services. (South Pacific Forum, 1995)

In the past, human resource development has been a priority area for aid and technical assistance and has also been given due attention by most island states governments. However, there is a narrow band of key posts at the senior levels of the public service most concerned with sector and project level planning. In a number of countries there has also been a high turnover of staff and much reorganization of planning responsibilities among ministries, which has meant many changes in the utilization of scarce skills. In the absence of well-defined policy frameworks and of continuity of policy and staffing, planning has tended to become increasingly ad hoc and dependent on narrower sets of ministerial and (at times donor) preferences. Sluggish growth in most countries of the region in the past decade has been reflected in low employment growth. Whereas, for some countries, outmigration has been a kind of safety valve, it has also represented a loss of young, trained and enterprising people.

Although there was considerable political and public service stability in the 1960s and 1970s, and even in the early 1980s despite increasingly constrained financial environments, the 1987 coup in Fiji and the more recent threatened secession of Bougainville have sent ripples around the region; ethnicity and long-submerged tribal rivalries have become an issue in crowded islands, and regional harmony has faltered. Particularly in the Melanesian states, there have been many changes of government, and throughout the region the senior levels of the public service have become more tied to political sponsors. In some of the Polynesian states, the ruling classes, who have long resisted political change, have also recently, reluctantly and partially embarked upon reform.

THE RURAL DEVELOPMENT PROGRAMME IN WESTERN SAMOA

Western Samoa is a concentrated country consisting of two main islands, Upolu and Savai'i, and two other inhabited islets. In an area of 2935 sq. km, the population of 163 000 has a density of 56 per sq. km but a low growth rate (0.5 per cent per annum) as a result of high rates of migration to New Zealand, American Samoa, Hawaii and California.

Agriculturally, the main technical determinants of potential in Western Samoa is the oceanic tropical climate, with daily mean temperatures ranging between 72F and 86F and with mean levels of humidity of 80 per cent. The country lies within the recognized South Pacific hurricane belt and in recent times hurricane Ofa, in February 1990, and the even more disastrous Val, in December 1991, caused enormous damage. Although tree crops suffered on a massive scale on both Upolu and Savai'i, such was the extent of damage to urban and rural infrastructure, communications and housing that these aspects of rehabilitation had to take precedence over replanting programmes. Estimates of the total cost of repairing damage to all assets (excluding forests) by Ofa alone were in the region of $140 million (World Bank, 1991, p. 319).

Over 80 per cent of the total land area is held under customary tenure in the overall traditional control of the local chiefs. The main staple crops cultivated on shallow-profiled yet fertile soils in this village land are taro (Colocasia esculenta), banana (Musa cavendishi), breadfruit (Artocarpus communis), yams (Discorea alata) and coconut (Cocos nucifera). Coconuts and cocoa are grown for local processing and export and taro has also been an important export crop in recent years. For the past ten years or so (until very recently) bananas sales were confined mainly to the internal market, although they were once a significant export item for small-scale producers.

Although pigs and poultry have long been kept as scavengers in almost all villages, cattle were introduced to producers on village land only relatively recently. The major portion of the national herd, estimated at approximately 20 000 in the late 1980s, is on freehold land with the government-owned Trust Estates Corporation plantation's almost 8000 head at peak of operations.

The village is the basic unit of social structure, with members of each individual family or *aiga* owing allegiance to their chief or *matai*. Traditionally, *matai* regulated all productive and social activities and protected the interests of their individual *aiga* in the *fono*, the village council where all *matai* meet on a regular basis to discuss village matters. Traditionally, *matai* have power, or *pule,* over the use of resources and the disposal of production. In present-day Western Samoa this is reflected mainly in authority over access to land, but this is changing in response to pressures on good-quality land for cash cropping. Tenure or occupation is now more often than not determined by descent from those who first cleared and planted the land, regardless of *matai* title (O'Meara, 1983; World Bank, 1991, p. 319). As a New Zealand mandated territory under League of Nations/United Nations authority from 1914 to independence in 1962, Western Samoa has strong trading and cultural links with New Zealand. Over 40 per cent (by value) of imports came from New Zealand in 1993 and that country has long operated a relatively liberal approach to migration of Samoans. The resulting remittances have constituted a vital inflow into almost all the villages and *aiga* in the country for many years. Western Samoa was economically and financially vulnerable at independence in 1962 and has remained so ever since. In 1962, the economy was dependent on three products: copra, cocoa and bananas. The trade statistics for 1963 show this very well as copra, cocoa and bananas made up respectively 33.0, 31.7 and 31.3 per cent of total export values. Some 30 years later, coconut products were still the dominant export, but cocoa had declined markedly and exports of bananas had virtually disappeared. A positive trade balance was the norm up to independence; in 1962, a small negative balance was recorded for only the twelfth time in 48 years; thereafter the gap was to widen at an ever-increasing rate. In South Pacific terms, Western Samoa has a long history of post-independence planning and, between 1965 and 1994, seven development plans were produced. From the first Plan:

> There is general agreement that Western Samoa needs more than three eggs in its economic basket. There must be diversification within agriculture ... there is little scientific farming on the village level. The fact remains that since most of the nation's agricultural production and exports come from village agriculture ... productivity must be improved. (Government of Western Samoa, 1966, pp. 31 and 35)

And from the seventh Plan:

> In the foreseeable future the primary sector will continue to be the foundation of the Western Samoa economy and the principal source of employment growth ... returns to labour in the primary sector must be improved. This implies a shift towards more profitable crops. (Government of Western Samoa, 1992, pp. 56 and 57)

In the early plans, there was no clear policy towards the removal of the main constraints on agricultural development and (despite the relative success of pre-independence government-initiated schemes for village-level cocoa and banana export production) little apparent recognition of the potential role of the public sector in stimulating small-scale production. The Department of Agriculture was underfunded in the face of infrastructure and public works investment programmes and more directly socially oriented claims on resources, and in none of the first three Plans was the allocation for the agricultural sector budgeted at more than 25 per cent of total development expenditure.

The agricultural sector plan for the fourth Plan period (1980–84) placed considerable emphasis on the dualistic nature of agricultural production. The new initiatives, and new financial resources for the village sub-sector, were heavily concentrated in the Rural Development Programme (RDP), with main financial assistance from the European Union (EU) Micro Projects Programme, supported by aid from key bilateral donors, Australia and New Zealand. The assistance was planned to finance village-level initiatives on the basis of a 65 per cent grant and up to 30 per cent on loan finance through the local Development Bank, with the balance in the form of a minimum deposit of 5 per cent of total capital expenditure required from the villages concerned prior to disbursement. A total of 690 000 ECUs was disbursed from the one million ECUs made available from the EC/EU under Lomé I (1975–80) together with an indeterminable portion of approximately 300 000 ECUs from a separate line of credit to the Development Bank.

Although the RDP approach evolved slowly, by late 1980, 663 projects had been approved in 225 villages and of these 406 had moved into implementation. Half of the projects were for livestock development and 17 per cent for fishing. Banana projects took up a further 8 per cent and other crop development activities for taro, cocoa, vegetables, weed control, land clearing and plantation development constituted a further 21 per cent. The balance (4 per cent) was for village-level activities such as water supply or electrification not specifically related to crop or livestock production.

Although, from the viewpoint of the Department of Agriculture, the RDP was seen as an essentially output-stimulating programme for small-scale producers, it was also intended to fulfil the specific objective of 'planning from below' (Government of Western Samoa, 1975, p. 55). The writers of the rural development section of the fourth Plan considered that the planning from below approach was

> possibly a necessary condition for any village development programme. The fierce autonomy with which villages conduct their own affairs make it well-nigh impossible for imposed central planning ... to succeed without their direct participating. The programme has ... related very strongly to the traditional system of values by basing all projects on ... existing knowledge and insisting on the communality of projects. (Government of Western Samoa, 1980, pp. 98–9)

Conceptually, the approach of the RDP appears to have been not only consistent with, but also based on, a belief that it was possible to build an increased degree of financial independence on the existing characteristics of self-reliant local social structures. However, although the initial perception of 'need' may have been accurate, analysis of the planning procedures indicates that self-reliance did not extend to the preparation of individual projects in a form initially suitable for analysis or acceptable to the donors. Paradoxically, the necessary response to EU's concern as to the extent of effective participation required concerted and coordinated involvement by the main government departments involved. Participation involved increased dependence on and interference by government in village affairs, especially through the work of the designated official village chief, or *pulenu'u*.

In the event, the extent of effective participation by villagers in the RDP did not in many cases extend beyond the acceptance of the conditions for eligibility laid down by the government and the donors. Samoans at village level have long been adept at taking what was deemed to be valuable from external sources and absorbing it into existing patterns of social organization (Wilson, 1989). The RDP was not exempt from this response, which was most apparent in the way in which what had been conceived as a communally based intervention was in effect transformed into family or individualist mini-projects. These investments were not without communal benefits, but these were obtained in the main through traditional patterns of responsibility and reciprocity. This was most apparent in the funding of investments in livestock where the very attractive (to the villager) beef development model failed to make any significant impact in terms of either import substitution or the long-term building up of improved quality beef herds at village level. Experience with grants and loans for piggery development – which were also attractive to villagers – also demonstrated the extent to which the planners had insufficient understanding of the realities of village life. Funds were wasted mainly because the pig development model was not appropriate to the needs of villagers. Villagers, not unreasonably, took advantage of the opportunity for cheap capital formation but development was not advanced.

From the management and organizational perspective of government, the programme suffered from insufficient extension support at village level, in itself a result of underfunding and weak management of village-level advisory services during the period of the first four Plans. The RDP was in effect too finance-oriented; villages were encouraged to express their needs in a financial framework rather than in the broader framework of resources and constraints. Monitoring disbursement was given greater priority than monitoring effective delivery and use, not, unfortunately, an uncommon situation in aid programmes for countries large and small, despite the increased sophistication of the monitoring procedures on offer. The lack of effective monitoring contributed substantially to the failure of the programme which, despite well-meant intentions, made very little direct contribution to small-scale commercial development or self-reliance whether measured in terms of import substitution or of new and sustainable village-level initiatives.

Within the space of little more than eight years, a high-profile programme with a major aid component had declined to a position of relative insignificance. Although politically the RDP was associated with the economic and financial mismanagement which had aggravated, if not necessarily created, the acute economic crisis of the early 1980s, its demise reflected much more the neglect of process which characterized so much post-independence development planning in the country.

STABEX TRANSFERS TO THE SOLOMON ISLANDS

The Solomon Islands, which became an independent nation in 1978 and had a population of 285 000 at the most recent (1986) census, consists of a chain of six mountainous island groups, with many other small outlying islands. Population growth rate is the highest in the region at over 3 per cent per annum and total population was expected to have increased to around 320 000 by the end of 1994 (World Bank, 1991, p. 203). On the basis of International Monetary Fund (IMF) estimates, per capita GNP was about $570 in 1988, placing the Solomon Islands in the 'low-income' classification. Around 90 per cent of the population reside in small, dispersed villages. Agriculture accounts for about 50 per cent of GDP (Asian Development Bank, 1993, p. 304) although this is likely to be higher owing to an underestimation of the full contribution of the large subsistence sector to GDP.

The country displays the same characteristics of a small, open, trade-dependent economy as Western Samoa, with economic activity heavily influenced by external fluctuations. The level of externally determined financial flows, be they in the form of aid transfers, inflows of foreign investment or export revenues, have been of great importance to the Solomon Islands Government (SIG). In this context the discussion of the policies and processes involved in the operations of the EU Stabex scheme which follows is of central significance to the agricultural sector and the wider economy.

Stabex was established in 1975 as part of the first Lomé Convention (Lomé I), a cooperation treaty between the European Union (EU) and African, Caribbean and Pacific (ACP) countries for the period 1975–9. The most recent (fourth) Lomé Convention was signed in 1990 for the period 1991–9. The basic aim of Stabex, to remedy the harmful effects of the instability of export earnings, has not changed over the four conventions. Unlike the IMF's Compensatory Financing Facility, Stabex is a commodity-specific compensatory financing scheme. Export shortfalls are calculated on a commodity-by-commodity basis and payments made to recipient governments on a commodity, rather than aggregate, 'net' balance of payments approach.

Repayment is not required from small and/or island countries and, in this sense, Stabex transfers may be described as more of a 'soft' form of multilateral aid than simply an export revenue stabilization scheme. The earlier transfers (Lomé I and II) provided a supply of 'soft' aid funds to which little or no conditionality was attached and for which no end-use was prescribed. Funds, in turn, tended to be used for a variety of public financing purposes and provided a considerable measure of assistance in terms of both foreign exchange and revenue for development budgets (Hewitt, 1987).

Over successive conventions, conditions have been progressively tightened and new rules applying to Lomé IV made it clear that the sector that recorded the loss of export earnings must be given priority. An important factor in the operation of transfers, therefore, is the interpretation given by the EU to the concept of a sector. If the sector is to be defined in the broadest sense then this entails all production, distribution, processing and marketing activities. The rules of priority to the sector thus preclude the funding of activities focusing on diversification into non-traditional (non-agricultural) sectors and anything more than simple processing of agricultural products. Transfer of funds outside the agricultural sector is normally forbidden.

Under the current convention, priority for fund allocation must be given to the economic operators in the sector which has suffered the loss of earnings; diversification is restricted. There is clearly a potential conflict between this conditionality and national policies for diversification from low-earning commodities into more profitable ones. EU concerns over the possible 'misuse' of such fungible funds have resulted in a seemingly paradoxical stance whereby the Stabex objectives of the scheme seek to mitigate the (perceived) destabilizing effects of export instability, yet the rules of the scheme would appear to prevent ACP countries from alleviating one of the root causes of such instability: that is, export concentration.

The reasons for this change in the nature of conditionality were twofold. It was felt that, owing to the previous unconditional use of Stabex funds, only limited support was being given to the production of commodities for export and that the fungible nature of such transfers might in fact be detrimental to the long-term growth potential of recipient countries in that harsh decisions were being postponed by governments while funds continued temporarily to alleviate balance of payments problems. The other factor influencing conditionality was the changing practices of other donor agencies in line with the introduction of structural adjustment lending by the World Bank in the early 1980s. Copra and palm oil export revenue shortfalls have been the source of almost all transfers in recent years. As the annexe shows, forestry and copra sectors have been the major recipients (almost 50 per cent) of the disbursed (or allocated) funds.

Analysis of the 1980–92 period suggests that the scheme has been unsuccessful if evaluated in terms of its macroeconomic stabilizing objectives. There are, of course, a number of reasons why instability in the period 1980–92 was higher than in the earlier period: in particular, large fluctuations in world prices (demand factors) and export volumes (supply factors). However, it is possible to conclude that operations of the scheme were not effective in maintaining stability at pre-Stabex levels, for two operational reasons. First, Stabex transfers are normally received 12 to 18 months after the end of the shortfall year, and can therefore be received when the export earnings of the product concerned are on the increase again. The net result of this is to increase 'apparent' instability. A feature of the Stabex scheme in the Solomon Islands has been the late disbursement of funds; in some cases, the payments were made four years after the actual revenue loss and any stabilizing effect under such circumstances could only have been coincidental.

Second, early transfers made under Lomé I and II were subject to little or no conditionality. The annexe tables show that use of transfers was not strictly sector-tied. In 1986/7, copra revenue shortfalls accounted for almost 65 per cent of transfers and palm oil for the remainder, yet the copra sector received less than 25 per cent and the palm oil sector only 15 per cent of disbursed project funds. Forestry, on the other hand, received over 20 per cent of disbursed funds and the transport sector over 15 per cent. This seemingly unplanned and non-strategic allocation of funds was a major contributing factor to the tightening of Stabex conditionality and the subsequent delays in release of later funds.

Between 1986 and 1992, a total of almost SI\$4.7 million from Stabex transfers was channelled through the Commodities Export Marketing Authority (CEMA) specifically for stabilization of copra export returns. As implementors of a micro-stabilization scheme which endeavoured to stabilize the incomes of producers and, by stabilizing prices, to stabilize export receipts, CEMA's aims are very similar to Stabex macroeconomic objectives. From the results obtained from as yet unpublished research (M.T. Wilson, 1994) it would appear that copra export revenue instability over the period 1975–92 was determined largely by price variability and a positive interaction effect between price and volume. This would appear to lend weight to the argument that price stabilization is worthwhile because of the importance of price variability in generating copra revenue instability. When judged in the context of the contribution of price variability to revenue instability, and CEMA's ability to stabilize prices, the Stabex transfer funds would appear to have been effectively utilized.

However, the impact of any commodity stabilization schemes on macroeconomic stability depends on the relative contribution of exports of these commodities to the balance of payments. Despite price support, copra production declined steadily, from 33 000 tonnes in 1989 to under 23 000 tonnes in 1992 and from over 25 per cent of total export revenues in 1984 to a little over 5 per cent in 1992 (CBSI, 1993). The effect on macroeconomic stability of a micro-stabilization scheme which attempts to stabilize the prices of a commodity contributing less than 10 per cent (in recent years) to total export receipts is likely to be negligible. This, and the decline in production despite price support, raises the question as to the effectiveness of using SI\$4.7 million of Stabex funds for stabilization, especially when the opportunity costs (in terms of alternative uses) are so high.

Equally serious in the Solomon Islands context are the two major problems which arose from the delays followed by the tightening of conditionality which had a direct effect on policy formulation and the effectiveness of project planning and management. The prolonged negotiating period made it necessary for SIG to identify other sources of recurrent expenditure funding for ongoing projects, and to postpone new projects. With changes in the 'rules', current SIG projects funded from Stabex transfers in previous years were no longer eligible to receive further funding.

Effective policy making and planning is constrained by the development characteristics of the Solomon Islands (outlined earlier in this chapter) which in turn limit the ability of small dependent economies to adapt to changes in conditionality. These changes have served to highlight deficiencies in the capacity of the government to plan and monitor development activities. While the imposition of conditionality *may* foster 'good governance', changing conditionality created both administrative burdens and misunderstanding in a country with limited institutional capacity. The 'strengthening' of government institutions to cope with the added administrative burden should be a priority in light of these problems. Sectoral planning with respect to diversification would appear to have been inhibited by the conditionality attached to disbursement. A conflict in the share of funds for diversification and for the affected sectors may occur unless the opportunity costs of using funds in a specific way are estimated; that is, unless the quality and consistency of project appraisal are improved.

It is apparent that the quality of project formulation and the effectiveness of project planning and management are key factors determining whether Stabex funds are used effectively or not. The development of effective and sustainable monitoring and evaluation systems for transfer-funded projects is extremely important as these projects are the 'cutting edge' of Stabex. Current practice is for monitoring to be carried out by the recipient government and evaluation by the EU (or its consultants). Improved coordination of these operations is required in order to obtain the benefits of more effective approaches to prioritization and operational management.

IMPLICATIONS FOR PROJECT PLANNERS AND MANAGERS IN COUNTRIES LARGE AND SMALL

It is possible to draw three main lessons, or sets of implications, from the experience of Western Samoa and the Solomon Islands with one particular multilateral donor agency. The first relates to the role of the external aid agency as initiator and prime influence on the processes of planning and management. The second related area is concerned with the ways in which the programme as designed was used or interpreted by the recipient and the third reflects on the need to reflect more adequately the institutional and administrative constraints in sectoral, programme and project-level planning and management.

In both the Western Samoa and the Solomons cases, the external donor was the prime mover in establishing a country programme based on well established policy and process. Although this applies in particular to the Stabex programme, it also has considerable relevance in Western Samoa where the Rural Development Programme was the first of the EU's micro-projects in the region. At the planning stage, both programmes drew heavily on laid down procedures and experience elsewhere which were not necessarily relevant to the particular circumstances in the two countries. Methodologically, the new initiatives were heavily donor-driven and there was little or no possibility for the recipient government – and even less for the ultimate 'beneficiaries' – to have any serious input into the planning process.

In both cases, despite or possibly because of the lack of access at an earlier stage, the implementation of the programmes was amended by the recipients to reflect their own priorities. In Western Samoa this was particularly evident at the level of the individual village and family (but with the compliance of the government) to the extent that the 'developmental' intentions of the planners were overturned by what can only be described as rational opportunism at village level. In the Solomons (and during the same period for transfers into Western Samoa) Stabex was used as a funding instrument, maintaining existing programmes and providing much-needed but ad hoc overall balance of payments support. When new conditions on Stabex transfers were imposed in the Solomons, a combination of obstructionism and lack of capacity on the part of the government led to delays which were not in the best interests of new EU-supported initiatives to develop the small farm sector.

Both programmes appear to reflect a neglect of the more important institutional and administrative constraints on planning and implementation at the sector, programme and project levels. In this sense especially, but also in a number of others, the experience of two small countries in relation to one set of multilateral programmes has a number of lessons for larger administrations. Where aid budget allocation has been driven by a need to disburse agreed funds almost regardless of the capacity and capability to absorb them, the financial analyst and the less enlightened breed of project economist may still have too much power and influence relative to other professionals. Where programmes and projects are analysed on the basis of criteria and methodologies which do not adequately reflect a true understanding of developmental priorities at local level, we will unfortunately continue to make expensive mistakes in countries large and small, on relatively remote islands and in the middle of huge continents.

There are signs that we are beginning to learn from past errors and omissions, so it is hoped that, in the future, it may be possible to learn in a positive rather than negative way from the trials and tribulations of those who seek to improve the quality of life in the South Pacific.

ANNEXE

Table 11A.1 below lists transfers for 1977 to 1990. Group 2 transfers cover the period of largest transfers (SI$61.2 million) for 1986 and 1987 plus a final settlement for the 1981 claim of SI$711 000).

The sectoral analysis is made according to approximate divisions within the projects receiving Stabex funds during the Group 1 and Group 2 time periods. Some projects, such as the Smallholder Development Project, allocate Stabex transfers to the development of a number of crops so that any sub-division by crop can only be approximate (see Table A2).

Table 11.A1   Stabex transfer years: application years 1977–90

	Application year	Sector	Transfer ECU	Transfer SI$	Received year
Lomé I	1977	Copra	1 274 640*	1 368 067	1978
Lomé I	1978	Timber	761 245*	875 657	1979
Lomé I	1978	Copra	138 502*	159 318	1979
Lomé II	1981	Copra	565 092*	565 092	1982
Lomé II	1982	Copra	1 726 633	1 749 650	1983
Lomé II	1983	Copra	1 463 298	1 409 906	1984
Lomé II	1983	Timber	34 791	33 522	1984
Group 1			5 963 201	6 161 212	
Lomé II	1981	Copra	387 031	710 976	1986
Lomé III	1986	Palm oil	6 657 167	14 392 338	1986–7
Lomé III	1986	Copra	12 328 129	26 652 569	1986–7
Lomé III	1987	Palm oil	3 283 484	7 677 776	1988
Lomé III	1987	Copra	5 435 875	12 710 716	1988

Group 2			28 091 686	62 144 377	
Lomé III	1988	Copra	2 910 168	10 622 113	1993
Lomé III	1988	Palm oil	653 282	2 384 479	1993
Lomé IV	1990	Copra	3 555 653	12 978 133	1993
Lomé IV	1990	Palm oil	675 471	2 465 469	1993
Lomé IV	1990	Cocoa	363 379	1 326 333	1993
Group 3			8 157 953	29 776 528	
Total 1978–90			42 212 840	98 082 117	

Note: * Group 1 transfers were not paid into a special account at the CBSI as with later transfers. As only some of the monies appear in published SIG accounts, it is not possible to locate with any accuracy the source of transfers and their use in 'Stabex projects' for Application Years 1977, 1978, 1981, 1982 and 1983.

Source: Central Bank of Solomon Islands Annual Reports.

Table 11.A2   Main projects/organizations receiving Stabex funding

Project/organization	1986–91	1992	Sector
1. Forestry Department	13 643 512	8 567 895	Forestry
2. Commodities Export Marketing Authority	10 927 648	4 000 000	Copra
3. Solomon Islands Plantation Ltd.	8 884 903	NIL	Palm oil
4. Development Bank of Solomon Islands	4 500 000	NIL	Various
5. Marine Department	4 460 390	40 000	Shipping
6. Guadalcanal and Malaita road rehabilitation	4 364 635	NIL	Roads
7. Smallholder development project	2 145 500	1 370 000	Copra/cocoa
8. Microprojects/provincial development unit	1 796 297	453 341	Rural projects
9. Noro infrastructure	1 379 488	141 947	New town
10. Sasape marina	1 071 526	NIL	Fishing
11. Tourism development	1 043 080	224 692	Tourism
12. Rural transport project	599 232	3 174 000	Roads and wharves
13. Housing site development	NIL	1 334 000	Urban housing
14. Rural services project	907 763	802 685	Agriculture

Major projects	55 438 974	20 108 560	
Minor projects	5 479 267	1 077 905	Various
Studies/reserved	NIL	8 590 063	
Total	61 243 241	29 776 528	

Note: Main projects = funding over SI$1 million.

Source: Central Bank of Solomon Islands Annual Reports.

REFERENCES

Asian Development Bank (1993) *Key Indicators of Developing Asian and Pacific Countries*, Oxford: Oxford University Press.

Central Bank of Solomon Islands (1993) *Quarterly Review*.

Duncan, R. (1994) 'On Achieving Sound and Stable Economic Policies in the Pacific Islands', *Pacific Economic Bulletin*, **9**, (1), 21–6.

Government of Western Samoa (1966) *Economic Development Programme*.

Government of Western Samoa (1975) *Third Development Plan*.

Government of Western Samoa (1980) *Fourth Development Plan*.

Government of Western Samoa (1992) *Seventh Development Plan*.

Hewitt, A.P. (1987) 'Stabex and Commodity Export Compensation Schemes; Prospects for Globalisation', *World Development*, **15**, (5), 617–31.

Hughes, A.V. (1992) *A Question of When and How*, Development Planning Division of ESCAP, Bangkok.

Kakazu, H. (1994) *Sustainable Development in Small Island Economies*, Boulder Col.: Westview Press.

O'Meara, J. (1983) 'Why is Village Agriculture Stagnating?', Department of Anthropology, University of California.

Smith, B.J. (1987) 'Some Aspects of Economic Adjustment in Small Island Economies', in F. Holmes (ed.), *Economic Adjustment Policies and Problems*, Washington, DC: IMF.

South Pacific Forum (1995) Communiqué Forum Finance Ministers, 21 February, Suva: Forum Secretariat.

Wilson, F.A. (1989) 'Room for Manoeuvre? Economic and Cultural Perspectives of Aid and Food Import Dependency in Western Samoa', in J. Kaminarides, L. Briguglio and H. Hoogendonk (eds), *The Economic Development of Small Countries*, Delft: Eburon Press.

Wilson, F.A. (1994) 'Small, Beautiful and Vulnerable – Policy Options and Processes for Agricultural Development in Small South Pacific Countries', in J.D. Macarthur and J. Weiss (eds), *Agriculture, Projects and Development*, Aldershot: Avebury.

Wilson, M.T. (1994) 'Export Instability and EU Stabex Funds in the Solomon Islands', unpublished MA dissertation, University of East Anglia, UK.

World Bank (1991) *Pacific Islands Economies: Towards Higher Growth in the 1990s*, World Bank Country Study, Washington, DC.

12. Institutional capacity building for rural development: a case study from Zimbabwe

John Cusworth

INTRODUCTION

During the 1970s and early 1980s, rural development projects funded by the major donors were generally characterized by a style of management that had much to do with output delivery and relatively little to do with genuine local-level participation and long-term institutional development. The driving force behind most of these projects was new agricultural technology and a belief that, once farmers could gain access to this through credit, input supply and marketing systems, this would lead to self-sustaining growth and development in rural areas. Supported by simultaneous investments in infrastructure such as roads and water supplies, together with increased provision of health services, the process was designed to address the problems of low incomes and lack of basic human needs in the same comprehensive and integrated 'projectized' package.

The management and organization of such projects tended to be focused upon a set of predetermined targets the achievement of which became the primary objective of management. Numbers of farmers signed up for loans, kilometres of road built, wells sunk (for example) – these became the benchmarks for project evaluation. Furthermore, the need for a multidisciplinary approach to managing such projects and the inappropriate bureaucratic management structures of government departments resulted in the widespread establishment of 'project management units' (PMUs) which became islands of 'task'-based management within, or even outside, the normal institutional infrastructure.

This approach to effecting rural development has been widely documented and criticized for its lack of apparent success and for the long-term damage that it inflicted on the capacity of government departments and other existing institutions. While the presence of target-oriented mechanistic management approaches to rural development still exist in many places, there has been a steady shift in practice away from such projects based on predetermined 'blueprints' towards a more 'process'-based approach to project planning and implementation. However, donors may be constrained in their ability to follow through a commitment to a process approach to development owing to a need to plan for resource allocation within specific time periods and to be held fully accountable for the utilization of these resources.

It is arguable that, in practice, these constraints inhibit international donors from effectively supporting genuine participatory rural development except through allocation of grants to non-government organizations working at the local level, as in the case of South Africa before 1994. Some rural development projects funded by major donors with a declared commitment to a 'process' approach to development, such as the Southern Mindanao Agricultural Development Project (SMAP) in the Philippines, are still largely target- and budget-driven (Cusworth, 1994). This is not to say that such projects do not involve local communities and organizations and that their management is not committed to working with and through them. It is just that the need to dispense predetermined quantities of resources and to account for them on a systematic basis fundamentally undermines the process approach which, almost by definition, precludes predetermination of levels of resource allocation within specific time periods and against specific project outputs.

To a certain extent, the process approach to development presents donors with a problem. While they are anxious to support development initiatives identified and prioritized by local people and supported by local organizations, they are themselves bureaucratic organizations with operating procedures and plans which are fuelled by a budgetary system requiring financial disbursement against planned action. Ways may be found to get round this problem, but they will inevitably involve a shift in management style that will often be uncomfortable for those more used to a bureaucratic and mechanistic style. Any fundamental shift towards a more adaptive process approach is likely to meet resistance from some people in donor organizations and government and not least those concerned with budgets and accountability. Project managers also may be more comfortable with the control that *comes with* the traditional PMU structure. Nevertheless, there has been a growing recognition that PMUs and interventions outside the normal institutional framework within a country do not lead to sustained capacity for the promotion of rural development. Furthermore, other factors are also influencing approaches to rural development, the most important of these being the effects of economic structural adjustments (ESAPs).

The purpose of this chapter is not to discuss the detailed impact of ESAPs but rather to point to some implications they have for rural development generally. A main component of most structural reform programmes is the curtailing of central government expenditure associated with a reduction in the size of the public sector. This has important implications in that reduced government expenditure will almost inevitably involve a reduction in centrally sourced investment funds at the local level and an associated reduction in the provision of services. This is likely to put greater responsibility on local organizations and local resources to support development which may be accompanied by a deliberate policy of decentralization. It will almost certainly raise the prospect of local-level government being seen as a vehicle for planning and managing the development process after, in many countries, decades of neglect.

The more pivotal role for local authorities may provide the opportunity to develop fully the process approach to promoting rural development such as has been tried on a pilot basis in Zimbabwe. This remainder of this chapter examines the experience of the (UK) ODA and Government of Zimbabwe-supported Pilot District Support Project (PDSP) in that country.

PILOT DISTRICT SUPPORT PROJECT (PDSP) OBJECTIVES AND APPROACH

The PDSP ran for five years in Midlands Province of Zimbabwe, between 1989 and 1994. What follows is a summary of the ODA/Government of Zimbabwe (GOZ) evaluation studies undertaken in 1992 and 1994 with the aim of indicating what appear to be the key factors which determined the project's apparent success. The chapter concludes with comments on managing the process approach towards rural development which may add to the current debate on the issue.

The overall aim of the project was to support the Government of Zimbabwe's policy of promoting effective planning and implementation of development activities at provincial, district and local levels. The specific objectives of the project were as follows:

1. to strengthen the capacity of the rural district councils to plan, implement, coordinate, fund and maintain (on a sustainable basis) their own development programmes, working together with district representatives of central government departments;
2. to improve the capacity of the provincial-level institutions to promote and support effective planning, implementation and management;
3. to demonstrate the benefits of a decentralized development planning and management system.

The approach adopted towards achieving the project objectives owed much to the experience of a previous project supported by ODA in Northern

Zambia. It involved a significant departure from the more traditional approach to implementing rural development projects having an emphasis on delivering a set of project outputs such as roads, water points and clinics. Such projects are generally characterised by management which is target-oriented and with the accent on firm leadership and accountability to sponsors based upon a project plan focused on a predetermined implementation schedule. Before it began, it had no targets for the delivery of specific project outputs in terms of tangible assets. It had no formal timetable for the delivery of development assistance or expenditure on development initiatives. The approach to implementation was envisaged as a 'process' of institution building which could enhance the ability of local authorities to take control and ownership of their own development planning and management activities. Against a background of experience with local authority-driven development throughout many parts of Africa, the project was not considered to be without risk, therefore it was launched as a 'pilot' approach, with all the implications for monitoring and evaluation that this involves.

The project approach involved three main components within the context of an 'enabling environment': enhancement of the 'capacity' of the local authorities (rural district councils, RDCs), allocation of development funds 'directly' to the authorities and provision of a 'facilitation' service within the project area working at all levels throughout the provincial and district-level administration. These components are examined in further detail below.

THE ENHANCEMENT OF RURAL DISTRICT COUNCIL CAPACITY

This component involved three specific activities: the provision of transport and equipment, assistance with the development of management systems and the delivery of training. The provision of equipment, initially to the Gokwe South RDC, included a heavy goods vehicle and Landrover, workshop tools and machinery, computers and other office equipment. Almost certainly the most important items on this list were the vehicles. The availability of transport within a large rural area such as Gokwe District was an essential requirement if the local authority was to have any real significant presence in the area. The provision of a new transport facility under the PDSP project transformed the operational capacity of the Gokwe RDC almost at a stroke. However, simply providing the transport is only part of the story in terms of the project's overall aim of capacity building. While, in itself, the provision of transport enabled the council to increase its operational capacity, it could not do this on a sustainable basis without the development of management systems to operate and maintain the vehicles. The purpose of providing the vehicles and equipment was therefore twofold: first, to enhance capacity directly through providing the means to undertake activities and, second, to provide an opportunity to assist the council to develop its managerial capacity through the development of appropriate support systems.

Assisting the council to adopt appropriate management systems was a key activity in developing the RDC capacity. The approach used to achieve this was also described as a 'process'. First, there was recognition that the RDCs would be unlikely to adopt new management systems designed to operate and maintain the project's facilities on a sustainable and accountable basis if they had no resources with which to operate. More traditional approaches involve systems development rewarded by provision of resources once the systems have been put in place. Under the PDSP approach, it was the other way round. It is assumed that, for the effective development of management systems to take place, the capacity to do things must come first and that assistance towards achieving this is only likely to be effective *after* the organization itself has recognized the need and value of having such systems. The transport management system operated by the Gokwe South RDC provides a valuable case study which illustrates this approach and the effectiveness of the overall PDSP approach more generally.

The third element of this component of the project was 'training'. Enhancement of capacity involves not only the allocation of resources and the setting up of systems but also equipping people working in organizations with the knowledge and skills to operate the systems effectively and efficiently. Training of RDC staff was a major project activity delivered in a variety of forms, but mainly through workshops using participatory learning methods very much oriented to meeting internally perceived training needs. Much of the training for council staff, councillors and members of village and ward development committees was undertaken by a provincial training and advisory team (PTAT) which was set up with assistance from the project personnel based at provincial level.

The training function of the project has permeated throughout the organizations with which it has worked and in particular the RDCs. This is reflected in the management style of the RDC executive in Gokwe South. Current practice now involves the operation of a staff development and appraisal system under which each member of the executive is appraised regularly with a view to identifying opportunities for strengthening his or her skills.

THE ALLOCATION OF DEVELOPMENT FUNDS DIRECTLY TO THE RDCs

The second main component of the project was designed to allow the local authority to develop its capacity to plan and manage the implementation of development projects in addition to subsequently deriving benefits from the development initiatives to which the funds would be allocated. The mechanism by which the funds were allocated to the RDC is complicated, but essentially involved the Ministry of Local Government allocating money directly to the RDC via a temporary deposit account (TDA) of the district administrator (DA). Expenditure plans for individual projects were required to be approved initially by the RDC itself and the District Development Committee and subsequently submitted to the Provincial Development Committee (PDC). On approval by this committee, the provincial administrator would authorise the ministry to release centrally held funds for the project into the TDA. The funds in this account would be released to fund project expenditure undertaken by either the council itself or other government departments. Following project implementation, a project completion certificate would be issued after a site review by a joint team of government and council officials and this certificate would then be used by the ministry to reclaim the expenditure from the ODA.

The mechanics of actually managing the disbursement of the funds raises a number of issues but for our purposes here it is sufficient to establish that the principle involved in the approach was that the money was made available for use by the RDC for projects which the council had itself planned, approved and implemented. This was a major innovation, given that most funds for development projects and programmes in Zimbabwe are channelled to districts through the main government departments. Very little money for development purposes was previously directed to the RDCs and few had any significant development funds of their own because of their very weak revenue base.

The rationale for allocating funds in this way was to reinforce the capacity-building exercise. However, it was based on more than just the assumption that there was little point in assisting a local authority to develop its planning and management capacity unless it had some access to resources. The allocation of the funds was actually a major means through which the capacity-building exercise could be achieved. This is the 'learning by doing' concept which underpins so much of the methodology deployed under PDSP, the idea being that undertaking complex activities using new systems requires development gained through experience. Inevitably, this means that, even at the design stage, the project sponsors were aware that mistakes would be made and scarce development funds wasted. Most development projects have associated with them management infrastructures designed specifically to avoid such wastage (and management is judged by its ability to use funds effectively). In this case, 'management' had no direct control over the funds and was required to view funds initially being utilized poorly as part of the process of capacity building. This has important implications for managers and personnel involved with this type of project in terms of their qualifications, experience, management style and reward systems and some of these are discussed further below.

PROVISION OF A FACILITATION SERVICE

The provision of a facilitation service through the project's operations at all levels within the province and across a wide variety of organizations was the third major component of the PDSP approach to project implementation. This was the least tangible of the project components, but was certainly not in any way less important than the others. The facilitation process is one that is not easy to describe and is impossible to quantify. It might be described as the process of responding to the internally perceived development needs of individuals and organizations, assisting them in identifying means of meeting those needs and helping them to gain access to and follow those means in order successfully to bring about the desired change. It is not a directly interventionist role. The facilitation process may involve the setting of desirable objectives by the facilitators, but it is the organizations and the people within them which actually seek to attain those objectives.

In the case of PDSP, this can best be illustrated by the structure, location, style and make-up of the facilitation team. First, unlike the case of many more traditional projects, the project facilitation team, consisting of three expatriate technical cooperation officers (TCOs), had no designated set of counterparts. The project approach adopted here did not rely on the transference of skills to counterparts to carry on the work once the project closed. There was no 'project management unit', no project logo, project headquarters or infrastructure. The project vehicles used by the facilitators did not even have the project name on them. Everything possible was done to play down the identity of the project as an entity in itself.

All this does not mean that the provision of a facilitation service was achieved without controversy. In the early months of the project there were some problems with respect to the physical location of the TCO team and in the way it operated. There were also other problems in the early days when the role and function of the team were not fully defined by the team themselves or understood by many of the people with whom they were working. It is clear that developing and operationalizing the facilitation role is in itself a 'process'.

THE ENABLING ENVIRONMENT

It is important to emphasize that the PDSP approach involved three main components which were inexorably interrelated. To have adopted two out of three of the components would almost certainly have rendered the whole project ineffective, although there may be arguments for and against the balance between the components. For example, could the same have been achieved with rather fewer development funds and more facilitators or the other way round? But the important point is that, although the project involved a disparate set of activities, they were part of a 'package'. Moreover, the package was designed to be delivered as a process which marks this pilot project out as particularly innovative within the context of contemporary Zimbabwe. But the package could not have been delivered in the absence of the supportive institutional environment within which it was implemented. The level of commitment to the approach and goals of the project, particularly by the provincial and district administrations, but also by other key departments, provided a framework within which the project was capable of demonstrating its potential.

There was also a political dimension to this favourable environment. The prime minister's directive on decentralized development in 1984 and the more recent passing of legislation reforming the structure of local government provided a focus for supporting the role of local authorities. As indicated in the introduction to this chapter, the effects of the economic reform programme also provided impetus to this process in that increased emphasis was being given to the mobilization of local resources within districts as the result of a forecast reduction in central government expenditure flows.

Although the macroeconomic and organizational environment might be generally supportive of a project designed to build institutional capacity at the local level, much depended on the attitude and response to such an initiative by people working in the various participating institutions. It would be quite erroneous to give the impression that there was total support for the PDSP approach in all quarters. The shift in ultimate control over some development resources away from the well-established line departments towards the local authorities remains one area of contention, as does the balance of relative power and authority between the district administrator and the chief executive and chairperson of the local authority. These are current issues in Zimbabwe that are reflected much more widely and still remain to be resolved, if indeed they can ever be so. As so often, therefore, the enabling environment finally boils down to the level of commitment, attitudes and motivation of the key individuals involved in the process. In the case of PDSP, the level of commitment to the process by the provincial administration remained remarkably high over four or five years. The leadership role proved essential and was supported in turn by individual DAs and the local authorities which quickly saw their chance to take on a proactive role in planning and managing development within their districts.

ISSUES ARISING FROM THE PDSP PROJECT APPROACH

This section raises a number of issues which have arisen as a result of five years of PDSP project operations. Perhaps the first point to make is that the 1992 and 1994 ODA/GOZ reviews (Blunt *et al.*, 1992; Cusworth *et al.*, 1994) concluded that the project had been largely successful in achieving its direct and indirect objectives. But evaluations of projects such as this are always difficult. Who knows what the situation in Gokwe South district might have been even without the project? In the absence of information on this, it is tempting to assess the project only against the baseline pre-project situation. Against this criterion, the project could be judged to have been extremely successful, but is this the right benchmark? A number of factors suggest that Gokwe South might have made some considerable progress with respect to achieving development goals even in the absence of PDSP. There is a sense of the 'frontier' about the district. It has a reasonably favourable resource base and lacks the severe pressure on land which characterizes many other communal areas in Zimbabwe. For most of the past five years it has had based within the district a highly motivated team of government officials and some able councillors and council officials. Such a combination would presumably in any case have resulted in some well-directed development.

The reviews concluded that, while this might well have been the case, there is little evidence to suggest that the RDC itself would have developed its planning and management capacity to the degree it had without this or some other similar project initiative. The baseline situation would probably have been fairly similar to date, if the current status of many other districts in the province are anything to go by. It is probably reasonably safe, therefore, to agree with the review findings that the project has largely been successful in meeting its direct and indirect objectives, while acknowledging these other favourable factors. The factors that may have determined this success are examined below, component by component.

STRENGTHENING ENHANCEMENT OF LOCAL AUTHORITY CAPACITY

This project component was recognizably the most visible in the early stages of implementation, despite the delays incurred in procuring vehicles. The presence of the TCO team and the arrival of the vehicles had a major impact on the Gokwe South RDC and provided the basis for changing the management culture permeating the council administration. The concepts of pre-planning and accountability that characterize so much of the council's activities today began with the need to develop a sound transport management system. This is not to play down the impact of other resources provided under the project, but pooled transport depends so much on sound management because of its scarcity value and potential for misuse and abuse.

The issue of management culture is of particular interest. The management styles and the systems operated by Gokwe South RDC are clearly character-ized by a 'mechanistic' management style mainly associated with bureau-cratic organizational structures (Rondinelli *et al.*, 1990). While there is probably no argument with the fact that local government structures are bureaucratic in nature, there has been considerable speculation about whether such structures at the local level are ever likely to be appropriate vehicles for managing development, owing to their chronically weak management, their tendency towards political manipulation and possibly a cultural dimension which sug-gests that they are resistant to the adoption of recognizable (Western style) management processes (Hyden, 1983, pp. 148–51). This argument could be used to delay any process of decentralization. If, so the argument goes, local government is deemed chronically incapable, then things must be left to the private sector, NGOs or the stronger central government departments. The PDSP experience would tend to contradict this orthodoxy.

DIRECT ALLOCATION OF CAPITAL DEVELOPMENT FUNDS

This is perhaps the most controversial and innovative aspect of the PDSP project. In itself, the process of transferring the functions of planning and managing development projects to the district level makes much sense and few would argue against the increased participation by local people in the process. There are arguments against such an approach based on the theory that locally based initiatives are more likely to be hijacked by important and powerful local elites, who would control the allocation of resources to meet their own ends rather than use them towards the general good. It is difficult to determine whether this has happened under this project, but the review con-cluded that perhaps the opposite has happened and that some previously powerful and influential people had seen their influence diminish during the time of the project.

On the other hand, there was evidence that some articulate councillors had managed to associate themselves directly with the advent of specific projects within their constituencies using PDSP funds. But, then, perhaps this is the stuff of political reality and is to be expected. There might be a problem if the development projects were overly concentrated in a few favoured areas, but there is apparently no evidence of this. In fact, the village and ward planning systems developed with assistance from the project probably reduce the chances of this happening.

The pre-project situation was that the RDC in Gokwe South, as with most other local authorities in the country, would draw up a list of projects that it would wish to see implemented in the district. This would then be submitted to the Provincial Development Committee and subsequently to central government to be considered along with all the other bids from government departments under the Public Sector Investment Programme (PSIP) process. Owing to the limited availability of funds and the fact that projects submitted by districts rarely met the technical specification required, very little PSIP money was ever allocated to the RDC to fund its own projects. Consequently, there was widespread apathy concerning the whole process, with little time being spent in drawing up anything more than a 'wish list' for submission to the province. To some extent this was a vicious circle: the less effort put into the submission the more unlikely it would be that projects put forward would attract funding.

With the advent of the PDSP project and the allocation of funds directly to the RDC, the prospect of actually being able to fund projects from its own capital resources altered the situation dramatically. However, the process by which the council could receive approval for projects to go ahead remained broadly intact; that is, the council's list of projects still required formal approval at the provincial level. This was an inspired aspect of the project design, as it ensured that the council would need to follow its existing practice with respect to the planning process and at the same time facilitated support for the whole development administration process at both district and provincial levels.

Early rejection of the project 'wish list' opened up the opportunity for the facilitators to assist the district authorities to set up a planning system which would lead to the identification and formulation of projects in a systematic way. This was achieved through the establishment of ward and district-level resource profiles and prioritized development plans. It would be difficult to envisage how such a system could have been set up in the absence of the capital funds. They provided a very powerful motivating force which played a major role in directing the district authorities towards adopting good practice.

While the allocation of capital funds provided the necessary motivation for the adoption of good planning practice in the district, which eventually led to projects being approved for implementation, there remained the issue of managing the process of project implementation. In some respects this aspect of the project was the most risky. The local authority was not generally well renowned for its expertise in project management. In Gokwe South the RDC had a poor track record of financial prudence prior to the start of the project and apparently lacked expertise and experience in managing the implementation of projects. If, under the project, the council failed to adopt sound management systems for project delivery then the whole purpose of the project would be prejudiced. No matter how technically well managed the council executive might become in running its own affairs and no matter how sound its planning processes might become, if it failed to deliver the process of competent project implementation it might reasonably be argued that the project had failed overall.

The ODA/GOZ reviews concluded that the councils in Gokwe South and Mberengwa districts did in fact manage the implementation of projects in a reasonably efficient manner. Relatively complex projects, such as the establishment of clinics involving several government departments and contractors, apparently presented the most problems. However, this was considered to be due to a lack of experience and it was apparent that most key officials were aware of these deficiencies.

The significance of the local authorities developing the capacity to plan and implement projects under the PDSP has very wide ramifications for the future. Already donors are beginning to consider allocating capital development funds directly to these local authorities as the managing agent for their projects (the externally funded Water and Sanitation Project in Mberengwa, for example). If donors are prepared to channel their funds directly to the RDCs, the question may eventually arise as to how much of the PSIP might also be channelled in this way. The problem in the short run, however, is how to develop RDC capacity to undertake these essential development tasks. The PDSP experience suggests that doing this will involve a short-run cost in terms of poorly utilized funds. As indicated earlier, this may present a major obstacle to replicating this approach more widely. It is hard to envisage a responsible authority deliberately allocating scarce resources in a manner which acknowledges that there is a high risk that they will not be utilized effectively. It might even be argued that this would be negligent. However, as the experience of this pilot project indicates, in the longer term it may be the only way to achieve genuine capacity building. This issue is at the centre of any more general debate as to how best to approach the whole process of institutional capacity.

THE FACILITATION COMPONENT

Given that this project component is so intangible, it is very difficult to identify indicators against which the process can be reviewed and evaluated. The process is analogous to the cement amongst the brickwork which supports all the other activities within the organizational framework. While there is no doubt that this project component has been instrumental in determining its success, there are a number of issues which stem from it that may have implications for the future of this type of process project.

One relates to the location of the facilitators within the general institutional framework. For PDSP, the facilitating team was based in the offices of a planning department at the provincial headquarters. The team was not part of the department as such and did not fulfil any of its administrative functions. It was based there for purely technical reasons (and also because there was office space available). Inevitably, this gave rise to some initial confusion over the role of the facilitators and their compatibility with the department. To some extent the issue revolves around the nature of the facilitation process and its purpose. The strength of the approach to providing this service under PDSP appears to have been the way that the facilitators have been able to work at all levels within organizations and across organizational boundaries. They were able to do this because they were not formally part of any organizational structure themselves and as a team they were free-standing. Although they were required to have their work programmes agreed by the provincial administration, this rarely affected their operations, except in a supportive way. In this case the facilitators were all expatriates, which distanced them from the bureaucratic tentacles of the government administrative structure.

Perhaps the key issue here is one of whether the facilitation function can be undertaken by people working from within an organization or whether it can only be effective if it is provided by outsiders. Clearly, the PDSP experience suggests that it can be achieved by outsiders, but does this mean that it could not necessarily be provided by insiders? Perhaps the answer to this question lies in the behaviour of people working in organizations. It is generally suggested that most people working in government bureaucracies have a propensity for job security and risk minimization and a tendency to avoid ambiguity in their work. Organization theory supports this view and holds that most government institutions are dominated by a role culture which reinforces the behaviour of individuals along those lines (Handy, 1976). This is the great strength of government organizations, in that it ensures stability, reliability in maintaining the routine and permanency. At the same time, it does not readily lend itself to risk, change and innovation. This is to a large degree reflected in the way the organization rewards the people working within it.

If the theory referred to above is reflected in reality then it might suggest that attempting to require people working within a bureaucratic hierarchy to act as 'change agents' (or facilitators) may be a problem. It may prove difficult to find people with the necessary skills from within the organization and attempting to train people in this role is likely to meet with resistance. Simply designating people as facilitators from a cadre of people who are more comfortable with routine, who prefer to be clear as to what tasks they are to perform and who constantly strive to be 'noticed' as competent (but 'safe') by their superiors is likely to be ineffective.

If the facilitation role is an essential ingredient of the proven capacity-building 'package' as demonstrated through the PDSP experience, and if this is to be adopted more widely in the future, the issue of finding suitable people as facilitators and placing them in the organizational framework will be a central issue. It is tentatively suggested here that facilitators are unlikely to be found within the existing organizational structure. An implication of this is that they will need to be outsiders of some kind, but not necessarily expatriates, although there may be a role for them in this function, provided they have the appropriate skills. Outsiders in this context means people not expecting to find their way up the organizational hierarchy, who have already proved their competency, are happy to take risks and are not afraid of being associated with occasional failure. They will need to have excellent communication and interpersonal skills and to be highly motivated towards the task of capacity building and development.

CONCLUSION

This chapter summarizes the experience of a pilot rural development project based on the 'process' approach which has apparently been judged to have been successful in achieving its primary objectives of developing the capacity of local authorities to plan and manage development at local level.

Perhaps the main point of wider interest is the observation that, while the process approach requires an adaptive style of management from the facilitation team, much of the output from their work is the establishment of more or less 'mechanistic' management systems within the institutions with which they have been working. This observation may have implications for current debate on the merits of the process approach to project implementation in that, while few would argue that the approach has many strengths in terms of ensuring sustainable development, this process in itself must include the development of capacity to deliver project outputs which rely heavily on the more familiar project cycle management skills.

REFERENCES

Blunt, M. *et al.* (1992) 'PDSP Mid Term Review Report', Overseas Development Administration, July, restricted.

Cusworth, J.W. (1994) 'Rural Development Project Management: Changing priorities in management style' in F. Analoui (ed.), *The Realities of Managing Development Projects*, Aldershot: Avebury.

Cusworth, J.W. *et al.* (1994) 'PDSP Terminal Review Report', Overseas Development Administration, July restricted.

Handy, C. (1980) *Understanding Organisations*, Harmondsworth: Penguin.

Hyden, G. (1983), *No Shortcuts to Progress; African Development Management in Perspective*, London: Heinemann.

Rondinelli, D., Middleton, J. and Verspoor, A. (1990*) Planning Education Reforms in Developing Countries, The Contingency Approach*, London: Duke University Press.

13. Entrepreneurship development programmes in practice: a case study in evaluation

Malcolm Harper and Vijay Mahajan

INTRODUCTION

Entrepreneurship development programmes, or EDPs, as they are commonly known, have for over 20 years been an important component of India's attempts to promote new industrial enterprises. This form of training has become something of a movement, and the large numbers of courses which have been and continue to be given by the many institutions which offer them all share a common origin, they are very similar to one another in content and in structure, and they have the same objective, namely to enable people to start their own businesses.

In addition to its scale, longevity and relative homogeneity, the EDP training movement represents an unusual phenomenon in that it is firmly based on a particular piece of experimental research, and it combines behavioural and skills training. It is also unusual in that the desired outcomes are objectively measurable, in economic terms, and it has largely been funded from public sources, so that it both could, and one might argue, should have been rigorously evaluated.

THE ORIGINS OF ENTREPRENEURSHIP DEVELOPMENT PROGRAMMES

The seeds of the movement lie in the work done by McClelland and his colleagues in Southern India in the early 1960s, testing the two linked hypotheses that the need for achievement is an essential ingredient for entrepreneurial success and that achievement motivation can be developed. This experimental research was rigorously evaluated, using baseline and post-training data obtained from the people who were trained and approximately matched control groups in two towns, covering indicators such as hours worked, new activities started, investment and numbers employed; the trainees performed better than the controls by every indicator and in most cases the differences were statistically significant (McClelland and Winter, 1971).

These experiments were based at the Small Industries Extension Training (SIET) Institute in Hyderabad, and after McClelland had completed his work there a number of his local collaborators continued the work that he had started. Most of the original trainees, and the controls, had been people who were already in business, often working in family enterprises, but the SIET staff decided to apply the same methods for people who wanted to start completely new businesses. It was clear that this group needed more than achievement motivation, and new components were added to cover opportunity identification and some management skills; and, as it became clear that obtaining finance was the major problem for would-be entrepreneurs, instruction on the preparation of the particular form of feasibility studies that was required by Indian banking institutions was also included.

In 1970, the Industrial and Development Corporation of the State of Gujarat, which is incidentally the homeland of the Patel community who dominate the entrepreneurial scene in so many countries, took up the SIET EDP model. The Ford Foundation supported their early efforts and they soon attracted the attention of a number of national financial institutions. By 1978, a number of EDPs had been conducted in other parts of India, and in that year a specialized EDP institution was established in Gujarat. A number of other states followed suit and, in 1983, Dr V.G. Patel, the leader of the Gujarat movement, left the Gujarat institution in order to set up the Entrepreneurship Development Institute of India (EDI(I)), which has since then acted as the main focal point for trainer training and assistance to other states in India and, latterly, countries in Africa and other parts of Asia.

There are now some 700 institutions offering EDPs in India. They include the 11 specialized EDP institutions, several hundred small industry support institutions, 30 banks, a number of technical and management training colleges and almost a hundred non-government organizations which specialize in this form of training (Gupta, 1991, p. 16). Many of them employ specialized trainers who are accredited by the EDI(I) and are listed in a special register. Although there is no record of how many people receive EDP training every year, 77 557 men and women were said by the end of 1989/90 to have gone through the courses which have been sponsored by the Industrial and Development Bank of India, which include only a small proportion of the total (Industrial Development Bank of India, 1990, p. 4).

THE PROGRAMME STRUCTURE

The EDP coordinator follows a carefully designed schedule to prepare for each course, residing for some time in the area where the course is to be held. The programme is widely publicized and the 25 to 30 trainees who can be accommodated in one course are selected from the hundred or so applicants who are expected to apply. They go through a three-stage selection process, starting with a simple written application form, which is followed by a series of written tests which are intended to assess what are known as 'entrepreneurial traits', such as achievement motivation, attitude to risk, initiative, optimism and self-confidence. Those who pass these tests are then interviewed in order to assess their understanding of and commitment to the training.

The course itself consists of a total of 180 hours of training, which may be given in six weeks of full time attendance or may be spread over 12 weeks. The training starts with about 45 hours of so-called 'behavioural inputs', which are structured around the various instruments which were designed by McClelland to enable trainees both to identify and to strengthen their achievement motivation. These include thematic apperception tests in which trainees write simple stories in response to neutral pictures and then award marks for the extent to which images of achievement are built into the stories, with exercises which test trainees' attitudes to risk, and various other forms of self-examination and appraisal (Harper, 1984a, pp. 24–6; Jain, 1990). This is followed by approximately two weeks of work in the classroom and the field, identifying and appraising business opportunities and learning how to prepare a feasibility study. The most important part of this component, at least until the recent attempts to liberalize the economy, is the introduction to the vast range of regulatory agencies and support services which have been set up to protect and assist small enterprises but which tend to involve a maze of procedures and formalities, many of which in some parts of the country can only be overcome by judicious corruption.

Unlike most courses in Britain and elsewhere which are designed to help people start their own businesses, the Indian participants are not required to come to the course with any idea of what business they want to start; the trainer who is responsible for each course has to spend some time on advance preparation in the area where it is to be held, and one of her or his main tasks is to identify promising business opportunities for the participants in the forthcoming course, who have at that stage not yet themselves been identified.

The final two weeks of teaching are devoted to management skills. The formal training period is then followed by a follow-up period of varying intensity and duration, which is designed to help trainees to overcome the initial hurdles of the bureaucracy, such as various licences, premises and raw material supply allocations, electricity and water connections, as well as the elusive loans which, because they are often subsidized and subject to quotas, are generally also subject to long delays.

THE NEED FOR EVALUATION

The average cost of this training is said to be the equivalent of around £150 for each of the 30 trainees who typically attend a course. The trainees themselves contribute little or nothing to this cost, which is borne by one or other of the development banks or other sponsoring institutions. This seems a small amount by European standards, but it must be related to the typical daily wage for an unskilled worker in India of around 50 pence.

In spite of this relatively high cost, and the enormous numbers of people who have been trained, there appear to have been very few attempts to evaluate EDP training. Many agencies count their success by the number of trainees who complete business plans, and only a minority actually count the numbers of trainees who start businesses. 'Start-up' is variously defined, and the proportion who have started is said to vary between 25 per cent and 80 per cent, with the lower figures generally coming from the more remote rural areas, where the trainees and the environment are totally different from the trainees and the South Indian cities where McClelland carried out his original research. There has been virtually no use of control groups, nor any attempt to compare the cost of training with the economic benefits resulting from the businesses which have been started.

The need for more rigorous evaluation has been recognized for some time, by EDP training institutions, by sponsors and other commentators. S.K. Gupta, who was for some time centrally involved in the large EDP sponsorship programme of the Industrial Development Bank of India, writes, 'unfortunately the vast literature on Indian EDP does not include any scientific evaluation' and concludes, 'The Indian [EDP] is a typical case where the emphasis on numbers has made most conducting agencies unable to see the wood for the trees' (Gupta, 1991, p. 24). Dr V.G. Patel has written, 'there is therefore a major gap in the knowledge about the effectiveness of programmes' (personal letter, 25 November 1991). The need for rigorous evaluation is all the more urgent in the current period of structural adjustment, when every item of public expenditure has to give value for money, and public sector institutions are under pressure to reduce subsidies of all kinds.

It is important to be clear as to the purpose of evaluation, and the 'stakeholders' for whose use it is intended, since this must be the basis on which the evaluation measures are selected. Easterby-Smith suggests that evaluation can be used to prove (or disprove) the effects of training, to improve the training itself or actually to enhance the learning process, and that it is unlikely that more than one of these purposes can be achieved through a given evaluation methodology (Easterby-Smith, 1986, pp. 12–17). We are here concerned with attempts to discover the impact and 'value' of training, if possible through some form of cost–benefit analysis which treats the cost of the training as an investment which should yield a certain economic return if it is to be justified. This form of evaluation is of little use to the training institution, whose staff, like most tertiary-level trainers and educators, and most providers of any service, judge the value of what they are doing by demand from potential clients and the willingness of sponsors to cover the cost. There is in any case no attempt to disaggregate the impact of different components in a way that could help the trainers to improve future programmes. It is also of little or no use to the trainees, since they have already 'bought' the training, at the expense of their own time if nothing else, and they may not even know that the evaluation is being carried out; nor are they likely ever to see the results.

Such evaluation, if it can be done, and 'opinion remains divided on whether it [cost-benefit analysis of training] is worth attempting' (Easterby-Smith, 1986, p. 14), is designed to help those who sponsor the training to decide whether it is a good investment of their resources, and thus whether to maintain, increase or reduce their support, and whether to press the trainers to investigate ways of improving the training, or to leave well alone. This kind of evaluation may also be of benefit to potential future trainees, particularly if, as is being talked of in India and has already happened in the UK and elsewhere, they are to be asked to pay part or the whole of the cost of the training themselves. Clearly, someone who is planning to start a business, and is deciding how to deploy whatever funds he can raise, would in those circumstances want information on the results achieved by other trainees in the past in order to assess and compare the return on the possible training investment with other alternatives.

The evaluation being considered falls squarely into what is characterized (Easterby-Smith, 1986, pp. 22–4) as the 'scientific–pragmatic' model, as opposed to 'research naturalistic'. It can suffer from all the weaknesses and pitfalls associated with the use of control groups to isolate effects, the difficulties of quantitative measurement not only of current but also of past results, and the selection of appropriate measures of financial value to be compared with the costs to all parties, assuming that these costs themselves can be assessed with any accuracy. However, since one major, if not the only, objective of EDP training is to generate economic activity through new business formation, it can perhaps be argued that it is at least less difficult quantitatively to measure the results than for many other forms of training. Our readers must judge for themselves how well we have succeeded.

INTERNATIONAL EXPERIENCE

Institutions in Indonesia and the Philippines have also used variants of the Indian model of EDP and, although the achievement motivation component originated by McClelland has hardly been used at all in the so-called 'industrialized countries', there has in recent years been an increasing worldwide interest in the possibility of training people to start their own businesses, as opposed to training them only to seek employment with others. Over 300 colleges in the USA, for instance, offer courses in entrepreneurship as part of their business programmes, and 'enterprise culture' is by no means a solely British phenomenon.

Governments and international development agencies are aware that the apparent lack of successful indigenous-owned businesses represents a serious economic, social and indeed political problem for many poorer countries, and the Indian EDP experience has thus attracted some attention from outside the country. Indian training institutions, like their counterparts in Europe and elsewhere, are under pressure to reduce their dependence on government funding and they have vigorously promoted the Indian EDP model, particularly in Africa, as a means of addressing this problem.

The Indian EDP model is by no means the only form of training which has the objective of enabling people to start their own businesses, and evaluation methods which have been used for other business start-up programmes may be equally applicable to Indian EDPs. It may therefore be useful to examine what forms of evaluation other institutions outside India have used. The 'Interman' department of the International Labour Office carried out a survey of 107 institutions throughout the world which conduct business start-up training programmes and the findings included some information about the evaluation methods they used. Some 30 per cent of the respondents did not answer the evaluation question at all, and 27 stated that they relied on questionnaires filled in by the trainees at the end of the course. A further 29 counted the numbers of businesses started by trainees, and only 14 measured the results in terms of jobs, investment or profits achieved by the businesses started by trainees (International Management Development Network, 1992).

The United States Agency for International Development, which places great emphasis on the development of private enterprise in its aid programmes, appears to accept that it is not possible to obtain 'reliable measures of program benefit' (A.I.D. 1989, p. 30), for micro-enterprises at any rate, and that 'cost per program beneficiary' is the most practical measure. This can of course be compared with the cost of other programmes, but it takes no account of the relationship between the costs and the benefits and the Agency makes no mention at all of the use of control groups in the section on methods of evaluation.

There are, however, both from India and elsewhere, a few isolated examples of rigorous evaluation, which demonstrate that it is by no means impossible to overcome the classic evaluation problems of isolation of effects, or to measure the benefits and to compare them with the costs. This is hardly surprising, since new business starts are an economic activity, whose effects can be measured in financial terms and, although there may be intangible or at least hard-to-measure benefits such as the role model effect or the up and down stream impact of sales and purchases by the businesses, these need not present insuperable problems for the evaluator.

Two rigorous quantitative evaluations of 'start your own business' training programmes in Kenya and in Nepal, have been identified (Harper, 1984b, pp. 179–86) and there are no doubt many other examples. These evaluations, and a not dissimilar attempt at Cranfield for the government-sponsored Graduate Enterprise Programme, however, were undertaken at the initiative of the providers rather than of the sponsors, and it may be that it is not only in India that those responsible for official sponsorship of such training are more concerned with the numbers of people trained than with the resulting economic benefits.

It did prove possible to identify a small number of more rigorous evaluations of EDP in India. One study of the results of rural industrialization programmes states that the cost of training and other assistance amounted to the equivalent of approximately £90 per job created. The average annual income of those employed in or owning the enterprises was about £126, which appears to represent a reasonable return on the promotional investment, although there was no attempt to assess the additionality or the opportunity cost of the new employment (Acharya, 1990, pp. 63–6). Similar results are reported from an earlier study of EDPs in Assam, where the average annual income earned by those trainees who did start businesses was 107 per cent of the training cost per 'successful' trainee (Akhouri, 1978, p. 14). In general, however, as Gupta (1991) has suggested, the extensive literature on EDP includes very few rigorous evaluations, and the few writers who use control groups or other similar techniques are more interested in comparing the effectiveness of different methods of trainee selection or of minor changes in programme content than in evaluating the effectiveness of a programme as a whole.

EXISTING EVALUATION PRACTICE

The lack of evidence of rigorous evaluation studies in published material is not in itself evidence that such evaluations are not actually carried out, and it might even be argued that the more effective agencies are less likely to spend time and effort on publications, since they are more than fully engaged in running programmes. We therefore selected a small number of EDP institutions which are generally agreed to be among the most effective in India, or which appeared from their responses to a simple preliminary questionnaire to be evaluating their programmes more rigorously than most, and examined their internal documentation and actual evaluation practices in the field.

Some of these had stated in their responses to our questionnaire that they were evaluating their programmes with the help of control groups and cost–benefit analysis, but closer examination revealed either that they intended to do this in the future or that they were using the terms in a different sense from that intended. One agency, for instance, used the term 'control group' to describe trainees who had not started businesses, while others had compared the costs of different types of programme rather than comparing the costs with the resulting economic benefit. Among these latter, the International Centre for Entrepreneurship and Career Development in Ahmedabad, which specializes in EDPs for women, has compared the effectiveness of the achievement motivation component with the management and project preparation components. They found that women who had been exposed to both components were significantly more likely to start businesses than those who had only attended one or the other, but they did not go further than this in order to assess the effectiveness of their programmes in general.

The North Eastern region branch of the National Institute of Small Industry Extension and Training (the successor institution to the SIET Institute where McClelland carried out his original experiment) has devised a General Programme Effectiveness Index, or GPEI, which is actually no more than an aggregation of a sample of trainees' responses to a questionnaire about various aspects of EDP training, after they had completed the course. The sample only included the one-third of the trainees who had actually started their businesses, or were actively in the process of trying to do so, so the acronym is clearly something of a misnomer. This organization, like a few other EDP institutions, has collected data about the financial results achieved by their trainees' businesses, but they do not relate these data to the cost of the programmes in order to assess their cost-effectiveness.

Many of the staff of the EDP institutions showed during our discussions that they were aware of the need for more rigorous evaluation, and our enquiry aroused a great deal of interest, and only a little resentment, amongst the EDP 'community'. The very suggestion of attempting to isolate results, however, or of regarding EDP as a development investment in human capital which should earn a proportionate return, seemed somewhat alien. Like many development inputs, EDPs seem to have become accepted as an almost traditional component of all kinds of economic development programme, whether they are urban or rural, for women, for 'untouchables', tribals or other disadvantaged minorities, or for unemployed postgraduate engineers or retiring army officers.

EVALUATION EXPERIMENTS

It is tempting to assume that failure to evaluate is caused by lack of confidence in the results, but it can equally well arise from lack of time or resources, unavailability of data, ignorance of suitable techniques or lack of interest on the part of the sponsors. We therefore sponsored or ourselves undertook some modest experiments to test the feasibility of more rigorous EDP evaluation than is currently generally practised.

In one study, carried out by J.S. Saini of the Technical Teachers' Training Institute in Chandigarh, two samples of 126 EDP-trained and 120 untrained business owners were identified. They were approximately matched in terms of their family background, education, location and age and type of business, and the EDP-trained group had been trained in 29 different programmes, offered by a number of different institutions. The businesses had been started during the ten years from 1980 to 1990, at dates fairly evenly spread over the period. The two groups were compared according to a number of qualitative and quantitative factors.

These samples clearly did not include people who had not started businesses or who had failed, and the results thus relate only to the differences between two groups of people who succeed in starting and sustaining an enterprise, and not to success or failure in starting at all. The findings nevertheless demonstrate rather clearly that the trained group were more successful than the untrained, along several dimensions. The main finding relating to financial performance was that 86 per cent of the trained group claimed to have reached break-even point during their first year of operation, while only 48 per cent of the untrained group said that they had done this. The businesses owned by the trained group were generally around half the size of those owned by the untrained group, in terms of employment and turnover, suggesting perhaps that people with more substantial resources and ambitions are less likely to need or to make use of EDP training, and the growth rates were similar. It is significant, however, that the average investment in the businesses owned by the EDP trainees was one-quarter that of the untrained group, giving a capital output ratio and cost per job of half as much as the businesses owned by those who had not been trained. Since India, like most poor countries, has a vast labour surplus and capital is scarce, businesses which create jobs and add value for lower than average amounts of capital are surely to be preferred; the EDP trainees would seem, therefore, in this case to be more efficient users of resources than the untrained.

We also carried out studies in Assam and Rajasthan States, using approximately matched samples of around 30 people in each state who had been through EDPs run by the main training institutions in these states between 1984 and 1989, and 30 untrained people in the same states who had registered their businesses with the appropriate local government agency at the same times as the trainees. Here again, the samples were approximately matched in terms of age of the business and of its owner, education, father's occupation, activity of the owner before starting the business and the type of business. There were, however, more women in the trained than in the untrained samples, because EDP institutions make a special effort to recruit women and there have until recently been very few women who have started their own formal businesses in India.

Data were obtained from all four groups regarding the owners' earnings, the business profits, employee numbers, turnover and employee earnings. In both Rajasthan and Assam, the business profits and owners' earnings were significantly higher, at a 99 per cent confidence level, for the EDP-trained business owners than for the untrained, and the employee numbers were also significantly higher for the trained group in Rajasthan. The other differences were not significant, but the untrained group had not fared better than the trained group along any dimension.

We also made a simple incremental cost–benefit analysis of the programmes in Assam and Rajasthan, using the additional profits earned by the businesses as the benefits, and a very approximate estimate of the full overhead-inclusive costs of the EDP as the cost. It was assumed that it takes four years between the time of training and the actual date of establishment of the business, because of the long delays so commonly experienced even by EDP trainees who have the benefit of follow-up from the training institution, and the benefits were assumed only to last for a further five years.

Even on these very pessimistic assumptions, the internal rate of return on the EDP investment was 40 per cent in Rajasthan and 29 per cent in Assam. These figures are clearly very sensitive to reductions in the delay in start-up after training and, if the current liberalization of business registration and licensing requirements in India is continued, these delays, which are in any case worse in Assam and Rajasthan than in other more industrialized states such as Punjab and the Southern states, are likely to be significantly reduced.

LIMITATIONS AND CONCLUSIONS

These modest attempts at evaluation were seriously constrained by the short time that was available and by the lack of data. Our intention, however, was not so much to find out whether EDP training is or is not effective, as to demonstrate that it is possible, and indeed not very difficult, to evaluate entrepreneurship development programmes. Our samples were small, and we were not able to carry out longitudinal studies of either the trained or the untrained business owners; nor were we able to investigate the reasons why so many EDP trainees fail to start businesses at all. Nevertheless, our studies, for all their weaknesses, appear to suggest that EDPs do 'work', in that the people who have been trained in such programmes and then start businesses fare better than those who have not been trained. The crude cost–benefit calculation also suggests that the low proportion of trainees who actually start businesses does not make the training investment unprofitable in socio-economic terms. Even when the total cost of the training course, including the cost of training the participants who do not start businesses, is spread only over those who do start a business, the rate of return is substantially higher than for many public investments, and well over the minimum 20 per cent cut-off rate demanded by the World Bank for projects which it funds.

Our methodology of course omits to make any allowance for the benefit gained by the trainees who do not start their own businesses. One would have to be very sceptical indeed to suggest that the training actually damages their future earning capacity, and anecdotal evidence suggests that many 'failed' EDP trainees actually find jobs after the training even though they were previously unemployed, and some also start businesses long after they have lost touch with the training institution.

The overall verdict, so far as it goes, is thus a favourable one, and we must admit that we and our collaborators were highly sceptical of the value of EDP training before we undertook this study. There are of course many further questions that need to be answered, and it is impossible to conclude that a given training design, even one where the trainee selection methods, the trainer training and the structure, content and design are as standardized as the Indian EDP, will 'work' in any future situation just because it appears to have performed well for a given group in the past.

Some EDP institutions agencies have, for instance, attempted to apply the EDP training model to people working in the so-called 'informal sector' of petty traders, wayside mechanics, village handicraft workers and others. This form of enterprise is, in India, as in every other poor country, a far more important source of employment than the type of business which we studied, but it is by no means self-evident that the same training methods which appear to be effective for entrepreneurs who wish to start formal businesses will be equally useful for the operators of informal enterprises. Quite apart from the difficulty of measuring the results, the problems arising from the illiteracy of the trainees, the illegality of many of their businesses and their very small scale, which necessarily limits the returns to training, mean that the funds spent on such programmes are unlikely to earn as high a return as those spent on training for people intending to start formal enterprises. The numbers who can be trained are also bound to be tiny in relation to the many millions of people who work in the informal sector. McClelland himself stressed that this training would be unlikely to be effective unless the basic business infrastructure was in place, and our investigations cannot be said to have proved him wrong.

It is also possible to argue that, in India at any rate, where bureaucratic procedures and the subsidized and thus regulated access to services means that success in 'working the system' is often a more important determinant of business success than successful marketing, low prices or good quality, the follow-up component of EDP training is what is critical. It would be interesting, but very difficult, to omit the follow-up component for an experimental group of trainees, and to compare their subsequent performance with that of a group who received the complete 'package', but this is only one of the many further experiments which might be carried out.

The main conclusion from this investigation, therefore, is that it is possible rigorously and quantitatively to evaluate Indian EDPs, and indeed any business start-up training programme, and it is surprising that such evaluation is so rare, not only in India, particularly when the results appear at any rate to be rather favourable. Training institutions, and their public sector paymasters, are notoriously reluctant to evaluate their activities, particularly in financial terms. There is, however, increasing pressure everywhere, and not only in India, for all institutions to show that they are providing value for money, and it has also been suggested by some of the financial institutions which sponsor EDPs that trainees might in the future fund their training with a loan, just like any other business start-up cost; these trends may encourage more trainers to evaluate their programmes more rigorously, whether they do it for their own professional satisfaction or because their customers demand evidence of performance.

REFERENCES

Acharya, B.T. (1990) *Rural Industrialisation, a Catalyst in Action*, Bombay: Himalaya Publishing.

A.I.D. (1989) 'Evaluation Special Study No. 66', United States Agency for International Development, Washington, DC.

Akhouri, M.M.P. (1978) 'Self-employment through Entrepreneurship Development Strategies – an experiment in Assam', *National Labour Institute Bulletin*.

Easterby-Smith, M. (1986) *Evaluation of Management Training and Development*, Aldershot: Gower.

Gupta, S.K. (1991) 'Entrepreneurship Development Programmes in India', *Small Enterprise Development*, **1**, (4).

Harper, M. (1984a) *Entrepreneurship for the Poor*, London: IT Publications.
Harper, M. (1984b) *Small Business in the Third World*, Chichester: John Wiley.
Industrial Development Bank of India (1990) *Development Banking in India*, Bombay: IDBI.
International Management Development Network (1992) *Networking for Entrepreneurship Development*, Geneva: International Labour Office.
Jain, G. (1990) 'Curriculum Development of EDP in India', mimeo, EDI(I), Ahmedabad.
McClelland, D. and Winter, D. (1971) *Motivating Economic Achievement*, New York: Free Press.

14. Evaluating assistance to small enterprises: institutional financial sustainability and the survival and growth of borrowers

Patrick Ryan

INTRODUCTION

During the past two decades an increasing number of development projects have been focused on promoting the small enterprise (SE) sector in an attempt to try and realize the potential of the sector, which had been largely ignored under earlier development strategies. The aim of assistance to SEs was to increase income and employment generation, foster indigenous entrepreneurship, create a seedbed of new indigenous enterprises, increase the opportunity for women to engage in income-generating activities, facilitate the adoption of local appropriate technology, improve linkages between the formal and informal sectors and help to reduce the concentration of economic activity in urban areas (see Page and Steel, 1984; Harper, 1984; Levitsky, 1986; UNDP *et al.*, 1988). Interest in the sector has increased further recently as its importance has been recognized, particularly in terms of job creation, for countries undergoing adjustment and the transition to a predominantly private sector market economy.

Small enterprise sector assistance projects have tended to address the main supply-side constraints affecting the sector. These include inadequate access to institutional credit, poor infrastructure, inadequate access to raw materials, managerial problems, a lack of skilled labour and inappropriate technology (Page and Steel, 1984). The most common form of assistance has been the provision of special lines of credit because it was believed that inadequate access to institutional credit was the most binding constraint on SEs. This type of credit-based assistance to SEs has been delivered through a variety of intermediaries, including commercial banks, development banks and specialist SE financing institutions. The effectiveness of this type of assistance has been the subject of much discussion, with two crucial issues at the centre of the debate. First, what is the most effective institutional arrangement for delivering this credit and, second, how effective has the credit actually been in promoting SEs?

This chapter will focus on these two issues in the context of evaluating the performance of a specialist finance institution established in Malawi to provide credit and technical assistance to SEs. It is drawn from a wider study (Ryan, 1993) which looks at the performance of the Small Enterprise Development Organisation of Malawi (SEDOM) from its inception in 1983 to 1991. SEDOM is fairly typical of the type of specialist credit-oriented institution established during the 1980s to provide finance and technical assistance to SEs. It was started by the government of Malawi (GoM) in early 1982, with financial support and technical assistance from the European Union (EU). It is registered as a trust and operates as a government-owned, non-profit-making body, under the Ministry of Trade, Industry and Tourism (MTIT). SEDOM was established to address the five major supply-side problems identified by the MTIT as being constraints on SE development in Malawi: inadequate access to institutional credit, insufficient workshop space, difficulties in the procurement of raw materials and machinery, problems with production management and business records and problems with planning and marketing (MTIT, 1982).

SEDOM was also expected to contribute to wider development objectives including the creation of more locally owned businesses and a Malawian entrepreneurial class, the generation of employment and income through the promotion of labour-intensive enterprises in both rural and urban areas, the development of a pool of semi-skilled workers, the improvement of the economic structure of rural areas and the reduction of regional, urban and rural disparities in the location of non-farm economic activities. SEDOM's activities were also expected to generate foreign exchange savings and to accelerate the transfer of technology to Malawian entrepreneurs (MTIT, 1982).

This chapter is focused on two aspects of SEDOM's performance. The first relates to the financial sustainability of the institution. That is, what is the cost of the services provided and to what extent are these costs covered by internally generated income or from external subsidies? Second, with respect to the borrower, the chapter will assess how effective SEDOM's lending has been in generating employment, in creating a seedbed of new enterprises and in developing an indigenous entrepreneurial class. In order to achieve this, the chapter will present empirical evidence about the survival and growth rates of SEs which borrowed from SEDOM. The study asks several questions: how many of the SEs that received loans from SEDOM are still operating; how many of those still operating have actually grown in terms of increased numbers of employees; and what type of enterprises have the highest survival and growth rates? The chapter will also attempt to identify the distinguishing features and characteristics of these successful enterprises. These questions are important because they give an indication as to whether or not the credit is achieving the broader objectives of creating sustainable employment and providing a seedbed of new indigenous entrepreneurs and enterprises. The bottom line is that, if borrowing enterprises do not survive and grow, the desired social and economic benefits will not be achieved.

The second section below begins with a brief review of the literature relating to financing SEs and extends to a review of the different methods of evaluating the performance of lines of credit. The third section provides a description of SEDOM and its lending activities and then analyses the financial performance of SEDOM with a view to assessing financial sustainability. The fourth section presents empirical data relating to survival rates of enterprises which have received term loans from SEDOM. In the fifth section, survey data of manufacturing enterprises are analysed, focusing on the issue of growth; the final section draws together the main lessons illustrated by SEDOM's experience.

DEVELOPMENT ASSISTANCE TO SMALL ENTERPRISES: ISSUES AND PROBLEMS

Access to Credit and Institutional Support

The provision of credit has been one of the major instruments used by governments and donors to promote SEs and rural development in developing countries. The rationale for this type of intervention was that SEs lacked the investment resources necessary to increase production and incomes, and were denied access to formal sources of credit, either because they were seen as high-risk and possessing no collateral, or because the financial markets were not working. The institutions and instruments used to finance SEs were similar to those used to finance smallholder agriculture. This model, described by Ellis (1994) as the 'old credit model' was characterized by state banks, development finance institutions and commercial banks using a variety of instruments to deliver credit. These included subsidized interest rates, recipient targeting, loan portfolio regulations and the use of central bank guarantees and refinancing schemes.

The experience of this model in many countries has been poor and its limitations have been widely documented (Adams, 1992; Adams and von Pischke, 1992). Two of the main problems encountered were poor loan recovery rates and high transaction costs. In addition, many programmes failed to reach the specified target group and often reached the wrong minority, with the benefits being captured by wealthy farmers or businessmen (Yaron, 1994).

One of the major criticisms of this approach is that it was primarily 'supply led'; that is, that funds originated from the central bank and donors rather than from local savings in the rural economy (Yaron, 1994). Yaron argues that the neglect of savings mobilization meant that many agricultural banks and specialist SE financing institutions were often only 'disbursement windows' and were too dependent on new injections of donor or government finance.

As a result of these problems, the past decade has seen the emergence of a new strategy. One of the most important features of this strategy is that lending institutions should be sustainable in the long term, meaning that internally generated income should cover operating costs and that they should not be dependent on subsidies. To achieve this, the organization should have a sound savings base and the interest rate for lending should cover the cost of the interest rate paid to savers, the cost of making the transaction and a margin to cover default (Ellis, 1994). Another important feature of the new strategy is to try and organize borrowers into groups and to use the idea of group responsibility and peer pressure to ensure improved loan recovery. The use of groups is also seen as a method of reducing transaction costs since the banks will only process one group loan application. There is a considerable volume of literature now emerging describing 'successful' examples of organizations, particularly in Asia, employing these ideas (Huppi and Feder, 1990; FDC, 1992; Yaron, 1994).

An important issue to arise from the apparent success of the 'new model' relates to the future role of 'old model' institutions. How can organizations like SEDOM become more financially self-sustainable without relinquishing their developmental role entirely? Following on from this, if, in order to survive, specialist SE institutions are forced to drop many of their development functions, who will take them up? What will happen to the people and enterprises considered to be unprofitable borrowers? Can the success of the 'new model' be replicated to the degree necessary to replace 'old model' institutions and is the new approach, which has been primarily based on supporting informal sector microenterprises, appropriate for more 'formal' small and medium enterprises?

Impact Evaluation Methodological Issues and Approaches

Various methods have been used to evaluate the performance of lines of credit and assistance to SEs, with no agreement as to which method is the most appropriate. An interesting example of an attempt to evaluate the economic impact of a special credit programme was carried out by Bolnick and Nelson (1990) in Indonesia. The survey data were collected in 1983 and focused on the changes in the condition of more than 1500 small enterprises over the period 1979 to 1982. The enterprises had all received term loans from commercial banks under a special credit programme. The authors are critical of previous attempts to evaluate the programme which used a before-and-after approach from a non-random sample, and argue that credit impact cannot be measured either by before-and-after comparisons or from simple comparisons of recipient with non-recipient. They argue that a proper evaluation requires estimating the differential of before-and-after changes for credit recipients versus comparable non-recipients. It is this method that surmounts the empirical hurdle of fungibility, to obtain an estimate of additionality due to the credit programme. Very few studies have managed properly to isolate the incremental effect of credit by measuring differential changes between borrowers and non-borrowers and, for a variety of reasons, including cost, convenience or lack of a comparable control group, many studies have relied on before-and-after information on programme beneficiaries, with the 'before' based on recall of recipients (Bolnick and Nelson, 1990). On the basis of their experience they conclude:

> the credit impact literature has been plagued by methodological problems, often to the point of invalidating evaluation results. A proper measure of credit impact requires a clear conceptual base, a practical survey design, and an appropriate sample. Where expediency dictates compromise, it is better to measure impact properly over a restricted domain than to end up with nothing but descriptive statistics. (Bolnick and Nelson, 1990, p. 301)

Adams (1988) is critical also of attempts to measure the effects that loans have on enterprises by looking, for example, at changes in physical output. He argues that the key problem is to isolate how much of the change is attributable to the loan. The question is how to prove that the activity would not have taken place without the loan, and how to isolate the impact of a loan on borrowers' actions from other forces affecting the borrowers' behaviour. He is also critical of the emphasis placed on the borrower in impact studies such as the Bolnick and Nelson study discussed above, and argues that they address questions that realistically *cannot be answered* and are *emphasizing the wrong issues*. He suggests that the focus should be on how the programmes affect financial intermediaries and financial markets, and on what changes in the institutions' performance have occurred as a result of the programme. He argues that the main functions of financial intermediaries are:

> to provide a flow of financial services to an increasing number of individuals and firms. These services include making loans to a few individuals and providing deposit facilities to a much larger number of people. A financial system must be able to sustain the quantity and quality of these services over prolonged periods. (Adams, 1988, p. 363)

He also argues that reliable access to a financial system is important for small borrowers, the implications of this being that intermediaries should cover the cost of operations, recover most of their loans, protect or increase the purchasing power of their loan portfolios and innovate to reduce transaction costs. In terms of evaluating intermediaries, Adams suggests the following criteria: the number of people who have regular access to formal financial services, the level of transaction costs, quality of services and the level of savings mobilization stimulated by the programme (Adams, 1988).

SEDOM: INSTITUTIONAL GROWTH AND SUSTAINABILITY

SEDOM began its lending operations in September 1983. The growth of lending is illustrated in Table 14.1 which shows that the number of loan approvals grew rapidly from 46, valued at Malawi Kwacha (MK)[1] 0.3 million, in 1983, to 513, valued at MK4.3 million in 1990. The largest number of approvals was made in 1986, with 798, and the largest amount approved was MK5 million in 1989. By the end of 1990, SEDOM had approved a total of 4190 loans, valued at MK20.1 million. Table 14.1 also shows the growth of loan disbursements to a cumulative total of almost MK16.9 million by 1990. During the period, total loan repayments increased from MK235 000 in 1984 to MK1.2 million in 1987, and a cumulative figure to 1987 of almost MK2.9 million. The total portfolio balance had grown to MK12.6 million by 1990.[2]

SEDOM's lending portfolio consists of two types of loans: 'mini loans' for amounts between MK500 and MK3000, and larger 'term loans' for amounts between MK3000 and MK75 000. As at the end of July 1988, term loans accounted for 61 per cent of the portfolio by value, and 18 per cent by number. Mini loans accounted for 39 per cent by value but 82 per cent by number. The mean size of term loans was MK13 900 and of mini loans MK1600. Table 14.1 shows that the mean size of all loans has increased steadily, from MK3300 in 1984 to MK9900 in 1989 and MK8500 in 1990. This reflects SEDOM's decision to increase the lending limits of term loans from MK30 000 to MK75 000 in the late 1980s in response to the requests of entrepreneurs to borrow larger amounts, which were partly stimulated by inflation.

In July 1988, 62 per cent of all loans in the current portfolio were made to projects situated in the more populous and economically developed Southern Region, while the Central and Northern regions attracted 25 and 13 per cent, respectively. Fifty-three per cent of the loan portfolio was made to rural areas, valued at MK4.0 million, with 47 per cent, valued at MK3.5 million, to urban areas. Mini loans were generally made to 'micro-enterprises' run by individual entrepreneurs, often on a part-time basis, and employing between

Table 14.1   SEDOM lending statistics, 1983–90

Performance indicators	1983	1984	1985	1986	1987	1988	1989	1990	Total
Loan applications									
Number	209	473	1 094	1 371	1 135	N/A	N/A	N/A	4 282
MK000s	2 773	3 731	3 714	4 729	5 132	N/A	N/A	N/A	20 079
Loan approvals									
Number	46	220	736	798	718	652	507	513	4 190
MK000s	308	731	1 139	1 482	2 793	4 261	5 050	4 357	20 121
Average value of approvals	6 695	3 322	1 548	1 857	3 890	6 535	9 961	8 493	—
Loan disbursements MK000s	166	603	1 327	1 551	2 079	3 571	3 664	3 891	16 852
Loan repayments MK000s	12	235	499	906	1 203	N/A	N/A	N/A	2 855
Portfolio exposure	N/A	N/A	1 540	2 396	3 766	6 274	9 201	12 610	—
Loan arrears (%)	0.0	2.4	3.5	8.7	13.9	22.1	23.2	26.1	—

Source: Compilation of SEDOM lending statistics, August 1991.

one and three people. Term loans were also made predominantly to sole proprietors and tended to employ an average of six people, with a few enterprises employing more than 30.

SEDOM's loan portfolio contained a broad range of activities. In 1988, the largest single activity category was clothing and tailoring, which received 21 per cent of loans, while maize milling, clay products, food processing and saw milling received 13, 11, 8 and 8 per cent, respectively. However, the largest single sector in terms of loan value was maize milling, which received 18 per cent of all loans.

Institutional Growth and Financing

To support this rapid growth of lending, SEDOM underwent a sustained period of institutional growth. In addition to the head office in Blantyre in the Southern Region, regional offices were opened in the Central and Northern regions in 1984. This was followed by the opening of several sub-regional offices in 1990. Table 14.2 shows that, during this period, total staff grew from 43 in 1984, to 205 in 1991, and that support staff has grown at a faster rate than professional staff. The ratio of professional staff to the number of support staff has grown from 1:1.4 in 1984 to 1:3.6 in 1991.

Table 14.2   SEDOM total staff numbers, selected years

Staff category	1984	1987	1990	1991
Management	4	5	7	9
Professional client contact staff	14	33	36	36
Support/administration staff	25	54	102	160
Total	43	92	145	205
Ratio of professional/support staff	1:1.4	1:1.4	1:2.4	1:3.6

Table 14.3 shows that internally generated income grew steadily, from MK0.25 million in 1984 to MK1.62 million in 1989/90, while total expenditure grew from about MK0.6 million in 1984 to MK5.1 million in 1990. The resulting operating deficit was supported by recurrent expenditure grants from the GoM and the EU and other donors, totalling MK11.8 million. Without this recurrent grant, the operating deficit would have risen from MK0.6 million in 1984 to MK3.5 million in 1990. By 1990, the contribution of internally generated income, made up of loan interest and industrial estate rental, to expenditure (excluding technical assistance) was 36 per cent. Although this is a significant improvement on 1987 and 1988, when

Table 14.3   SEDOM's income and expenditure account (31 March) (MK000s)

	1984	1985	1986	1987	1988	1989	1990
Income							
Loan fund interest	16	80	203	316	519	853	1 337
Other income	9	30	53	48	93	136	285
External grants	504	493	803	1 060	1 806	2 421	2 441
GOM grants	101	153	159	186	196	320	1 115
Total income	630	756	1 218	1 610	2 614	3 730	5 178
Expenditure							
Personnel & housing	155	235	358	595	1 057	1 334	1 731
Travel & subsistence	42	102	220	495	1 018	730	746
Communications	29	42	62	101	364	348	327
Technical assistance	345	279	394	372	449	690	676
Training & entrep. devel.	0	31	129	243	392	297	420
Trade fair & craft mkting	0	0	2	115	256	234	92
Provision for bad debts	8	13	52	51	90	700	525
Depreciation	0	16	57	63	116	133	234
Miscellaneous	11	24	28	51	282	217	394
Total expenditure	590	742	1 302	2 086	4 024	4 683	5 145
Operating surplus/(deficit)	40	14	(84)	(476)	(1 410)	(953)	33
Operating surplus/(deficit) excluding grants	(565)	(632)	(1 046)	(1 722)	(3 412)	(3 694)	(3 523)
Internal income (%)*	10	24	28	21	17	25	36

Note: *   Internally generated income expressed as a percentage of total expenditure, excluding technical assistance.

only 17 and 15 per cent, respectively, of expenditure was recovered by internally generated income, it is clear that SEDOM is unlikely to generate the required level of internally generated income to cover its operational costs in the foreseeable future.

One of the major areas of recurrent expenditure growth was personnel and housing costs, which grew from MK0.16 million in 1984 to MK1.7 million in 1990. This amounts to 27 per cent of total costs in 1990. If the cost of technical assistance is included in 1990 then personnel costs had risen to 40 per cent of total recurrent costs. This rapid growth of personnel costs has significant implications in terms of SEDOM's ability to continue to deliver services in a cost-effective and sustainable manner. A further important feature of SEDOM's total costs is the contribution SEDOM was expected to make to other development objectives. For example, Table 14.3 shows that SEDOM had spent MK1.5 million on training, entrepreneur development and MK0.7 million on trade fair and craft marketing.

SEDOM has received considerable support from the EU, GoM and other donors in financing this level and style of operations. By 1990, SEDOM had received a total of MK14.2 million for loan fund capital and MK2.1 million for recurrent expenditure from the donors. The GoM contributed a total of MK2.2 million for recurrent expenditure. The EU loan capital was a grant which SEDOM lent to enterprises at 16 per cent, thus giving a spread of 16 per cent to cover costs. However, even with this spread, it is clear from the information presented in Table 14.3 that SEDOM has not managed to reach a position of near cost recovery and, with the existing cost structure and style of operations, it is difficult to see SEDOM moving from a grant-dependent institution to financial sustainability in the near future.

One of the key elements in the financial sustainability of an institution is loan repayment and arrears. Table 14.1 shows that, between 1984 and 1990, the official arrears rate grew gradually, from 2.4 to 26.1 per cent. The implication of this for SEDOM's liquidity position is important because the loan interest figure shown in Table 14.3 is interest charged, not actually received. Thus any delay in receiving interest income because of non-repayment further weakens the liquidity position of SEDOM.

Institution Building and Sustainability

It was clear at its inception that SEDOM was expected to move eventually towards cost recovery and self-sufficiency at the earliest possible date: 'in order to reduce and eventually eliminate Government assistance and to enable SEDOM to raise funds in its own right, SEDOM will move towards imposing cost covering charges for all services rendered. (GITEC, 1984). In addition, SEDOM commissioned in 1985 a consultancy report on financial planning and control with the specific brief to determine when SEDOM could expect to become self-sufficient. The report concluded that, given the current growth of lending operations, SEDOM should be able to cover costs on its income and expenditure account by the year 1994/95 (Peat Marwick, 1985). While it appears that SEDOM was expected to become a self-sustainable institution, it was not made explicitly clear how this was to be achieved at the same time as providing development-oriented assistance. It is not surprising, therefore, that the financial data presented in this chapter show that such expectations were totally unrealistic and that the objective of SEDOM recovering its own costs and becoming financially sustainable while providing the current level and style of services was not achievable. The source of this problem is at the planning and design stage, where conflicting goals require SEDOM to 'defy the laws of finance' (Adams, 1992).

If donors and governments see the development objectives of such schemes as significant, the cost of such activities must be recognized as development costs at the outset and planned for. In this situation, sustainability of the project should not be seen in terms of cost recovery from internally generated income, but rather in terms of securing continuous subsidized funds in order to realize the broader economic returns. It is not realistic to expect SEDOM to make small loans to rural areas, at subsidized rates of interest, as well as finance the cost of promotional training and support services, and still expect it to be cost-covering. If SEDOM is expected to become self-financing then a change in the style of operations is necessary in the form of making larger loans at higher rates of interest, reducing the level of follow-up and technical assistance and entrepreneur training. If, on the other hand, SEDOM is expected to continue to operate in the existing style, an acceptable level of financial deficit should be planned for. The financial cost to the project needs to be offset against the economic benefits to the economy of enterprises being financed. This raises several questions, such as what is the acceptable level of financial subsidies; how is this finance secured over the life of the project and how does one identify and measure the impact of the lending? Also what level of social and economic benefits justifies this subsidy and how can these benefits be quantified?

The idea of long-term subsidized finance of recurrent costs and loan fund capital for financial intermediaries is anathema to current thinking. Adams (1992) argues that creating reliable, sustainable financial intermediaries that integrate borrowers into the mainstream financial system is the best way to assist small entrepreneurs in the long term. To judge SEDOM by this criteria would show that it does not cover its cost of operations, and therefore does not provide a reliable service, because it is dependent on grants from donors for its survival. It also does not mobilize savings. From this perspective, perhaps one of the most damaging aspects of creating specialist donor-dependent institutions is that, because of the very existence of institutions like SEDOM, pressure to encourage commercial banks and other formal financial sector institutions to increase their participation in this area may be reduced. As a result, small entrepreneurs in Malawi may be no nearer being integrated into a reliable and sustainable formal financial sector than they were at the beginning of the 1980s.

To conclude, it would appear that SEDOM had been successful in rapidly increasing the volume of its lending, in establishing a nationwide administrative network and in disseminating information and awareness of opportunities in the sector. However, it was extremely donor-dependent and unlikely to become self-sustainable, given the current level of operations, in the near future. Early development thinking justified this subsidy if it was likely to be a short-term subsidy, and if the economic and social benefits to the economy of the enterprises financed were large enough. The identification and measurement of some of these benefits is the subject of the rest of this chapter.

SURVIVAL RATES OF BORROWERS

One of the most commonly used indicators of loan portfolio performance is loan repayment rates. However, this is not necessarily a reliable indicator of the success of individual enterprises in the portfolio because loan repayments can be derived from many different sources. For example, there is clear evidence that many of SEDOM's borrowers repay their loans from the sale of agricultural output during harvest time. A monthly analysis of total loan repayments received by SEDOM during a year shows a marked peak in the three-month period around harvest time. This type of cross-subsidization also occurs with entrepreneurs who have more than one enterprise. SEDOM also receives loan repayments by standing order from civil servants and private sector employees who repay their loans from their salaries and wages. It is for this reason that survival rates are used as a more accurate assessment of whether or not SEDOM's lending is succeeding in realizing the socio-economic objectives discussed earlier.

There is surprisingly little information on how the enterprises financed by development projects perform and it is difficult to say what an acceptable survival rate is. This is not the case in most OECD countries, where there is an abundance of statistical data regarding the birth and death rates of small enterprises. In a comparative study of mortality rates of small businesses, El-Namaki (1990) found a surprisingly high number of small business failures early in the life of enterprises. Normally, this is compensated for by the birth of new enterprises. However, at certain times, depending on the state of the economy, death rates overtake birth rates. El-Namaki cites various studies which show that percentage cumulative mortality rates for small business in The Netherlands during a five-year period in the 1980s was 69 per cent. This may be compared with a 70 per cent cumulative mortality rate of manufacturing enterprises in Japan between 1981 and 1986 for enterprises employing between one and 49 people.

A similar picture is observed in the UK in 1993 as the economy was emerging from the recession. In the first six months of 1993, 25,883 businesses collapsed in England and Wales (Dun and Bradstreet Int, 1993). The same report also found that half as many more small businesses were failing compared to large and medium-sized companies. Results reported by the new UK Business Links organizations showed that survival rates of new enterprises after 18 months' trading varied from 85 per cent to as low as 55 per cent, depending on the region.

These figures show that there is an almost *natural* birth and death rate cycle for SEs and that some enterprise failure is inevitable. In fact, one could go so far as to say that failures should be expected since, if none of the enterprises financed by development projects fail, this may be an indication that the wrong target group is being supported: wealthier and more established entrepreneurs.

The data used to calculate survival rates are drawn from SEDOM's term loans which account for 61 per cent of lending portfolio by value, and is SEDOM's most important activity. The total number of term loans made by SEDOM between 1983 and 1988 was 320. These loans were made to 254 enterprises with a total value of nearly MK3.3 million and were distributed over 17 industrial activity categories using the two-digit International Standard Industrial Code (ISIC). For the purposes of this study, the loans have been grouped into five major ISIC categories: Primary Sector, Maize Milling, Manufacturing, Construction and Services.

Table 14.4 shows that the sector receiving most financial assistance was the manufacturing sector, which received 106 (42 per cent) loans valued at MK1.69 million (52 per cent). This sector includes enterprises engaged in food processing, tailoring and garment manufacture, wood products, printing, soap making, ceramics and metal products. Within this category, tailoring and food processing received MK0.38 million and MK0.62 million for 26 and 25 projects, respectively. Maize milling was the single largest activity, with approvals valued at MK0.95 million (29 per cent) made to 100 (39 per cent) enterprises. These loans were made primarily for the purchase of mills, hullers and engines, as well as for transformers to link remoter sites to electricity. Five per cent of loans by value also went to agriculture and 5 per cent also to construction; 9 per cent went to a wide range of services enterprises.

A simple 'still operating', 'not operating' categorization was used to determine survival rates.[3] Using enterprise survival rate as the performance indi-

Table 14.4   Distribution of term loans by broad ISIC categories (MK000s)

Category	Number	%	Value	%
Agric/fishing/mining	17	7	146	5
Maize milling	100	39	946	29
Manufacturing	106	42	1 692	52
Construction	10	4	163	5
Services	21	8	292	9
Total	254	100	3 239	100

cator, the following questions were asked. What was the overall survival rate and what type of enterprises had higher survival rates? Did enterprises existing prior to obtaining the loan have higher survival rates than new enterprises established with the assistance of the SEDOM loan? Were enterprises receiving loans with full-time entrepreneurs more successful than enterprises with part-time entrepreneurs?

Of the 254 enterprises receiving one or more loans from SEDOM between September 1983 and February 1988, 180 (71 per cent) were found to be still operating in August 1991, while 74 (29 per cent) were found to have ceased operating (Table 14.5, cols 4 and 6). As might be expected, Table 14.5 shows a changing pattern of survival over time, with 50 per cent of enterprises receiving loans in 1983 still operating eight years later in 1991. This percentage increases steadily to 82 per cent in 1988. Other possible factors influenc-

Table 14.5   Survival rates by age of loans

Year	(1) Number of enterprises	(2) %	(3) Still operating	(4) %	(5) Not operating	(6) %
1983	20	8	10	50	10	50
1984	35	14	23	66	12	34
1985	49	19	36	73	13	27
1986	48	19	34	71	14	29
1987	91	36	68	75	23	25
1988	11	4	9	82	1	18
Total	254	100	180	71	73	29

Note: The chi-squared test shows that these results were not statistically significant at the 5 per cent level.

ing the results are that SEDOM may have made a higher proportion of bad loans in the beginning and passed through a learning curve, and improved in terms of knowing who to lend to and how to appraise applications. These results may also reflect the harsh and variable economic conditions in the 1980s when many of these loans were made.

Table 14.5 shows that seven out of ten enterprises receiving loans were still operating at the time of the survey. Interpretation of these figures is difficult but they appear to be comparable with the European survival rates mentioned earlier. This appears to be quite a reasonable achievement, given the particularly difficult economic conditions existing in Malawi during the 1980s.

The rest of this section will analyse survival rates in terms of the following:

- activity category – to ascertain what type of enterprises were being supported in SEDOM's seedbed;
- new or existing enterprises – to ascertain whether SEDOM was succeeding in creating new entrepreneurs and enterprises;
- full and part-time entrepreneurs – to ascertain whether SEDOM was succeeding in developing an indigenous entrepreneurial class and what were the characteristics of these entrepreneurs.

Survival by Activity Category

Table 14.6 shows quite a marked difference in survival rates between the sectors. Approximately 90 per cent of enterprises receiving construction loans survived and 80 per cent of maize mills survived, while only 67 and 66 per cent of services and manufacturing enterprises, respectively, survived. The lowest survival rates were obtained from agriculture, fishing and mining, with 48 per cent.

One possible explanation for the higher survival rates of maize milling enterprises is that maize mills are less complex enterprises to operate and manage. Maize mills process the grain brought to them by their customers, who pay cash. The millers have therefore no raw materials to buy or to transport, and have neither to finance stocks nor to give credit. They also have low overheads, employ on average only two people and use machinery that is comparatively easy to maintain. The main potential problem for this type of enterprise is a shortage of maize. However, this has been such a politically sensitive area during the past decade that every effort has been made by the GoM to ensure availability of adequate supplies. Construction enterprises have also performed well and this may be because the loans were for working capital for large building contracts; thus the loan was secured against an existing contract.

Table 14.6   Survival rates by activity category

Enterprise category	(1) Number of enterprises	(2) %	(3) Still operating	(4) %	(5) Not operating	(6) %
Agric/fish/mine	21	8	10	48	11	52
Maize milling	100	40	80	80	20	20
Manufacturing	102	40	67	66	35	34
Construction	10	4	9	90	1	10
Services	21	8	14	67	7	33
Total	254	100	180	71	74	29

Note: These results are statistically significant using the chi-squared test at the 5 per cent level of significance.

By comparison, manufacturing enterprises are often in new activity areas, with uncertain markets, dependent on problematic supplies of imported machinery and materials, and demanding additional management skills such as stock control and labour management. Also manufacturing enterprises tend to be more exposed to liquidity problems as a result of purchasing material inputs on a cash basis and being forced to sell their output on credit. This problem is aggravated by their weak market bargaining power, due to their size, and the low purchasing power of rural and township customers who are forced, by their low incomes, to offer payment by instalments.

It is difficult to draw conclusions on the service sector since it comprises such a diverse mix of enterprises, including electrical and mechanical repair workshops, hotels, petrol stations and veterinary services. The primary sector's poor performance can be explained by the fact that five loans were made to quarrying, stone crushing and charcoal and all of these failed. The agriculture and livestock loans on their own had a survival rate of 67 per cent.

Survival Performance by New or Existing Enterprises

Although one of SEDOM's objectives was to create new enterprises, it was not restricted from lending to existing enterprises. Table 14.7 shows that 54 per cent of loans went to new enterprises and 46 per cent to existing enterprises. This seems a reasonable mix, given that it was thought that loans to new enterprises would be a higher risk. It was also expected that loans made to existing enterprises would have higher survival rates than loans to new enterprises, since existing enterprises were likely to be more established and have a more experienced entrepreneur. This is important for lending organizations attempting to establish a mix of loans so as to ensure that they have an adequate proportion of performing safer loans in their portfolio to compensate for the smaller, riskier loans.

However, the evidence does not clearly support the hypothesis that a higher proportion of existing enterprises are likely to survive. Table 14.7 shows that, of the loans to new enterprises, 74 per cent were still operating compared to 68 per cent of existing enterprises. There are several possible explanations for this result. It may be that existing enterprises have had more time to fail, or it may be an indication that existing enterprises tended to borrow from SEDOM once they were in financial difficulties, and have been refused access to other sources of finance. Another possible explanation for this is that the majority of new enterprises borrow primarily for working capital and not for investment in plant and machinery for expansion.

Table 14.7   Survival rates of new and existing enterprises

Category	(1) Number of enterprises	(2) %	(3) Still operating	(4) %	(5) Not operating	(6) %
New enterprises	136	54	100	74	36	26
Existing enterprises	118	46	80	68	38	32
Total	254	100	180	71	74	29

Note: The chi-squared test showed no significant difference at the 5 per cent level.

Survival Performance of Enterprises with Full- or Part-time Entrepreneurs

As mentioned earlier, one of SEDOM's main objectives was the creation of a Malawian entrepreneurial class. One of the problems SEDOM has faced in achieving this aim is the reluctance of borrowers to give up full-time employment and become full-time entrepreneurs. This is understandable, given the insecurity of the Malawian economy during the 1980s, but it does create a problem which has been experienced in many developing countries: that of absentee management. Table 14.8 shows the extent of this problem. Out of the 254 enterprises receiving loans, only 51 per cent were full-time entrepreneurs while 49 per cent had owners with full-time employment elsewhere.

As a result of absentee management, it was expected that enterprises with full-time entrepreneurs would perform better than those with part-time. How-

Table 14.8   Survival rates of enterprises with full- and part-time
              entrepreneurs

Category	(1) Number of enterprises	(2) %	(3) Still operating	(4) %	(5) Not operating	(6) %
Full-time	130	51	90	69	40	30
Part-time	124	49	90	73	34	27
Total	254	100	180	71	74	29

Note: These results were not statistically significant using the chi-squared test at the 5 per cent level.

ever, Table 14.8 does not conclusively show that this is the case. Of the 130 loans to full-time entrepreneurs, 69 per cent were still operating, compared to 73 per cent of the 124 loans to part-time entrepreneurs. One difficulty in interpreting this result and relating it to absentee management is the fact that some of the initial 124 part-time entrepreneurs subsequently became full-time, once the enterprise was established. It may also be that other factors are more important in explaining success than absentee management, for example the character and education of an entrepreneur.

ENTERPRISE GROWTH RATES: A SAMPLE SURVEY OF FIFTY MANUFACTURING ENTERPRISES

One of the problems of using survival rates as an indication of success is that this gives no indication of the level of operation of surviving enterprises. It is conceivable that all the enterprises could be operating at a low level of production on a part-time or seasonal basis. For this reason it is useful to look at the growth rates of surviving enterprises. One of the most important objectives of SE lending in developing countries is to develop an indigenous manufacturing sector. It is for this reason that this part of the study focused on the 112 manufacturing enterprises in the total of 254 enterprises. Details of the random stratified sample of 50 enterprises is given in Table 14.9.

Initially, it was planned that, in order to determine the growth of surviving enterprises, data relating to sales, profits, fixed assets and employment would be used as indicators. However, after testing the questionnaire it became apparent that respondents were not prepared to give either the necessary time required or the level of financial detail to achieve this. In many cases, this information did not exist, given that to establish growth it was necessary to

Table 14.9   Details of final sample by two-digit ISIC

Activity category	No. of enterprises	%	Loans (MK000s)	%
Food processing	10	20	187	25
Tailoring/knitting/leather	13	26	195	26
Timber/wood products	9	18	102	14
Printing/publishing	3	6	63	9
Soap/chemicals	2	4	18	2
Clay/cement/lime	4	8	86	12
Metal products	9	18	86	12
Total	50	100	737	100

obtain information at two points in time, near the beginning of the enterprise's life and at the time of the study.

As a result of these difficulties, employment only was used as a measure of growth. The advantage of using employment is that it is one of the few indicators that entrepreneurs could consistently recall at both the current point in time and at the time the loan was received, without referring to records. For existing enterprises, the number employed at the time of the loan approval has been used as the base level, while for new projects the number employed in the first year after the loan was approved has been used. Growth rates were calculated using the simple annual average growth rate formula.

Characteristics of the Sample

Of the 50 enterprises in the sample, 40 were owned and managed by sole proprietors, four were registered companies, one was family-owned and one was owned by partnership. This confirms, what appears to be a significant feature of the small-scale sector in Malawi, that the majority of entrepreneurs tend to work on their own (READI, 1989). This characteristic may be restrictive in terms of limiting an entrepreneur's ability to raise more equity and may lead to higher debt–equity ratios. However, it does have the benefit of avoiding potential disputes and organizational problems between shareholders and partners. Indeed, a feature of SEDOM's work is that comparatively little time is spent in registering enterprises under company or cooperative acts, or in trying to sort out enterprise ownership and management disputes.

The average age of the entrepreneurs in the survey was 43.7 years, with 50 per cent falling between the age of 40 to 50; 24 per cent were between the ages of 30 and 40, the youngest being 33, and 18 per cent over 50, the oldest being 58. Hence SEDOM does not appear to be a vehicle for young people below the age of 30 to obtain loans. It was not clear whether this is because people of this age group are not coming forward with applications, or whether there has been a conservative loan approval policy within SEDOM. A similar pattern was seen in the READI (1989) survey, which found that there were relatively small numbers of youthful or elderly entrepreneurs, with 56 per cent of entrepreneurs falling into the 30–49-year-old category. Of the 31 entrepreneurs interviewed, 52 per cent responded that they spent 40 hours or more per week on their business, while 24 per cent said that they spent fewer than 40 hours, ranging from one to five hours per week. These tended to be engaged in other income-generating activities, mainly farming and full-time waged employment.

An additional interesting fact to emerge from the survey was the tendency for an entrepreneur to have more than one enterprise in different activities, rather than for growth and expansion to occur in one enterprise. This tendency for diversification may be partially explained by the small size of the domestic market and the reluctance of entrepreneurs to take partners or form companies, and also by the desire to spread risks by diversifying into different activities.

Growth Rates of Sample Manufacturing Enterprises

Of the 50 manufacturing enterprises in the sample survey, 31 (62 per cent) were still operating at the time of the survey, while 19 (38 per cent) had ceased operating. The survival rate of 62 per cent compares with a survival rate of 65 per cent obtained from all term loans (see previous section). The survey data show that the average age of all the enterprises in the sample was 6.8 years, while the average age of the 31 surviving projects was 8.6 years. The average age of the 19 projects that had ceased operating was 3.8 years. Thus, on average, 38 per cent of enterprises failed within the first four years of operation.

Table 14.10 shows that, of the 31 surviving enterprises, 68 per cent had positive growth rates, 6 per cent showed zero growth and 26 per cent showed negative growth. Of the 21 enterprises that grew, 66 per cent grew between 1 per cent and 30 per cent per annum, and the remaining 34 per cent grew at a rate above 34 per cent. The results are somewhat distorted by the fact that some enterprises had a small number of employees in the base year, often only one or two, and a small number of years' operation. The results were also strongly influenced by large growth in a few small firms. The 31 surviving enterprises currently employed a total of 656 people, compared to a total of 362 at the time the loans were approved.

Table 14.11 analyses these results by the seven ISIC activity categories used in the sample. The analysis shows that all the garment enterprises in the

Table 14.10　Growth rate of surviving enterprises

	Number	%
Positive	21	68
Zero	2	6
Negative	8	26
Total	31	100

Table 14.11　Growth rates by ISIC category

	Positive growth	%	Negative or no growth	%	Total	%
Food processing	4	57	3	43	7	23
Garment/leather	4	100	0	0	4	13
Timber/wood	5	83	1	17	6	19
Printing/publishing	2	67	1	33	3	10
Soap/chemicals	1	50	1	50	2	7
Clay/cement/lime	1	50	1	50	2	7
Metal products	4	57	3	43	7	3
Total	21	68	10	32	31	100

sample exhibited growth, as did 83 and 67 per cent, respectively, of timber and printing enterprises. Only 57 per cent of food processing and metal projects grew, compared to 50 per cent of lime and soap projects, though the latter two were only represented by two enterprises in each category.

One interesting point to emerge from the analysis of growth rates was the difference in regional performance. Table 14.12 shows that 81 per cent of surviving enterprises in the Southern Region grew, compared to 50 per cent and zero per cent of enterprises registering growth in the Central and Northern regions. This result appears reasonable, given the fact that the Southern Region is the most populous and economically active, followed by the Central Region, which contains the capital city of Lilongwe, and the Northern Region, which is the least developed and populated.

Table 14.12   Growth rate by region

	Positive growth	%	Negative or no growth	%	Total	%
North	0	0	2	100	2	6
Centre	4	50	4	50	8	26
South	17	81	4	19	21	8
Total	21	67.7	10	32.3	31	100

Note: These results are statistically significant using the chi-squared test of significance at the 5 per cent level.

CONCLUSIONS

This chapter has attempted to evaluate the performance of a specialist financing institution established to provide credit to small enterprises. It has focused on two important issues: first, on what is the most effective method of delivering credit and how institutions involved in this process can be financially sustainable; second, on how effective the credit has been in creating enterprises that actually survive and grow, thereby contributing to employment generation and the growth of indigenous enterprises and entrepreneurs.

The chapter has shown that SEDOM has been successful in rapidly increasing the volume of its lending and establishing a nationwide network to disseminate its services. However, it has experienced the problems of most 'supply-led' finance institutions in that it is extremely donor-dependent and is unlikely to become financially self-sufficient while it maintains the current style and level of operations. In its defence, the chapter has argued that SEDOM's poor performance in this area has been caused by the way it was conceived at the planning stage, rather than by poor operational performance. As with many development finance institutions, SEDOM was expected to make small, costly and risky loans to people who were unable to borrow from commercial banks because the banks viewed the activity as inherently unprofitable. On top of this, SEDOM was charged with achieving many development objectives as well as performing other costly functions, including the provision of technical assistance, entrepreneur training, marketing and trade fairs. All this was to be achieved while moving towards financial sustainability, charging subsidized interest rates.

In short, such institutions were expected to perform an impossible task and it is not surprising that they have experienced problems and continue to depend on outside funding and subsidies. These subsidies were originally justified in the short term if the economic and social benefits resulting from the loans were sufficiently large. In this respect, the chapter has shown that SEDOM was reasonably successful, as 71 per cent of enterprises receiving loans survived and 68 per cent of the survivors grew in terms of the number of employees. The question of whether these benefits justify the subsidy to SEDOM cannot be conclusively shown by the data used in this study. However, the data do show that there was a group of potential and existing entrepreneurs that did benefit from SEDOM's activities.

The SEDOM case illustrates many of the problems of the 'old credit model', which has now been largely discredited and superseded by the 'new credit model' and the discipline of the market and financial liberalization. However, the question is: will the dominance of the market and the quest to eliminate subsidies entirely lead to a situation where a large proportion of existing and potential entrepreneurs are denied access to credit? Renewed attempts to coax the commercial banks into this process by using groups and NGOs as intermediaries may also be difficult, given that the banks are facing increasing levels of competition as a result of financial liberalization.

The one recent sign of hope is the apparent success of financial innovations based on group credit and savings mobilization. However, the question here is: can this success be replicated to the degree necessary to replace 'old model' institutions and to service more formal sector small enterprises, given that the success to date has been primarily based on supporting informal sector micro-enterprises. A key question in all of this relates to the future of development finance institutions like SEDOM and how they can adapt to the changing environment. These questions have not been fully answered here, but they do present elements of an important future research agenda.

NOTES

1. The prevailing exchange rate at the beginning of 1988 was MK4.58 to £1 and MK2.5 was equal to US$1. The Malawi Kwacha had depreciated to MK5.01 to £1 and MK2.6 to US$1 by the beginning of 1991.
2. Total approvals for the period amount to MK20.1 million, compared to MK16.9 million disbursements. This difference is explained by the fact that many approved loans were not drawn and the projects were not implemented. The difference is also due to the delay in implementation caused, for example, by difficulties in importing machinery. The time lag factor explains why for 1985 and 1986 disbursements are higher than approvals.
3. An enterprise was classified as surviving if it was actually operating on the day of the site visit, or if there was evidence that the enterprise was still operating at a low level but not on that specific day.

REFERENCES

Adams, D.W. (1988) 'The conundrum of Successful Credit Projects in Floundering Rural Financial Markets', *Economic Development and Cultural Change*, **36**, (2), 355–68.

Adams, D.W. (1992) 'Building Durable Rural Financial Markets in Africa', *African Review of Money, Finance and Banking*, **1**.

Adams, D.W. and von Pischke, J.D. (1992) 'Micro-enterprise Credit programs: Déjà Vu', *World Development*, **20**, (10), 1463–70.

Bolnick, B. and Nelson, E. (1990) 'Evaluating the Economic Impact of a Special Credit Programme: KIK/KMKP in Indonesia', *Journal of Development Studies*, **26**, (2).

Dun and Bradstreet Int. (1993) 'Press Release', 30 June.

Ellis, F. (1994) *Agricultural Policies in Developing Countries*, Cambridge: Cambridge University Press.

El-Namaki, M. (1990) 'Small Business – The Myths and the Reality', *Long Range Planning*, **23**, (4), 78–87.

The Foundation for Development Co-operation (FDC) (1992) *Banking with the Poor*, Brisbane: The Foundation for Development Co-operation.

GITEC (1984) 'SEDOM, Phase 1 Final Report', GITEC Consultancy Report for the Ministry of Trade, Industry and Tourism, Lilongwe, Malawi.

Harper, M. (1984) *Small Business in the Third World*, Chichester: John Wiley.

Huppi, M. and Feder, G. (1990) 'The Role of Groups and Credit Co-operatives in Rural Lending', *The World Bank Research Observer*, **5**, (2), July, 187–207.

Levitsky, J. (1986) 'Assessment of Bank Small Scale Enterprise Lending', World Bank Industry Department, mimeo, Washington, DC.

MTIT (1982) 'SEDOM Inception Reports', Ministry of Trade, Industry and Tourism, Government of Malawi, November.

Page, J. and Steel, W. (1984) *Small Enterprise Development: Economic Issues from African Experience*, World Bank Technical Paper No. 26, Washington, DC.

Peat Marwick (1985) 'SEDOM Short Term Consultancy in Financial Planning and Control' (unpublished report).

READI (1989) 'Rural Enterprises and Agrobusiness Development Institutions Project', Government of Malawi/USAID, June.

Ryan, P.W. (1993) 'An Evaluation of Small Enterprise Lending: Evidence from Malawi', DPPC, University of Bradford, Research Monograph No. 5, April.

UNDP, Government of Netherlands, ILO and UNIDO (1988) *Development of Rural Small Industrial Enterprise: Lessons from Experience*, Vienna.

Yaron, J. (1994) 'What Makes Rural Finance Institutions Successful?', *The World Bank Research Observer*, **9**, (1), January, 49–70.

15. Income generation and micro-enterprise projects: why do they not reach the poorest women?

Uschi Kraus-Harper

INTRODUCTION

In recent years women have come more into the focus of attention of national and international organizations promoting micro and small business in so-called 'developing countries'. An increasing number of business start-up programmes, entrepreneurship development programmes and the like are being conducted for women, especially the more educated, middle-class women in urban areas. For the poorer women, many voluntary organizations formerly engaged in charitable activities, such as health programmes, or mother and child care programmes, have taken up income-generating projects, credit and saving programmes and basic business training programmes.

The interest in women in the context of development assistance goes back to the discussions initiated during the 'UN 'decade for women' (1975–85). During this period, many 'women in development' programmes and projects were started, and research projects began to look into all manner of women's issues. Due to this, development workers and planners have become aware that it is often a poor woman herself, and not so much her husband, who is investing in change towards a better livelihood for her family. For India, for example, the authors of the World Bank country report, *Gender and Poverty in India* (1991) write that

> studies show that the poorer the family, the more it depends on the economic productivity of a woman [because] first, women's earnings increase the aggregate income levels of these poor households, and second, as numerous studies have shown, Indian women contribute a much larger share of their earnings to basic family maintenance and increases in women's income translate more directly into better child health and nutrition status. (pp. xv and 1)

The *Wall Street Journal*, certainly not a feminist publication, found women in developing countries to be worth a first-page report:

This changing perception extends all the way to the big development agencies and multilateral banks in Washington, which are increasingly funding women-led small businesses and farming projects based on an assumption that women – more than men – are the critical players in the fight to relieve poverty. (*Wall Street Journal*, 22 June 1994)

More women are becoming de facto heads of households as men leave their families for economic or social reasons; rural men, for example, go to earn money in the cities and often fail to send money home. Women, therefore, need to be given a fairer chance to generate income or to improve ways of gaining access to the means through which this generation can take place.

Awareness about 'women's roles in economic development' goes hand-in-hand with small-scale enterprise promotion programmes increasingly directing their efforts towards what is called the 'grass-roots level' where women's economic activities are mostly to be found. Farbman and Steel (1992) wrote that 'women now make up about half the clients of small enterprise assistance programmes'. By 1995, this number had surely increased, especially since small enterprise promotion is increasingly related to, or at least linked with, savings and credit programmes which are often based on women's traditional groups savings systems.

There is, at least at development programme level, a great deal of overenthusiasm about what self-employment, micro or small enterprise promotion can do to improve poor women's (and poor men's) lives. The present writer has experienced this enthusiasm at international conferences, during field assignments in several countries and while teaching international short course participants in the UK. Of some 160 government and non-government organizations that have sent participants to courses on which the writer has taught during the last five years, at least 90 per cent promote or run small-enterprise or income-generating activities for women. Most of these programmes have started in recent years, and it is fair to say that, on the whole, programmes to promote women's income-generating activities have not been shown to be very successful and, still less, to be sustainable.

When Buvinic (1986) wrote about the 'misbehaviour of projects for women in the Third World', one of the reasons she mentioned was (and in many cases still is) the 'welfare approach' of many women in development programmes, which includes everything from family planning, mother and child care and nutrition to income generation components and is based on a 'hand-outs' and 'hand-holding' approach to poverty alleviation. Eigen (1992) analysed women's income-generating programmes in Kenya and found the same 'welfare approach' still prevalent. She concluded that it was impossible to tackle all problems in one single programme and that it is therefore important to 'disaggregate the focus in accordance with specific objectives and in response to the target group one is trying to reach'.

However, in order to 'disaggregate the focus', one must know the target group one is trying to reach. Most development workers and others working in adjacent fields appear to see 'the poor' too much as just one homogeneous group of people below a certain income level. In 1991, the present writer collected life-stories and much other qualitative data about the 'inclinations towards enterprise and self-employment' amongst 40 women in four poor communities in Orissa, the poorest state of India. One of the main objectives of the research was to find a tool that would help to 'disaggregate the focus'.

DO POOR WOMEN WISH TO BE SELF-EMPLOYED?

The two central research questions that evolved during the first months of the field research were: do poor women wish to run enterprises; in other words, what are their inclinations towards self-employment and enterprise; and what is there in the women's social and economic environment that hinders, pushes or pulls them to wish to run an enterprise of their own? In searching for answers to these and other related questions, five types of inclinations were revealed by analysing women's activities and by asking them about their dreams and plans for the future. By comparing field data with the literature about entrepreneurship and change, it was also possible to define a number of important sociological factors that were influencing women's inclinations towards self-employment and enterprise, namely the culture, especially the 'enterprise culture', family and economic situation, availability of time, skills, work experience and exposure, social and professional networks, 'artificial networks' or change agents, financial support, availability of land and availability of employment. A summary of the findings about the five types of inclinations is given below.

1. The negative–despondent woman: this type of woman has a negative–despondent inclination towards enterprise; she cannot and does not want to be self-employed although she needs money desperately and employment is not within her reach. The negative attitude of this woman is not only related to enterprise; it dominates her whole life.

2. The negative–pragmatic woman: this type of woman has a negative–pragmatic inclination towards enterprise. Her family depends on her income, as she is the main or only income earner. She is earning a low but regular wage through employment, usually as a domestic helper or as an unskilled day labourer with some sort of agreement with a contractor. She does not see self-employment as a desirable alternative to her current employment.

Table 15.1   Key elements of constructed types

Factors	Negative–despondent woman	Negative–pragmatic woman
Personal	Any family status; negative attitude to life in general; 'fate' is responsible	Any family status, but no male income provider; family depends on her
Enterprising activities	Not involved in any type of employment/self-employment; s.e. not desirable and feasible	Earning low but regular wage through some sort of empl.; s.e. not desirable
Enterprise culture	Whatever 'enterprise culture' is around her has no relevance to her attitude	Whatever 'enterprise culture' is around her is not relevant to her attitude
Family and economic situation	Belongs to the poorest of poor; likely to have young children; family may have experience in enterprise but do not support her	Family lives in hardship; she is main income earner
Time	Plenty of time to spare because of poverty	No time to spare because of empl. and household
Skills	Domestic; maybe vernacular; but 'I do not know anything', 'I cannot do anything'	Domestic; any vernacular skill even if marketable not used; prefers low but secure income
Work experience and exposure	If any at all, unskilled labour without possible exposure to something new	No experience with self-employment; any exposure is not likely to influence perception of s.e.
Social and professional networks	Isolated within her community; women's groups may exist but she is not a member of any	Not likely to be involved in active women's group; employers are important network
Artificial networks and change agents	If intervention programme in village then she has not been affected by their activities	Does not want change: wants security; also thinks herself too old or too tired
Financial support	May have received financial support but this was used for immediate survival needs	Lack of finance not reason for not being self-employed
Land and employment	Her family is landless; any empl. is not within reach for her	Family is landless; she is lucky to have fairly regular wage work or empl.

Note: s.e. = self-employment; exp. = experience; empl. = employment; iga = income generating activity; neg. = negative; pos. = positive; artif. = artificial.

Positive–uncertain woman	Positive–pragmatic woman	Positive–ambitious woman
If living with family, someone earns the main income and provides for her	Any family status; provides substantial part of the family income	Any marital status, but husband abandoned her or is dead
If alone and no infant, earns very low occasional wage; s.e. desirable but not feasible	Income is the focus and not the activity; will take up empl. or self-employment because of need	Is self-employed or has concrete idea of s.e. activity and only lacks finance
If other women around her are in enterprise, this has positive impact on her perception	She is involved in traditional activities of women in her community	Is from caste of community with 'enterprise culture' or with more 'gender equality'
A bit better off; someone earns quite regular wage; family may oppose her self-employment wishes	Lives in hardship; family support her activities because they need her	Is among the better off; family is supportive
Has time to spare	She may have spare time during some seasons, depending on her activity	Household duties not centre of attention; if not yet in s.e., busy with other things
Domestic; maybe vernacular; but keen to learn new skills: 'Teach me a skill'	Domestic and vernacular, which she uses for income generation	Has skills with which she can produce or sell a marketable good
The kind of s.e. activity she would like to do is always related to previous (work) exp.; exposure to something new intimidates her	Has worked from early childhood; exposure to something new increases positive perception of self-employment	Any previous work experience has helped her to start her self-employment; exposure to enterprise or work from early childhood has given confidence
Is passive member of women's groups	Likes to 'network'; is involved in women's social activity, if existent, and in group	Strong social network; if in women's group then likely to be leader
If change agents work in her community, her perception of desirability has been influenced	In s.e. often because of positive pull and support from such network	Often experienced either neg. push in private life or pos. pull from change agents
Finance not available or perceived as unobtainable	If available, she has made use of it	If better off, likely to have bank loan; if poorer, loan through 'artif. network'
If family owns land then not enough for subsistence; empl. very limited or only casual	If from rural area, would prefer to own land and farm; would take empl. if available	Is landless; even if empl. was available, she prefers to be self-employed

3. The positive–uncertain woman: she has a positive inclination towards self-employment but she is not quite sure whether she can do it or how she can do it. She is likely to say, 'I would like to do something but I don't know what' or 'I would like to do this or that but ...'. What is most important is that, although she has a positive inclination, she has not undertaken any step towards turning her wish into a practical experience.
4. The positive–pragmatic woman: this woman has a positive inclination towards self-employment but her being positive has a pragmatic quality: she has to earn money and she welcomes almost any opportunity to do so. Income is the focus, not the activity or enterprise, although this does not mean that she is not interested in what she is doing.
5. The positive–ambitious woman: the positive–ambitious woman is investing great effort in starting a very specific self-employment activity or in expanding or diversifying her current enterprise.

Table 15.1 shows in a summarized form how the selected social and economic factors influence the inclinations of these five types of women.

CHANGING PERCEPTIONS

Each of the five types summarized above is based on a number of propositions or hypotheses, which in themselves provide material for much further discussion. Most can be gained, though, when these individual types are compared with each other. Even a brief contemplation of the summary above reveals the *transitory* character of each of the five types. In the positive case, a woman may 'move on': from being despondent to being more confident and consider the possibility of venturing into something new: maybe a job or self-employment. The woman thus may become either negative–pragmatic because she finds a relatively secure job and prefers it to self-employment, or positive–uncertain because she cannot find any adequate job and needs more assurance, advice and/or access to financial means. Once the causes of the uncertainty have been removed, she may venture into self-employment, and may become a member of a successful group enterprise, or become a business owner with employees. Whether a woman 'moves on' or not depends upon her personality (which was not analysed); it depends upon the social and economic circumstances she lives in, that is factors such as her family situation, her location, her skills, her network and the availability of financial resources. It also depends upon 'critical events' or 'pushes and pulls' that initiate change.

Knowledge about these changing perceptions and what initiates them is essential for any kind of 'social engineering', or the initiation of social development programmes and projects. A comparative analysis of the various real types that make up the constructed types of women presented above indicated the pattern of change described below.

Moving out of Despondency

The negative–despondent women in the sample seemed to be trapped in what Robert Chambers has called the 'deprivation trap'. For a woman, this trap can be intensified by the mere fact of her gender, more so in societies where the status of women is very low. This seems to work on two levels: a social and economic level, with isolation, powerlessness and all the other factors that make up the 'deprivation trap', and a psychological level with the woman's own assumption of being a lesser being, through which the existent power-lessness and isolation are reinforced and internalized.

In the perception of women in this condition, nothing is deemed to be feasible, yet under certain circumstances their perception towards life in general can change, can become more positive. In respect to enterprise, they are then likely to join the many positive–pragmatic women who run micro-enterprises in every corner of the world, because employment, or the plot of agricultural land they may prefer as a source of income, is not accessible to them.

A group of like-minded women had been the catalyst for change: among a group of like-minded women, some of the negative–despondent women had started to move out of isolation and powerlessness. But, and this is important, these women had secured their very basic needs (regular food, secure housing) or had family members who had secured these needs. The women who had not moved out had been those with small children and without any means to secure the basic needs, or without any support from their family or a network of friends or neighbours. These women were usually quite isolated within their community.

Two inferences can be made from this. First, before a despondent woman changes her negative perception of self and life in general, her children's and her own livelihood have to be secured. The (by now) famous old Chinese saying (transferred to a woman) says, 'If you give a woman a fish she will eat it and be hungry again tomorrow; if you teach a woman how to fish she will be able to maintain herself and her family.' It needs to be looked at from a gender perspective. Before the woman can hold a fishing rod or net she needs the physical strength to do so, she needs, to use a technical language, a certain minimum calories intake. The woman is also likely to have small children; the poorer the woman, the more likely this is. With three little hungry children around her, it is difficult for her to hold the fishing rod and sit by the river patiently waiting for the fish that will feed her and these children.

Second, belonging to a group of like-minded women gives a woman more confidence to overcome the 'deprivation gap'. To take the Chinese saying again: the woman also needs to see – to become aware – that it is only custom and not moral or other law that restrains a woman from taking up a traditionally male occupation like fishing. And she needs the 'psychological strength' to convince her traditional community and social network of the same because otherwise this network will exert its control function and make sure that she moves within prescribed boundaries.

From an enterprise development intervention perspective, the negative–despondent women are not (yet) among the 'target group' because they are not (yet) inclined to run an enterprise activity. From a general development perspective, it can be said that any intervention that offers training and financial assistance for micro-enterprise as a means of poverty alleviation, without enabling women to increase their own self-reliance and their inner strength, will not serve their needs.

Is Negative Pragmatism Unchangeable?

Some women in the sample were not interested in earning more money through enterprise, because they did not believe that by being self-employed they *could* earn more than through their current badly paid wage-work. Compared with other 'pragmatic' women, they had no specific skills, and all of them were the sole or main income earners of their families, without a supportive social network.

Employment opportunities for women (and men) in most developing countries are scarce; and the few opportunities available for women are usually badly paid. One could therefore hypothesize that women will take up any opportunity to become self-employed instead of being underpaid and, perhaps, humiliated by employers. But the millions of extremely badly paid, mostly female, domestic helpers, for example, in every corner of the world, indicate that the relatively secure income is more important to them.

What can be concluded from this is that, if a woman's family depends on the income that she earns through miserable, badly paid but relatively regular wage-work, she is likely to prefer the security and not venture into self-employment. Women like these are not the 'target group' for enterprise development intervention programmes. Any intervention that tries to improve their lot will have to be on a more economic–political level, by helping these women to demand better working conditions and wages.

Becoming Certain

How does a woman with a positive, but uncertain, inclination towards enterprise become certain that she wants, or is able, to start or expand her enterprise? The many positive–uncertain women in the sample had small children and no extended family to take care of them so that they could venture out and find employment or self-employment. Other women said – and the observations confirmed this – that they had no skills and would not know what to do. During the whole period of field research it often seemed to the researcher that women were not aware of the opportunities around them; they could not perceive the possibility of doing things in a different way, less so doing completely new things.

At least four of the external socioeconomic factors considered in this research influence (either individually or in combination) a woman's uncertain inclination towards enterprise: lack of child care facilities, lack of finance, lack of 'marketable' skills and lack of exposure to opportunities. Any intervention programme planned to assist this type of woman to start an enterprise activity that seeks to provide a regular income would first have to analyse and remove the reasons for the uncertainty.

Who Moves from Pragmatism to Ambition?

The typical positive–pragmatic woman is someone who has to earn money and welcomes any opportunity to do so; income is the motivating force and not the activity or the enterprise itself. These women will be found in the many income-generating groups or cooperatives – and they will leave these groups if they find a better paid enterprise or job. Many of the rural women in the sample repeatedly said that they would prefer to have their own land and live off that land.

The enterprise activities of most of these women are either tedious or produce very little income (or both); there is nothing to be enthusiastic about. Given the poor environment of these women, the poverty of their customers, the limitation of their skills, there is little scope for growth. And those women who were ambitious had a higher level of formal education and had been exposed to different environments; they also had a supportive family. Two hypotheses can be deduced from the analysis of the lives of these women.

1. Poor rural women are farmers; they see the ownership of agricultural land as a way out of poverty, at least to secure the family's basic needs. If they get access to land, off-farm enterprise will always be a sideline, seasonal activity; it has to fit into their farming activities and not vice versa.

2. The primary concern of poor enterprising women is to earn enough money to feed their families; enterprise is only one, if often the only, possibility to do so.

For any enterprise development intervention this seems to indicate that if these women are to be the 'target group' of a programme, this intervention cannot be enterprise-centred, that is centred around the needs of a single enterprise. It has to be person-centred, providing a woman with the means to tackle, if needed, her multiple seasonal, petty or part-time activities. A person-centred approach also means that the intervention has to be concentrated where the woman is.

To help women to get cultivable land is, of course, beyond what most enterprise development interventions can do. But if cultivable land is what most poor rural women want, land that they own, that their husbands cannot sell, then more development intervention efforts should be redirected to help these women to achieve this goal.

From Ambition to Success

The reason why some positive–ambitious women in this study had not succeeded in starting the enterprise they were so ambitious to start was that they did not have the money to do so. But money had not been the only reason why others had been successful. All of them had marketable skills, most had some work experience and many of them would earlier have been classified as positive–pragmatic women. Ambition came with being exposed to enterprise, with some initial experience of success and increasing confidence. These women had gained strength from their own self-reliance; they were now able to approach a bank, to talk to a houseowner, to deal with customers (although mainly female customers). The main factor that may hinder their further success as businesswomen is the boundaries of their gender prescribed by culture and society. The successful, positive–ambitious women do not need enterprise development intervention projects; they need an economic–political environment that caters for the needs of small enterprise in a gender-sensitive way.

CONCLUSIONS

So why is it that income generation and micro-enterprise projects do not reach the poorest women, at least not in a sustainable way? The findings from the research discussed here point at a number of reasons. One very important reason is that money is not the main factor, yet more and more programmes specialize in providing access to credit for individual women or women's groups to alleviate poverty and enable them to start enterprise. In a recent ESCOR-funded study report, Hulme and Mosley wrote:

> our study supports the claim that interventions in financial markets can make a significant contribution to improving the income of poor people. ... However, this work found little evidence that such interventions can reach 'the poorest of the poor' as has been claimed by the Bangladeshi institutions [Grameen Bank, BRAC] and many proponents of 'micro-credit' schemes. The innovative schemes that we have studied have assisted many hundreds of thousands of poor people: however, the bottom two or three deciles of the socio-economic pyramid ... are unable to access even targeted financial interventions and will require other forms of assistance if their situation is to be ameliorated. (Hulme and Mosley, 1994, p. 7)

Education, training in vocational skills, exposure to market situations and to new ideas, confidence building, 'empowerment' of women – all these require much more commitment and patience from project-implementing organizations and from their staff than the mere provision of funding. They require that we know more about the women we claim to work for. The very poor women in this study, for example, all had time to spare and many of them expressed a desire to use their time more productively, yet researchers and many practitioners in the 'women and development' field (Young, 1993; Hilhorst and Oppenroth, 1992; Jumani, 1991; Downing, 1991) claim that women's multiple household roles and duties overburden them with work.

One of the most common ways of promoting women's income generation is to form women's groups or to work with existing groups. The findings of this research indicate that, while such groups may be very good starting points or 'springboards', they are not likely to become the more successful growth-oriented enterprises as most of the group members are 'positive–pragmatic' women who will leave the group to earn more whenever it suits them.

Another important finding is the lack of skills, not only 'marketable skills'. While it is true that most women have some traditional skills in agriculture or in what may be termed 'home economics', many very poor women in this study did not have any such basic skills: they did not have knowledge of food preparation other than the simplest cooking or of food preservation, basic sewing, or keeping chickens or a cow. Poverty had prevented them from learning even the most basic and very traditional skills.

REFERENCES

Buvinic, N. (1986) 'Projects for Women in the Third World: Explaining their misbehaviour', *World Development*, **14**, (5), 653–64.

Downing, J. (1991) 'Gender and the growth of micro-enterprise', *Small Enterprise Development*, **2**, (1), 4–12.

Eigen, J. (1992) 'Assistance to Women's Business – evaluating the options', *Small Enterprise Development*, **3**, (4), 4–14.

Farbman, M. and Steel, W.F. (1992) 'Research Issues for Small Enterprise Development', *Small Enterprise Development*, **3**, (2), 26–34.

Hilhorst, S. and Oppenroth, D. (1992*) Financing women's enterprise. Beyond barriers and bias*, Amsterdam: Royal Tropical Institute with IT Publications.

Hulme, D. and Mosley, P. (1994) 'Conditions for the Effectiveness of Loans to Small Businesses and Farms in Developing Countries', unpublished ODA/ESCOR Report, 7.

Jumani, U. (1991) *Dealing with Poverty. Self-employment for poor rural women*, New Delhi: Sage.

Young, K. (1993) *Planning Development with Women. Making a world of difference*, London: Macmillan.

Index

adjustment *see* structural adjustment
Africa *see* Ethiopia; Madagascar;
    Malawi; Sierra Leone; Zimbabwe
agricultural development
    and the growth strategy 79
    Sierra Leone 161
    Western Samoa 171–5
    see also rural areas, development
agricultural enterprises, survival 225, 226
agriculture, and women 243–4
aid
    problems 98–9
    to the South Pacific 169–70
    see also projects
aid agencies
    attitudes to sociocultural factors 105,
        106–8
    co-ordination of policies 161–2, 164
    and participatory rural appraisal 109–
        10
    and the process approach 117–18,
        120–21, 135, 184
    and project development 179
    see also European Union; ODA;
        World Bank
air pollution
    control 7–13
    dose response functions 15–17
    economic costs 6, 7, 10–13
    effects 8–13, 15–17
anti-poverty strategy of development 79,
    82
appraisal systems
    for projects *see* evaluation, of
        projects; projects, appraisal
    for staff 187
artificial markets (valuation method) 30
Assam, entrepreneurship development
    204, 207
assessment, of environmental impacts
    27–8, 29, 37, 56–7

Bangladesh, Flood Action Plan 129–32
basic needs strategy of development 79–
    80, 81–2
benefit transfer studies 9
benefits of projects
    equity in 133, 156
    perceptions 160
bilateral agencies *see* aid agencies
blueprint models 115–16, 126, 131, 132,
    134–5, 183–4
    and contracts 119
    and donor control 115–16, 179
    problems 127–8
    project types 117, 129
Bo/Pujehan rural development project
    156–62
borrowers *see* entrepreneurs
Britain *see* United Kingdom
business *see* entrepreneurship

capital
    and discounting 36–7
    see also credit; human capital;
        investment
carbon dioxide, economic costs 9, 12
CBA *see* cost–benefit analysis
Chambers, R. 99, 100, 108–9, 111, 241
change, management of 124–6
childhood experiences *see* sociocultural
    factors
class *see* sociocultural factors
classical contracts 118–19
cocoa, export of 180, 181
commodity stabilization schemes 175–8
community involvement *see* local
    government; participatory rural
    appraisal; popular participation;
    process approach
conditionality, of Stabex funds 176–8
conservation *see* environmental conser-
    vation

constant natural capital approach, to
sustainable development 23–4, 25
construction enterprises, survival 225,
226
consultation *see* local government;
participatory rural appraisal;
popular participation; process
approach
consumption growth, and discounting
35–6
contingent valuation 8, 30, 43–4, 50–51
case studies 48–50
in litigation 45–6, 51
methods 44–6, 51–3
problems 46–8
of recreational services 21, 30
contracts, and the process approach
118–19
control and command instruments *see*
direct regulation
copra, export instability 176–8, 180,
181
cost–benefit analysis 4, 5–6
alternatives 28–9
benefits 20
and the constant natural capital
approach 23–4, 25
criteria 22–3
definition 26, 28
distributional weights 31–3, 36, 37
of entrepreneurship development 202,
204, 206, 207, 208
and market liberalization 66–7
and the non-declining welfare
approach 23
problems 20, 27, 28
and sustainable development 37–8
see also benefit transfer studies;
discounting; environmental and
social cost–benefit analysis
cost recovery *see* financial sustainability
countries in transition
economic policies 57
and environmental impact assessments 68, 71–2
environmental policy instruments 4,
65–6, 70–72
and privatization 59, 62
and structural adjustment *see* structural adjustment

see also less developed countries
credit
institutional providers 211–12
evaluation 214–16, 220–33
financial sustainability 213–14,
215–16
statistics 216–18, 219, 223, 224
see also Malawi, Small Enterprise
Development Organization
repayment 222
for women 236, 237, 238–9, 244–5
see also capital; investment
cultural identity *see* sociocultural factors
culture, and management styles 141
cyclones *see* hurricane damage

damage function studies 9
decade for women 235
decentralization 185, 190, 192
decision making zones 126
deep ecological view, of sustainable
development 22
deforestation 4–5
see also forests
deprivation gap 241–2
design
of projects *see* projects, design
of surveys 47–8, 52–3
developed countries, growth rate 80
developing countries *see* countries in
transition; less developed countries
development
aid *see* aid
definition 23
and education 85, 87, 88–9, 91–2, 93
and environmental quality 4–5
models *see* blueprint models; process
approach
and popular participation *see* participatory rural appraisal; popular
participation; process approach
role of government *see* government,
role in development; local
government
and skills *see* skills
sociocultural factors *see* sociocultural
factors
strategies 77–93
and taxation 86, 87–8, 90–91
and technological progress 84–5

and trade *see* trade
see also projects, development;
    sustainable development
direct regulation
  and environmental control 66
  see also environmental policy
    instruments
discounting 34–7
distributional concerns *see*
  intragenerational justice
distributional weights, in cost–benefit
  analysis 31–3, 36, 37
District Support Project, Zimbabwe
  185–96
diversification
  and entrepreneurship 230
  and Stabex 176, 178
domestic markets
  liberalization 57, 58
  environmental impact 60–61
donors
  control of projects 115–16, 179
  see also blueprint models
dose response functions, in air pollution
  15–17

ecological view, of sustainable development 22
economic instruments *see* environmental
  policy instruments; taxation
economic structural adjustment *see*
  structural adjustment
economic valuation
  of environmental assets 3, 5–6, 14,
    26–7, 38–9
  of environmental impacts 29–31, 48–
    50, 67
  techniques 8–9, 30, 31
  see also contingent valuation; hedonic
    prices; travel cost; willingness to
    pay
education
  and development 85, 87, 88–9, 91–2,
    93
  for women 245
educational projects, sociocultural
  factors 105
effect matrices 28
effect on production (valuation method)
  30, 31

EIA *see* environmental impacts,
  assessment
emigration *see* outmigration
employment
  and the growth strategy 77–9
  as a measure of growth 229
  for women 237, 238–9, 242
  see also human resources
employment strategy of development 79
empowerment *see* participatory rural
  appraisal; popular participation;
  process approach
England *see* United Kingdom
entrepreneurs
  characteristics 229–30, 237–44
  growth rates 228–9, 230–32
  starting up 200, 201, 204, 208
  survival 222–8, 230
entrepreneurship development 203
  and diversification 230
  evaluation 201–9
  India 198, 203
    cost–benefit analysis 202, 204, 206,
      207, 208
    costs 201, 204
    evaluation 201–2, 204–9
    and the informal sector 208–9
    origins 198–9
    programme 200–201
  Malawi 212, 221–2
  for women 207, 235, 236, 245
  see also small scale industries
environment
  existence value 22
  and human welfare 21, 25
  and recreation 21
environmental assets, economic
  valuation 3, 5–6, 14, 26–7, 38–9
environmental concerns 21, 25
  and project appraisal 4
environmental conservation
  effects of discounting 34
  and project planning 130
  projects, sociocultural factors 105–6
  see also non-renewable resources;
    pollution; renewable resources;
    tropical rainforests
environmental impacts
  assessment 27–8, 29, 37, 56–7
  and market liberalization 67–72

control, policy instruments 4, 65–6, 70–72
economic valuation 29–31, 48–50, 67
of income inequalities 64
of market failures 63, 71
of market liberalization 60–65
of price rises 63
of privatization 62–3, 70, 71
environmental investments, rates of return 4, 5
environmental policy instruments 4, 63, 65–6, 70–72
environmental quality
and development 4–5
preferences 5–6
environmental and social cost–benefit analysis 27–8, 29, 30, 37–8
see also cost–benefit analysis; social cost–benefit analysis
equity, of project benefits 133, 156
ESAPs *see* structural adjustment
ESCBA *see* environmental and social cost–benefit analysis
Ethiopia, tsetse fly control 48–9
ethnicity *see* sociocultural factors
Europe
costs of air pollution 12–13
see also industrialized countries
European Union
foreign aid 173–4
Stabex 175–8, 179, 180, 181–2
evaluation
of entrepreneurship development 201–9
of projects 101–6, 114–15, 124, 214–16
India 198–9, 201–2, 204–9
Indonesia 214–15
Malawi 220–33
Sierra Leone 161–4
sociocultural aspects 101–6
Solomon Islands 178, 179–81
Western Samoa 174–5, 179
Zimbabwe 191–6
existence value, of the environment 22
expenditure patterns, and project development 159
export instability, compensation for 175–8, 179, 180, 181–2

facilitation services, for project development 189, 193, 195–6
farming *see* agriculture
finance *see* capital; credit; investment; projects, funding
financial sustainability, of credit institutions 213–14, 215–16, 218, 220–22, 232–3
fiscal measures *see* environmental policy instruments; taxation
fisheries
development, Sierra Leone 161
exploitation of 169, 180, 181
survival of enterprises 225, 226
Flood Action Plan, Bangladesh 129–32
foreign aid *see* aid
foreign trade *see* trade
forests
exploitation of 4, 169, 180, 181
see also tropical rainforests
funding, of projects 91, 188–9, 192–4

gender
awareness, and projects 104, 133
and participatory rural appraisal 110
see also women
Gokwe *see* Zimbabwe
government
role in development 84–8, 89–90
Bangladesh 131
Sierra Leone 156, 162
Western Samoa 172–3, 174
Zimbabwe 185–6, 190, 193
see also direct regulation; environmental policy instruments; European Union; local government; ODA
Great Britain *see* United Kingdom
groups
borrowing 214, 233
saving 236
see also income, generation; networking; self-help institutions
growth
and income inequalities 87
measures 229
growth rate
of industrialized countries 80
of small scale industries 228–9, 230–32

growth strategy of development 77–9,
    83, 88
  see also new growth theory

health, effects of pollution 6–7
health projects, sociocultural factors 105
hedonic prices (valuation method) 8, 30,
    50
higher education, and development 92
human capital (valuation method) 30, 31
human development strategy 83
human resources
  development 170
  and development strategies 77–93
  and structural adjustment policies 88–
    9
  see also education; employment;
      skills; women
human welfare
  and the environment 21, 25
  see also intragenerational justice
hurricane damage 169, 171

identification of need, and project
    development 122
implicit markets (valuation method) 30
income
  generation
    and the anti-poverty strategy 79
    for women 235–45
    see also groups; self-help institu-
      tions
  inequalities
    environmental impacts 64
    and growth 87
    see also intragenerational justice
  patterns, and project development
    159–60
India
  entrepreneurship development *see*
    entrepreneurship development,
    India
  irrigation planning 132–4
  ODA projects in 121–4, 126
  senior management in 144–50
  women
    productivity 235
    and self employment 237–44
Indonesia, credit for small scale industry
    214–15

industrialized countries, growth rate 80
informal sector, and entrepreneurship
    development 208–9
infrastructure development 161, 183
instrumental view, of sustainable
    development 22–3
interest rates, rises 80
intergenerational justice, and sustain-
    able development 23, 25–6, 27, 35,
    37
interviewers, effects on surveys 52
intragenerational justice 86–7, 156
  and the basic needs strategy 80
  and the growth strategy 78
  and project design 133
  and sustainable development 21, 25–
    6, 27, 32–3, 35, 36
  and taxation 86
investment
  and development 84–5, 86
  see also capital; credit
irrigation
  Philippines 135
  planning, India 132–4
  and soil conservation 133–4

Japan, small scale industries, survival
    rate 223
justice *see* equity; intergenerational
    justice; intragenerational justice

labour
  availability, and project development
    158–9, 163
  migration, effects 78, 167, 168, 172
labour surplus economy 78
land, for women 243–4
lead pollution, economic costs 7, 10
leadership
  of projects 102–3, 157–8, 164–5, 174,
    185–96
    see also blueprint models; manage-
      ment; popular participation;
      process approach
  of villages 171–2
leisure *see* recreational services
less developed countries
  economic problems 80–81
  and environmental impact assessment
    68, 71–2

environmental policy instruments 4, 65–6, 70–72
and privatization 59
and structural adjustment *see* structural adjustment
and valuation methods 30–31, 48–51
see also countries in transition
liberalization, of markets *see* market liberalization
linkage capabilities
and development 84–5
see also networking
loans *see* capital; credit; investment
local development *see* rural areas, development
local government, control of development 185–96
Lomé Conventions 173, 175, 176, 177, 180

McClelland, D. 198–9, 200, 201, 203, 209
Madagascar, tropical rainforest conservation 49–50
maize milling enterprises, survival 225, 226
Malawi
entrepreneurship development 212, 221–2
Small Enterprise Development Organization 212–13, 214
economic development of entrepreneurs 228–9, 230–32
evaluation 220–33
financial sustainability 218, 220–22, 232–3
growth 217, 218–20
objectives 212
statistics 216–20, 223, 224
survival of entrepreneurs 222, 223–8, 230
management
of change 124–6
effectiveness 137–8, 149–50, 188–9
definition 138–9
positivist approach 140–41
skills for 142–4, 146–9, 150, 187, 188–9, 191–2, 200–201
and social action theory 137, 141
of projects 104, 114–15, 121–2, 124–6
of risk 123, 195, 196, 200
roles 144–6
sociocultural factors 141
staff turnover 170
styles 137, 140–41, 192, 195–6
systems, development 186–7
see also leadership
manufacturing enterprises
growth 228–9, 230–32
survival 225, 226, 230
market failures, environmental impacts 63, 71
market liberalization 56–9
and cost–benefit analysis 66–7
and environmental impact assessment 67–72
environmental impacts 60–65
and environmental policy instruments 4, 65–6, 70–72
market prices, as a valuation method 30
markets *see* domestic markets; trade
MCA *see* multi-criteria analysis
Melanesia *see* Solomon Islands; South Pacific
micro-credit *see* credit
migration, of labour, effects 78, 167, 168, 172
mining enterprises, survival 225, 226
Ministry of Overseas Development *see* ODA
models, of development *see* blueprint models; process approach
monetization *see* economic valuation
Mosse, D. 110–11
multi-criteria analysis 28–9, 30

National Irrigation Agency (Philippines), and the process approach 135
natural capital *see* constant natural capital
need, identification, and project development 122
net present values 26
Netherlands, small scale industries, survival rate 222–3
networking 126
for women 237, 238–9, 241–2
see also groups; linkage capabilities; self-help institutions

new growth theory 84–8
  and human resource development 89–
    91
  see also growth strategy of develop-
    ment
NGOs *see* aid agencies
nitrogen oxides 10, 12, 13
non-declining welfare *see*
    intergenerational justice
non-governmental organizations *see* aid
    agencies
non-renewable resources
  exploitation 24, 38–9, 62, 64
  see also renewable resources

ODA
  evaluation of projects 114–15
  Indian projects 121–4, 126
  and the process approach 114–15,
    117–18, 120–21, 135
  Zimbabwean projects 185–96
operations management 144–7, 150
outmigration 168–9, 170, 171, 172
Overseas Development Administration
    see ODA
ozone pollution, economic costs 7, 10

Pacific *see* South Pacific
palm oil, and export instability 176, 180,
    181
participatory rural appraisal 46, 99–100,
    108–11
  see also popular participation; process
    approach
particulates 7, 10, 12, 13, 16–17
personnel management 144–9, 150, 187
Philippines
  National Irrigation Agency, and the
    process approach 135
  water pollution control 49
Pilot District Support Project, Zimba-
    bwe 185–96
policy instruments *see* environmental
    policy instruments
pollution
  and contingent valuation 45–6
  control, policy instruments 65–6
  economic costs 6–7, 10–13
  effects on health 6–7
  effects of market liberalization 64

effects of privatization 62, 63
  see also air pollution; environmental
    concerns; particulates; water
    pollution
Polynesia *see* South Pacific; Western
    Samoa
popular participation
  in projects 97, 98, 99–100, 108–11
  in rural development 155–65, 173–5
  see also process approach
population
  growth 24–5, 79
  pressure 168–9, 175
  projects, sociocultural factors 105
positivist approach, to management
    effectiveness 140–41
poverty *see* anti-poverty;
    intragenerational justice
PRA *see* participatory rural appraisal
preference surveys *see* contingent
    valuation
preventive expenditure (valuation
    method) 30, 31
price rises, environmental impacts 63
prices *see* market prices
primary education *see* education
privatization 58–9
  environmental impacts 62–3, 70, 71
process approach
  and contracts 118–19
  and cooperation between villages 134
  limitations 134–5, 184, 194
  management 121–2, 124–6
  and the ODA 114–15, 117–18, 120–
    21, 135
  principles 116–17, 128
  in the project cycle 122–4
  and project planning 130–34
  and relationships 120–21
  and rural development projects 135,
    185–96
  and water resources development
    128–35
  and women 133
  and the World Bank 128
  see also participatory rural appraisal;
    popular participation
productivity, and development 84–5,
    235
programme lending 91

project cycles 117, 122–4, 129
projects
  appraisal 4–6, 123, 193
    concerns about 114
    and contingent valuation 48–51
    screening for sustainability 37–9
  benefits of 133, 156, 160
  blueprint models *see* blueprint models
  concepts of 103
  and contracts 118–19
  control, by donors *see* donors, control
    of projects
  design 117, 122–3, 164, 190, 221, 232
    and intragenerational justice 133
    and participatory rural appraisal
      109–11
    and social assessment 98
    sociocultural factors 102–3, 106–7,
      164, 165, 174
  development
    and aid agencies 179
    and conditionality 176–8
    and expenditure patterns 159
    facilitation services 189, 193, 195–
      6
    and income patterns 159–60
    and labour availability 158–9, 163
    and local leadership *see* leadership,
      of projects
    and local resources 159–60
    problems 114, 194
    and seasonal changes 158–9, 163
    and self-help institutions 160, 163,
      165
    Solomon Islands 178, 180–81
    Western Samoa 173–5
    Zimbabwe 192–4
  evaluation *see* evaluation, of projects
  funding 91, 188–9, 192–4
  and gender awareness 104, 133
  identification of need 122
  implementation 124, 185, 194
  local control *see* leadership
  management 104, 114–15, 121–2,
    124–6
  planning 122–3
    Bangladesh 129–32
    and environmental conservation
      130
    India 132–4

    Malawi 221
    Sierra Leone 155–65
    and women 133
    Zimbabwe 185, 192–4
  popular participation in *see* popular
    participation
  process approach 130–34
  sociocultural assessments 100–107
  success factors 125–6
property values *see* hedonic prices
public sector
  Bangladesh 131
  South Pacific 169–70
  Zimbabwe 144–50
  see also government; local govern-
    ment
Pujehan *see* Bo/Pujehan

quantification, of environmental impacts
  27, 28, 37
questionnaires, design 52

rainforests, conservation 49–50
Rajasthan, entrepreneurship development 207
recreational services, contingent
  valuation 21, 30
regulation *see* direct regulation;
  environmental policy instruments
relational contracts 119
remittances
  from abroad 167, 168, 172
  see also outmigration
renewable resources
  exploitation 4–5, 38–9, 62, 63, 64,
    169
  sustainable yields 24
  see also non-renewable resources
replacement costs (valuation method)
  30, 31
resources *see* human resources; non-
  renewable resources; renewable
  resources
resources, valuation *see* economic
  valuation
risk management 123, 195, 196, 200
rural areas
  development
    and the anti-poverty strategy 79
    and contingent valuation 48–50

models *see* blueprint models; process approach

planning 155–65

popular participation in 155–65, 173–5

process approach 135, 185–96

and transport 186–7, 191–2

see also agricultural development; Bangladesh; participatory rural appraisal; Solomon Islands; Western Samoa; Zimbabwe

effects of labour migration 78, 167, 168, 172

Rural District Councils, Zimbabwe 186–9, 191–2, 193–4

Samoa *see* Western Samoa

sampling methods, for surveys 52

scenario descriptions, in contingent valuation 46–7, 53

seasonal changes, and project development 158–9, 163

secondary education, and development 91, 92, 93

SEDOM *see* Malawi, Small Enterprise Development Organization

self-employment, *see also* small scale industries

self-help institutions
 and project development 160, 163, 165
 for women 245
 see also groups; income, generation; networking

senior management *see* management

service sector enterprises, survival 225, 226

shadow prices 29, 37

Sierra Leone, project planning 155–65

skills
 and development 88–9, 92, 163
 for management 142–4, 146–9, 150, 187, 188–9, 191–2, 200–201
 for women 238–9, 245
 see also entrepreneurship development; technological transfers

Small Enterprise Development Organization *see* Malawi, Small Enterprise Development Organization

small scale industries
 activities 218, 223
 characteristics 229–30
 credit for 211–12, 213–16, 233
 evaluation 214–16, 220–33
 growth rates 228–9, 230–32
 problems 212
 and sociocultural factors 105–6
 survival 222–8
  by activity 225–6, 230
  by age of enterprise 226–7, 230
  of part-time entrepreneurs 227–8
 for women 235, 236, 237–44
 see also entrepreneurship development

smoke pollution, effects 16

social action programmes 89, 92

social action theory, and management effectiveness 137, 141

social assessment, and project design 98

social class *see* sociocultural factors

social cost–benefit analysis 33
 see also environmental and social cost–benefit analysis

social development specialists, role 106

social prices 4

sociocultural factors
 attitudes of aid agencies 105, 106–8
 and development 97–8, 192
 and management 141
 in project design 102–3, 106–7, 164, 165, 174
 in project evaluation 101–6
 and project types 105–6
 in women's development 237, 238–9

soil conservation, and irrigation 133–4

Solomon Islands
 economic situation 175
 forestry 169
 population pressure 169, 175
 project development 178, 180–81
 and Stabex 175–8, 179, 180, 181–2
 trade 175–8, 179, 180, 181

South Pacific
 economic situation 167, 168–70
 outmigration 168–9, 170
 public sector finance 169–70
 see also Solomon Islands; Western Samoa

South Pacific Forum 168, 169–70

specification techniques *see* environmental impacts, assessment
spot contracts 118
Stabex 175–8, 179, 180, 181–2
stabilization *see* structural adjustment
staff, management 144–9, 150, 187
staffing, public sector 170
stakeholders *see* popular participation; process approach
statistical design, and contingent valuation 47–8
strategic environmental assessment 68–70, 71–2
   see also environmental impacts, assessment
structural adjustment 57, 80–81, 82–3, 91, 169, 176, 184–5, 201
   effects 81–2
   environmental impact 61, 70
   and human resources 88–9
   and privatization 59
   and small business 211
sulphur oxides
   economic costs 10, 12
   effects 13
surveys
   design 47–8, 52–3
   of management skills 144
   see also contingent valuation
survival, of entrepreneurs 222–8, 230
sustainability, of credit institutions 213–14, 215–16, 218, 220–22, 232–3
sustainable development
   constant natural capital approach 23–4, 25
   and cost–benefit analysis 37–8
   definition 22–6
   instrumental view 22–3
   and intergenerational justice 23, 25–6, 27, 35, 37
   and intragenerational justice 21, 25–6, 27, 32–3, 35, 36
   and population increase 24–5
   screening for 37–9
   and technological progress 24–5
sustainable waste disposal 24
sustainable yields, of renewable resources 24

task management 144–7, 150

taxation, and development 86, 87–8, 90–91
technical cooperation officers 189, 191–2
technological progress
   and development 84–5
   and the growth strategy 78–9
   and sustainable development 24–5
technological transfers 93
third world *see* countries in transition; less developed countries
timber *see* forests
time preferences, and discounting 35
trade
   changes in 80, 81
   and development 84–5, 86, 90–91
   and export instability 175–8, 179, 180, 181–2
   and market liberalization 57–8, 59, 64
   Western Samoa 171, 172
training *see* education; entrepreneurship development; skills; technological transfers
transport, and rural development 186–7, 191–2
travel cost (valuation method) 9, 30, 44, 50
tropical rainforests, conservation 49–50
tsetse fly control, Ethiopia 48–9

underdeveloped countries *see* countries in transition; less developed countries
unemployment *see* employment
United Kingdom
   costs of air pollution 12–13
   small scale industries, survival rate 223
United Nations, decade for women 235

valuation *see* cost–benefit analysis; economic valuation
villages
   cooperation in water utilization 134
   leadership *see* leadership
vocational skills *see* skills

wage differentials *see* hedonic prices
Wales *see* United Kingdom
waste disposal, sustainable 24

water pollution
    control 13–14, 49
    economic costs 13
    effects 6, 13–14
water resources
    development, and the process
        approach 128–35
    planning 128–9
weights, distributional 31–3, 37
welfare approach, to women's develop-
    ment 236
Western Samoa
    economic plans 172–5
    economic situation 171–2
    hurricane damage 169, 171
    outmigration 168, 171, 172
    remittances from abroad 168, 172
    rural development 171–5, 179
    trade 171, 172
willingness to accept, (valuation
    method) 44, 50
willingness to pay, (valuation method)
    29, 44–5, 48–9, 52–3
women
    and agriculture 243–4

attitudes to self-employment 237–44
    and development 110, 235–45
    education for 245
    employment for 237, 238–9, 242
    entrepreneurship development 207,
        235, 236, 245
    income generation 235–45
    networking 237, 238–9, 241–2
    and project planning 133
    skills for 238–9, 245
    see also gender
World Bank
    attitude to sociocultural factors 105
    and participatory rural appraisal 109
    and the process approach 128

yields, sustainable 24

Zimbabwe
    decentralization 185, 190, 192
    Pilot District Support Project 185–96
    Rural District Councils, development
        186–9, 191–2, 193–4
    senior management in 144–50